Environment Reporters in the 21st Century

Environment Reporters in the 21st Century

David B. Sachsman,
James Simon, and
JoAnn Myer Valenti

Transaction Publishers
New Brunswick (U.S.A.) and London (U.K.)

Library of Congress Catalog Number: 2010004006
ISBN: 978-1-4128-1415-7
Printed in the United States of America

Library of Congress Cataloging-in-Publication Data

Sachsman, David B.
    Environment reporters in the 21st century / David B. Sachsman, James Simon and JoAnn Myer Valenti.
        p. cm.
    Includes bibliographical references and index.
    ISBN 978-1-4128-1415-7
    1. Environmental protection--Press coverage. 2. Mass media and the environment. 3. Reporters and reporting. I. Simon, James, 1952- II. Valenti, JoAnn Myer. III. Title. IV. Title: Environment reporters in the twenty-first century.
PN4888.E65S37 2010
070.4'493337--dc22

                                                    2010004006

Contents

Foreword by Bud Ward   vii

Preface   xi

Acknowledgments   xvii

Part I: Environment Reporting

1.   The Environment Beat   3

2.   Studying Specialized Environment Reporters   37

Part II: The Environment Reporters of the 21st Century

3.   The Environment Reporters   53

4.   The Work Environment   73

5.   Covering the Environment   93

6.   Wrestling with Objectivity and Fairness   115

Part III: The Craft: Telling the Environment Story

7.   On the Beat: Environment Reporters at Work   145

8.   Environment Reporters in a Time of Change   179

Appendix A: The Survey   195

Appendix B: Sources Used by Environment Reporters   219

Appendix C: Three Factors in Environmental Reporter Analysis:
Objective/Fair Reporters, Workplace Critics, and Advocates/
Civic Journalists   227

Index   229

Foreword

Environmental reporting is on the fast track.

No, make that environmental journalism or, better yet, journalism overall.

Change is everywhere: Fewer metropolitan daily newspapers publishing fewer copies with fewer news pages and for fewer readers spending less time ferreting out the day's hard news. And they are doing it for shrinking subscription revenues and, what's worse, for dwindling display and classified advertising dollars.

The question isn't whether journalism and news reporting—and with them reporting on the environment and natural resources—are changing, and changing fast. They are. The question involves just where that fast track is going.

Journalists are taught—and it's in their DNA—to be skeptical. All readers and audiences too should be skeptical if anyone tells them they *know*, know beyond a doubt, where journalism in the United States is headed over the next several decades. They don't, can't actually.

It's pretty clear that what has come to be known as the mainstream media, and to have its own acronym (MSM), is undergoing extraordinary and truly unprecedented change. It's imposed from without in the wake of wilting pressure from new online information sources; crippling consolidation of media ownerships; sagging readership and viewership from among key demographic groups and in particular those of keenest interest to retail advertisers; and paring back of newsroom staffs and reporting resources.

It's no secret either that the financial challenges facing major "legacy" news organizations—some of them unquestionably brought on by themselves and resulting from their long-comfortable local monopolies—predate and in some cases even exceed the added pressures, as bad as they are, resulting from the worldwide economic collapse at the end of the first decade of this new century.

It's not unrealistic to picture this painful transition as the first stage of what likely will be a decades-long evolution—an "epochal transformation" in the words of the Project for Excellence in Journalism's first "State of the News Media" report in 2004.

Where it will end, no one quite knows.

So into this mix comes the specialized journalistic field dealing with coverage of news—scientific, economic, policy, public health, political, and more—about environmental and natural resources. And into that mix comes the colossus of global climate change and all its implications, viewed by many reporters and others as likely to be "the story of the century."

And it all comes at a time of enormous upheaval in the halls of environmental journalists, on whose narrowing shoulders, one might submit, rest the prospects for the informed citizenry so critical to effective policy making in our still works-in-progress democratic society.

Picture it this way: Think of a huge mansion. That's the house of journalism. All right, it's a severely dilapidated one at that. Environmental journalism, notwithstanding the enormity of the issues it embraces (think oceans, land, atmosphere and beyond), constitutes one small room. No, make that one tiny closet of that mansion.

Or view the vehicle of journalism instead as a limousine, and environmental journalism as a tiny glove compartment.

The mansion might be crumbling, the limo headed for a cliff. We can perhaps fix the closet or the glove compartment, but to what avail?

You get the picture.

So into this mosaic comes *Environment Reporters in the 21st Century*. As it was going to press, the astute authors knew well not to go too far into predicting what for anyone, at this point, is surely an unpredictable future. What they do instead, and rightly so and well indeed, is provide us a roadmap, a fact-filled foundation, telling us from whence we came.

A former chairman of the U.S. Senate's Committee on Environment and Public Works, the late Vermont Republican Robert T. Stafford, was fond of telling stories. A favorite involved a tourist to his state who, approaching a fork in the road, asked, "Does it matter which road I take to get to Montpelier?" The senator's brisk reply was classic Vermont: "Not to me, it don't."

What does matter, and matter a lot, the good senator would be among the first to acknowledge, is what happens next with journalism—the path or paths it takes—and, in particular for those valuing our stressed ecosystems, with environmental journalism. The years of diligent and conscientious work reflected in these pages by David B. Sachsman, James Simon, and JoAnn Myer Valenti, shine a bright light with which tomorrow's media—in whatever form and number they may take—now have a better chance of leading the way.

It's a moving picture, one rapidly changing and certain to continue to do so. A city today with two dailies may become another one tomorrow with but one. A "daily" publishing seven times a week for decades and longer may soon be publishing but three or four. More and more of the nation's best and brightest journalists are being forced to forsake the comforts of a regular paycheck, health care, and other fringe benefits, joining countless peers before them (and more to come) in the new "niche journalism" ... with all its potential, promises and perils.

Want to know for sure where environmental journalism is going in this twenty-first century, a time period so critical, the best scientists are increasingly warning us, not only to the planet's atmosphere, but also to the world's oceans? Want to be in the best possible position to help steer that future, and not just sit by idly watching and lamenting it?

Then, it's essential that we know the baseline, that is, where environmental journalism and environmental reporters and editors stand now.

Know thyself, the ancient Greeks taught us. Through the accumulated details in these pages, we—both environmental reporters and others recognizing the value of informed reporting to public understanding and to our society—can indeed do that.

The challenges they and we face are abundant. Let's all be part of the solutions.

Bud Ward
Editor, *The Yale Forum on Climate Change & The Media*
http://www.climatemediaforum.yale.edu
January 2010

Preface[1]

Environment Reporters in the 21st Century is the story of the men and women who do that reporting, the specialized journalists who because of their expertise, their experience, or their willingness, regularly wrote about environmental issues or covered an environment beat in the first five years of the new century. *Environment Reporters in the 21st Century* tells the story of a new journalistic beat, a beat that developed during the lifetime of the authors. This book also provides a view of American journalism at the very beginning of the 21st century, when newspapers and television were still the major source of news in America.

Was this a golden age of environmental reporting? By the end of the decade, newspapers and local television stations were in a state of economic decline, and the business of news was rapidly changing. But while the systems of delivery were changing and the economic recession was causing massive cutbacks, many newspapers and television news programs were still holding on, and newspaper and television companies were still vitally important sources of news.

The dominant finding of this project is that environment reporters working at daily newspapers and television stations at the beginning of the 21st century shared many individual and work-related characteristics with U.S. journalists in general. Environment reporters are journalists first, perhaps due in part to their similar backgrounds and to the basic professional training received by most journalists. The differences that exist between some environment reporters and U.S. journalists in general may be related to differences that exist in their college education.[2]

Who were the reporters covering environmental issues in the United States in the first five years of the 21st century? Did these environment reporters in print and television news differ from other journalists? Just as earlier studies of American journalists have provided a record that helps us understand the realities of news professionals, this work offers a layer of findings about those specialists who report on the environment. Such continuing research about journalists, their attitudes about what they do, and why they choose to specialize is useful both to the history of the profession and in order to move beyond anecdotal and stereotypic generalizations.[3] It provides the baseline data necessary for all future comparisons.

For more than two decades, research teams headed by David H. Weaver of Indiana University have conducted comprehensive national studies of U.S. journalists every 10 years.[4] The statistical profiles, each drawn from a sample of more than 1,000 working journalists, offer rich data showing how journalists have changed in terms of demographics, attitudes, and work routines. While the samples were large enough to allow the researchers to generalize about subgroups such as newspaper and television reporters, the samples could not offer insights into specialized subgroups such as beat reporters.[5]

From 2000 to 2005, researchers in Tennessee, Connecticut, and Utah sought to remedy the lack of information about the subgroup of reporters who cover environmental issues. These journalists provide a vital link between scientists and other experts studying environmental issues and the general public, who want to know about the natural world in which they live.[6] Previously, there had been no major project that looked at the personal characteristics of environment reporters, their attitudes, and their work routines. This study sought to fill that gap, both by reporting on those characteristics and then comparing them, whenever possible, to the national data generated by the Weaver group. This research provides the baseline data needed for the systematic study of American journalists and specialized reporters. This study, like most studies based on interview data, is descriptive in nature, providing information regarding a particular slice in time.

Our first proposition was that environmental journalists were similar to U.S. journalists in many individual and work-related characteristics, perhaps due in part to the similar backgrounds and basic professional training of most reporters. We also believe that differences between environment reporters and U.S. journalists in general may relate to variations in their education. In addition, we propose that the larger the newspaper, the more likely it will be to employ one or more specialized environment reporters, suggesting that bigger is better for specialized reporting. As recently as 2006, the *Los Angeles Times* employed "more than two dozen" reporters and editors who specialized in "coverage of science, technology, medicine, or the environment,"[7] and, like the *New York Times*, was a poster child for the concept of bigger is better. While this may no longer be true, since large newspapers like the *Los Angeles*

Times have been cutting their budgets in recent years, generally speaking, large newspapers appear to have the most specialized reporters. The question here is whether the same concept holds true for the more typical "large" newspaper, with a circulation of more than 60,000.[8]

Environmental concerns can vary widely across the different regions of the United States. Do regional differences affect how newspaper and television reporters cover the environment? Or, do journalists—who generally have received standardized professional training—bring a consistency to their work regardless of the issue or locale? This project began with an examination of New England environment reporters first published in *Science Communication* in 2002.[9] The research continued as a nationwide series of regional studies conducted over time in which all available newspaper and television environment reporters were interviewed in the Mountain West, the South, the Pacific West, the Mid Atlantic states, the Mid Central region, and the West Central states, in addition to New England.[10]

Who were the environment reporters in these seven regions, and for whom did they work? What were the similarities among environment reporters across these regions, and what were the regional differences? What were their job titles, and what were their duties? How satisfied were they with their jobs, and how much freedom did they have to pursue a story and decide which aspects should be emphasized? Which news sources did they say they use most often, and how did they frame their stories? How did they explain the science of the environment to the general public? Did they consider risk when writing environmental stories? How often did they say they use a risk assessment angle compared to other issues? What concerns did they have for the state of environmental reporting? Were they concerned that their colleagues may be exaggerating environmental risks, excessively frightening their readers and viewers? How did they differ from each other and how did they compare with U.S. journalists in general?[11]

Should environmental journalists be as objective as journalists in general or should they sometimes be advocates for the environment? Should environment reporters work with community leaders to solve environmental problems? Are objectivity and advocacy polar opposites on the same dimension, which never overlap for most environment reporters? Or are they separate dimensions that can intersect on some issues and in some circumstances? We looked at whether some reporters felt they should be as objective as other reporters, but also were open to being an advocate sometimes or working to solve problems (often called a civic journalism approach).

Data from this project may lay the foundation for basic theory building. The authors propose a theory of journalism education that argues that journalists are journalists first because of the similarities in their studies, training, and experience, and that differences among reporters may be related to variations in their education or factors that affect their choice of study. Such a theory of journalism education is worth pursuing, providing an explanation for the similarities that exist among American journalists regardless of their age, ethnicity, gender, or politics. This theory of journalism education may also provide an explanation for the general conflicts that exist between reporters and their sources, whose education and training differ.

In addition, this project found that newspapers employ more specialized reporters than do television stations, and that the bigger the newspaper, the more specialists. This suggests that bigger is better for specialized reporting. This *bigger is better theory of specialized reporting* does not always appear to be true, given some reported regional differences. However, the impact of size on specialty beats appears often enough to be worth pursuing, especially at a time when the fate of some of the nation's larger newspapers is under threat by corporate readjustments. If bigger really is better, then perhaps big newspapers should be sustained, despite the cost of operation.[12]

Environment Reporters in the 21st Century is divided into three parts. The first, Environment Reporting, includes a review of the literature and a detailed explanation of the methodology of the current study. Part II, The Environment Reporters of the 21st Century, describes the results of the present research. Part III, The Craft: Telling the Environment Story, provides in-depth accounts of environment reporters at work. Were the first five years of the 21st century a golden age of environmental reporting, given the cutbacks already occurring? The final chapter in the book, Environment Reporters in a Time of Change, puts this research in historical perspective, viewing it in terms of the economic decline of the newspaper business and of local television news.

The authors are grateful to Bud Ward, the founder and former editor of *Environment Writer* and the editor of the *Yale Forum on Climate Change & the Media*, for writing the foreword for this book.

The authors would like to thank David H. Weaver and his colleagues at Indiana University for providing this study with their survey instrument so that many of the questions asked of environment reporters could parallel those asked of U.S. journalists in general.

The authors would like to thank the many people, mostly students, who worked on this nine-year project at the University of Tennessee at Chattanooga, Fairfield University, and Brigham Young University. They conducted most of the surveys, entered much of the data, ran the numbers, prepared the charts and tables, and typed the final drafts of this book and the papers and articles that were its precursors. This project could not have been attempted, let alone completed, without the dedication of these individuals.

The authors would like to thank the following: Diana Andrew, Alison Brasher, Lauren Brown, Victoria Bryan, Kara Clemenz, Autumn Dolan, Weston Eighmy, Andrea Elkins, Ethan Evans, Courtney Fultineer, John Harker, Meredith Jagger, Sarah Thompson Kennedy, Patrick Ley, Heather Nation, Drew Neslin, Andrew Phillips, Tatiana Trevor, Victoria Vaughn, and Aimee Wilson at UTC; Pamela Brubaker and Nathan Thompson, graduate students in the Department of Communications at BYU; Elizabeth Burns, Carolyn Canonica, Ethan Fry, Angela Schuster, and Andrea Vavasour, undergraduate students at Fairfield University, for their work as field interviewers and Lily Norton for her work as an editorial assistant; Professor James Shanahan of Boston University for his review of the first draft of the book; and Professor Irving Louis Horowitz, our publisher. The authors appreciate the overall support of the University of Tennessee at Chattanooga, Brigham Young University, and Fairfield University during the inception of and throughout this lengthy research effort.

Finally, the authors would like to thank the 652 environmental journalists who took part in confidential interviews for this study and the reporters and others whose on-the-record comments provide personality and perspective to this work.

Notes

1.   Earlier versions of elements of this preface were originally written by the authors and published in:

David B. Sachsman, James Simon, and JoAnn Myer Valenti, "Risk and the Environment Reporters: A Four-Region Analysis," *Public Understanding of Science* 13 (2004): 399-416.

David B. Sachsman, James Simon, and JoAnn Myer Valenti, "Regional Issues, National Norms: A Four-Region Analysis of U.S. Environment Reporters," *Science Communication* 28 (2006): 93-121.

David B. Sachsman, James Simon, and JoAnn Myer Valenti, "The Environment Reporters of New England," *Science Communication* 23 (2002): 410-41.

David B. Sachsman, James Simon, and JoAnn Myer Valenti, "Environment Reporters and U.S. Journalists: A Comparative Analysis," *Applied Environmental Education and Communication* 7 (2008): 1-19.

The final, definitive versions of the papers published in *Public Understanding of Science* and *Science Communication* have been published by SAGE Publications Ltd./SAGE Publications, Inc. All rights reserved.

2.   Sachsman, Simon, Valenti, "Environment Reporters and U.S. Journalists," 18.
3.   Sachsman, Simon, Valenti, "The Environment Reporters of New England," 410-11.
4.   David H. Weaver, Randal A. Beam, Bonnie J. Brownlee, Paul S. Voakes, and G. Cleveland Wilhoit, *The American Journalist in the 21st Century: U.S. News People at the Dawn of a New Millennium* (Mahwah, N.J.: Lawrence Erlbaum, 2007).

     David H. Weaver and G. Cleveland Wilhoit. *The American Journalist: A Portrait of U.S. News People and Their Work* (Bloomington: Indiana University Press, 1986).

     David H. Weaver and G. Cleveland Wilhoit. *The American Journalist in the 1990s: U.S. News People at the End of an Era* (Mahwah, NJ: Lawrence Erlbaum, 1996).

5.   Sachsman, Simon, Valenti, "Environment Reporters and U.S. Journalists," 1.
6.   Tony Atwater, Michael B. Salwen, and Ronald B. Anderson, "Media Agenda Setting with Environment Issues," *Journalism Quarterly* 62 (1985): 393-97.

     Paul Rogers, "Complexity in Environment Reporting is Critical to Public Decision Making: '…The Craft is Now Firmly Entrenched as a Key Beat in American Journalism,'" *Nieman Reports* 56 (Winter 2002): 32.

7.   Robert Lee Hotz, "Large Newspapers," In *A Field Guide for Science Writers, 2nd ed.* Eds. Deborah Blum, Mary Knudson, and Robin Marantz Henig (New York: Oxford University Press, 2006), 57.
8.   Sachsman, Simon, Valenti, "Environment Reporters and U.S. Journalists," 1-2.

     Russ Britt, "Are job cuts death knell for America's newspapers?" *Market Watch,* March 17, 2008 accessed on January 13, 2008 at http://www.marketwatch.com/news/story/job-cuts-signaling-end-americas/story.aspx?guid={AC857D6D-5557-4EF9-BAF6-29A95C7BC540}.

9.   Sachsman, Simon, Valenti, "The Environment Reporters of New England," 410-11.
10. The states in New England were Connecticut, Maine, Massachusetts, New Hampshire, Rhode Island, and Vermont; those in the Mountain West were Arizona, Colorado, Idaho, Montana, Nevada, New Mexico, Utah, and Wyoming. Those in the Pacific West were the Pacific Northwestern states of Alaska, Oregon, and Washington, and California and Hawaii; and those in the South were Alabama, Arkansas, Florida, Georgia, Kentucky, Louisiana, Mississippi, North Carolina, South Carolina, Tennessee, and Virginia. The Mid Atlantic region included Delaware, the District of Columbia, Maryland, New Jersey, New York, Pennsylvania; the Mid Central consisted of Illinois, Indiana, Michigan, Ohio, West Virginia, and Wisconsin; and the West Central included Iowa, Kansas, Minnesota, Missouri, Nebraska, North Dakota, Oklahoma, South Dakota, Texas.

     Sachsman, Simon, Valenti, "Regional Issues, National Norms," 94.
11. Sachsman, Simon, Valenti, "Regional Issues, National Norms," 94.

     Sachsman, Simon, Valenti, "Risk and the Environment Reporters," 401-02.
12. Sachsman, Simon, Valenti, "Environment Reporters and U.S. Journalists," 18.

Acknowledgments

The authors of this book contributed equally to this work. Their names are listed alphabetically.

The authors are grateful for permission to include the following previously copyrighted material:

David B. Sachsman, James Simon, and JoAnn Myer Valenti, "Risk and the Environment Reporters: A Four-Region Analysis," *Public Understanding of Science* 13 (2004): 399-416. Copyright © 2004 Sage Publications.

David B. Sachsman, James Simon, and JoAnn Myer Valenti, "Regional Issues, National Norms: A Four-Region Analysis of U.S. Environment Reporters," *Science Communication* 28 (2006): 93-121. Copyright © 2006 Sage Publications.

David B. Sachsman, James Simon, and JoAnn Myer Valenti, "The Environment Reporters of New England," *Science Communication* 23 (2002): 410-41. Copyright © 2001, 2002 by David B. Sachsman, James Simon, and JoAnn Myer Valenti. Published with permission.

David B. Sachsman, James Simon, and JoAnn Myer Valenti, "Environment Reporters and U.S. Journalists: A Comparative Analysis," *Applied Environmental Education and Communication* 7 (2008): 1-19. Copyright © 2008 Taylor & Francis, LLC.

David B. Sachsman, James Simon, and JoAnn Myer Valenti, "Wrestling with Objectivity and Fairness: U.S. Environment Reporters and the Business Community," *Applied Environmental Education and Communication* 4 (2005): 363-373. Copyright © 2005 Taylor & Francis, LLC.

David B. Sachsman, "An Early History of Environmental Reporting and Public Relations," *SEJournal* 12 (2002): 1, 14-15. Copyright © 2002, 1973 by David Bernard Sachsman.

David B. Sachsman, "Commentary: Should Reporters Use Risk as a Determinant of Environmental Coverage?" *Science Communication* 21.1 (1999): 88-95. Copyright © 2004 Sage Publications.

David B. Sachsman, *Who Sets the Environmental Agenda?* Paper presentation, International Congress on Hazardous Waste: Impact on Human and Ecological Health, 1995. Copyright © 1995 by David B. Sachsman.

Forecast Cloudy, writ. and narr. Christy George, Oregon Public Broadcasting, October 25, 2007. Accessed April 1, 2009 from http://news.opb.org/forecastcloudy/#.

Seth Borenstein, "The Future of Science and Environmental Journalism." (Edited transcript); (2009, Feb. 12); accessed 3-2-2009 at http://www.wilsoncenter.org/events/docs/Borenstein%20Edited%20Transcript.pdf.

Peter Dykstra, "The Future of Science and Environmental Journalism." (Edited transcript); (2009, Feb. 12); accessed 3-2-2009 at http://www.wilsoncenter.org/events/docs/Dykstra%20Edited%20Transcript.pdf.

Elizabeth Shogren, "The Future of Science and Environmental Journalism." (Edited transcript); (2009, Feb. 12); accessed 3-2-2009 at http://www.wilsoncenter.org/events/docs/Shogren%20Edited%20Transcript.pdf.

Jan Schaffer, "The Future of Science and Environmental Journalism." (Edited transcript); (2009, Feb. 12) accessed 3-2-2009 at http://www.wilsoncenter.org/events/docs/Schaffer%20Edited%20Transcript.pdf.

The edited transcript from the Wilson Center event is published with permission of the Woodrow Wilson Center's Environmental Change & Security Program www.wilsoncenter.org/ecsp.

Lisa Palmer, "What Lies Ahead as Mainstream Outlets Shrivel?" *Yale Forum on Climate Change and the Media*, (2009, February); accessed 3-2-09 from http://www.yaleclimatemediaforum.org/2009/02/potential-abounds-but-will-they-delivernew-media-and-coverage-of-environment/.

"The New Washington Press Corps: A special report on the rise of the niche," *Project for Excellence in Journalism*, (2009, Feb. 11); accessed 3-2-09 from http://journalism.org/print/14681.

Peter Nelson, *Ten Practical Tips for Environmental Reporting* (Washington, D.C.: International Center for Journalists, 1995), vii–viii, x, 13-15, 29-30. ICFJ manuals can be found at www.icfj.org/publications.

Part I

Environment Reporting

1

The Environment Beat[1]

Researchers have long been interested in the work habits and attitudes of journalists, including specialized reporters such as environment and science writers. As early as the 1930s, scholars began studying the characteristics of science writers: who they were, how they were trained, and their impact on science and the mass media.[2] By the 1980s, this experienced, well-educated group of journalists, who had a non-adversarial relationship with their sources, reported they were devoting nearly a quarter of their time covering environment and energy subjects, primarily in breaking news or feature stories.[3] While many environmental stories were written by science writers, a separate environment beat was emerging. By the early 1990s those attending the annual convention of the Society of Environmental Journalists were writers interested in politics, land use, transportation, and economics, as well as science.[4]

From the 1930s to modern times, the nature and focus of reporting changed. A review of the history of how the media presented engineering research to the public from the 1930s through the 1950s applies equally well to the environmental issues of the time. Media then celebrated engineering accomplishments, featured famous engineers, discussed failures and problems overcome, identified engineering progress with prosperity, and emphasized practical applications of research findings. Most notably, corporations (DuPont, General Electric, AT&T, and Westinghouse) sponsored or served as underwriters for broadcast series on both radio and television that dramatized engineering achievements, even venturing into descriptions of mathematical principles and mechanics. "Audiences may be sometimes interested in techniques and principles but they are almost always interested in how people...succeed," researcher Marcel LaFollette reported to an audience of scientists, journalists, and others attending the American Association for the Advancement of Science conference in Seattle, Washington in 2004.[5] Likewise, a study of environmental coverage found that environment reporting in the 1940s often was dominated by corporate public relations efforts.[6]

By the late 1960s, however, while corporate public relations may still have dominated news stories on engineering, environmental reporting was based on conflicting statements from a wide variety of sources, ranging from environmental activists to government officials and business leaders.[7]

America's environmental news sources were engaged in a communication war—a war that continues today.[8]

From the Archives:
An Early History of Environment Reporting and PR

This excerpt from the Introduction to the 1973 Stanford University Ph.D. dissertation Public Relations Influence on Environmental Coverage (in the San Francisco Bay Area) was published in the form below by *SEJournal*, the publication of the Society of Environmental Journalists, in Fall 2002.[9]

Throughout most of the Sixties, unless a river was on fire or a major city was in the midst of a weeklong smog alert, pollution was commonly accepted by both the press and the general population as a fact of life. Until the late Sixties, conservationists were thought of as eccentric woodsmen and environmentalists were considered unrealistic prophets of doom.

Times have changed. By the early 1970s, environmental problems concerned many Americans. Mass media coverage of environmental issues has changed. Newspapers, magazines, books, and broadcast outlets offer the public a stream of information and opinion, much of which treats ecology seriously if not intelligently or completely. By the early 1970s, both the media and the general population were aware that there is such a thing as an "environmental issue," and many mass media outlets transmitted environmental information and opinion to their publics.

What Rachel Carson had written about in *Silent Spring* in 1962 finally became a hot news story in 1969. Perhaps it was the dramatic Santa Barbara Channel-Union Oil leak that caused print and broadcast editors to begin taking seriously their own local problems of air and water pollution, overcrowding, and the loss of natural resources. It was in 1969 that the *New York Times* created an environment beat—a practice that would be followed by major newspapers across the nation. It was also the year that *Time* and *Saturday Review* began regular environment sections, *Look* devoted almost an entire issue to the ecology crisis, *Life* greatly increased its coverage of the topic, and *National Geographic* offered a 9,000-word article on man's environmental problems. At the start of the new decade, the CBS Evening News with Walter Cronkite was presenting an irregular feature called "Can the World Be Saved?" and Paul Ehrlich's *Population Bomb* was a best-seller.[10]

It was no accident that the public and the media until the late Sixties accepted pollution as part and parcel of industrial society. Corporate public relations promoted this view, and skillfully kept the public satisfied. The press rarely heard the bad news of industry pollution but often received good-news releases concerning industry pollution controls and the many benefits offered to the community by local industry.

After World War II, International Harvester built a new plant in Memphis, Tennessee. Located in open fields, the Memphis Works burned coal and its big smokestacks spewed smoke, soot, and cinders. New homes were then constructed adjacent to the plant, and at the first hint of complaints (the air pollution was so bad that wash hung out to dry turned black, and windows had to be permanently closed), company spokesmen went door to door assuring homeowners that something would be done. Before the homeowners could go to newspapers or public officials, they received a letter from the Works manager stating that the company was searching for a solution. For three long years, no pollution controls were installed, and reporters did not write about the pollution. The people were apparently kept happy by the company's claims that it had spent $68,000 on improvements. Much of this money was used to purchase 17 acres around the plant as a green belt to catch low-level debris—a very good investment. Finally, the company installed a device to trap most of the residue coming from the plant powerhouse. The final expenditure of $71,900 gave International Harvester a reputation as a company concerned for the public interest. To mark the installation, the company held a community meeting and press conference glorifying its efforts to solve air pollution. The first newspaper story ever carried on the issue was headlined: "IH Spends $71,900 to Be a Good Neighbor."[11]

After World War II, in those isolated instances in which a few citizens fought corporations concerning questions of land use, they faced skillfully designed corporate public relations campaigns, and local media that generally accepted the industry arguments. To build a 90-acre research center in a residential neighborhood in Wayne Township, New Jersey, United States Rubber needed to bring about a change in the community's zoning ordinance. Stressing that buildings would be set back from property lines, the tract would be landscaped, and there would be no offensive odors, traffic problems, or water pollution, the company began a massive public relations campaign with a release to the press. Personal letters were written to local opinion leaders and community and state officials, booklets explaining rubber research were widely distributed, residents were invited to visit other rubber labs, and company spokesmen met with various civic groups. With the press, local government, and an estimated 90 percent of the people in its pocket, the company had little trouble quashing a suit filed by 10 property owners to prevent the change in zoning.[12]

In the International Harvester and the United States Rubber cases, only the corporations were producing press releases. By the late 1960s, the picture had changed. The media now received environmental releases not only from industry and industry-related institutions, but also from government agencies and officials, citizen-action pressure groups, and other institutions such as universities. The rise of environmental awareness in the 1960s is perhaps due to what Richard W. Darrow, then president of Hill and Knowlton, the largest public relations firm, called the Great Ecological Communications War—a war between conflicting public relations forces.[13]

At least in part, the environmental information explosion is due to the realization by politicians that ecology is a safe issue (unlike war, poverty, or taxes) and the use of public relations techniques (by officials, environmental activists, and others) to expose the crisis. President Lyndon B. Johnson was one of the first national political figures to realize that being against pollution is good public relations.

Johnson said in his message to Congress, February 8, 1965: "In the last few decades entire new categories of waste have come to plague and menace the American scene. These are the technological wastes—the by-products of growth, agriculture and science... Almost all these wastes and pollution are the results of activities carried on for the benefit of man. A prime national goal must be an environment that is pleasing to the senses and healthy to live in... Our government is already doing much in this field. We have made significant progress. But more must be done."[14]

As other government officials began to talk about the environment, the press began to treat ecology as a serious government story, and the general public began to become increasingly aware that vital questions were involved. At the same time, environmental activists began flooding the media with releases, some media began environmental investigative reporting, and public awareness was heightened by a series of ecological disasters. More and more, government officials realized that environmental action was more than a fad, and slowly they realized that they would have to add actions to their words.

As Walter J. Hickel explained: "When I took office in 1969 as Secretary of the Interior, pollution was no longer a joke; this fact was made clear by the nature of my confirmation hearings. The subject was aggravating millions of Americans; frustration and hostility were growing. The nation was desperately looking for leadership, and I decided that we should take the lead."[15]

The environment is in part a government story. Government officials and agencies are directly involved in decision-making that will determine the future quality of life, and they are responsible for a great amount of the public relations environmental material received and used by the mass media. Their words and deeds are regularly covered by the press.

Not only did the established, environmental activist groups learn that good public relations made for solid press coverage, but the many new activist groups also realized that public relations was the key to reaching the public. By the early 1970s, there were dozens of national groups, and a separate citizen action organization for every local issue—all trying to reach the public through the press.

Other institutions are also involved. Universities have information departments, as do many foundations. Educational institutions, especially, are now centers of discussion and study concerning environmental matters, and speeches and research often become press releases.

Finally, the environment is in part a business story, and corporate America is involved in a Great Ecological Communications War. As Darrow told the 1971 Economic Council of the Forest Products Industry: "The hour is later, Communications Time than it is Mountain Standard Time, for you and me and our colleagues at the control points of industry. We will do those things that earn us attention and gain us understanding, or we will live out the remainder of our professional lives in the creeping, frustrating, stultifying, stifling grasp of unrealistic legislative restraints and crippling administrative restriction. A public that ought to understand us—and thank us for what we are and what we do—will instead clamor for our scalps."[16]

To answer this call and win the public relations war, corporate America is using the press release as the primary weapon.

The American mass media are faced with the overwhelming task of sorting through the barrage of environmental information and deciding what news to carry about environmental issues.

Author's Note:

I continue to believe that the 1960s was the key decade for the development of modern environment reporting and the battle between conflicting public relations forces. The 1960s marked the rise of the federal government as the most important source of environmental news, and the rise of television as a powerful, "visual" news medium. The Santa Barbara Channel-Union Oil spill was covered by television as a human-interest story of young people trying to save oil-soaked birds on the beach. The moving pictures of students in tears with dying birds in their arms were seen "up close and personal" by young and old across the nation. While most environment reporters then and now work for print media, the impact of television on the growth of the environmental movement deserves recognition.

Much has been written about the changes in America between the beginning and the end of the 1960s—in civil rights, women's rights, and in our response to the war in Vietnam, as well as in culture, music, and style. Our world today is so much a product of changes that took place in the 1960s that it may be hard to imagine the world as it existed in the 1940s, 1950s, and early 1960s. Rachel Carson's *Silent Spring* in 1962 gave us a new way of considering our environment, and we have never been the same.

David B. Sachsman
Copyright © 2002, 1973 by David Bernard Sachsman.

Today almost every news reporter may be called on to cover breaking stories about the environment. The police reporter or general assignment reporter arrives at the scene of an accident—an overturned truck—and learns that some kind of spill is involved that cannot easily be cleaned up. The road is closed in both directions, a special clean-up crew is on its way, and a normal two-hour traffic delay accident story is now a six-hour closed-highway toxic-spill accident story.[17]

Government: The Dominant Source

Even more common than the accident story is the government environmental story. Government is the dominant source for environmental news.[18] The federal government breaks environmental stories almost every day, state government agencies are major sources of environmental news, and many local government meetings have at least one environmental item on the agenda. Government reporters, whether they cover the president, the governor, or the city council, must be prepared to cover environment stories. And local beat reporters, who cover everything that happens in their areas, from zoning board meetings to leaking underground storage tanks (at gas stations), have more than their fill of environment news.[19] Some daily newspapers and a much smaller number of local television stations employ specialized environment reporters, that is, reporters who because of their expertise, their experience, or even just their willingness, have been given a regular (though often part-time) environment beat. But even at those newspapers and TV stations that employ environment specialists, the first-day story of the spill, the accident, or the city council meeting is almost always covered by the reporter on the scene, the general assignment reporter, the government reporter, or the local beat reporter.[20] Specialized environment reporters usually don't get there until the second day—or until an evacuation has been ordered. There are just too few of them to be everywhere at once.[21]

Many Different Beats

Thirty years ago the environment beat often was part of the science beat, the province of the specialized science reporter at larger newspapers.[22] Today the environment belongs to reporters on many different beats, who recognize that ecological issues overlap their areas. So many environmental issues spill over to the business pages that the environment often is a business story as well as a government story, or an accident story, a local beat story, an outdoors, nature or hunting and fishing story... and, yes, a science and health story.[23] Some journalism texts stress the need to frame environment stories broadly and the need for environment reporters to be knowledgeable about a wide range of topics that extend well beyond threats to nature.[24]

Environment specialists do become knowledgeable in many of these areas, and they bring to their media an intense focus and a level of in-depth coverage beyond that possible on the first day of most breaking stories.[25] Because they are few in number, they touch only a handful of the environmental items handled by their media. But where these specialists exist, they make a difference, helping readers and viewers differentiate between environmental claims and legitimate threats to the public health, between manipulated statistics and carefully conducted research.[26] These specialists provide a model of environmental reporting worth being emulated by the general assignment reporters, government reporters, and local beat reporters who cover most of the breaking stories.[27]

A Model of Today's Environmental Specialists[28]

The *Salt Lake Tribune*'s environment reporter, Judy Fahys, describes her job as "helping people to find and understand information they need to live better." Her aim, she says, is to provide her readers with insights into the politics and science behind environmental issues.

Reporting on climate change, she says, is a "tough job, a really big responsibility, and an important challenge." She says she works hard to make climate change accessible to people. "Journalists are good at reporting stories that are easy, like the dialogue and spin around political stories," she said. Reporting on environment issues requires a commitment to facts, and takes time. It's easier to write about politics, the former Washington

D.C. reporter believes, because politics is all about opinions, not a lot of facts. Science information is different. "Science is a process, there are no answers or static facts." And since science is "always open to debate" being nimble sacrifices depth. She acknowledges that there are time-tested themes in science, but "it's always debatable." Yet, particularly with complex issues like climate change, "debate doesn't tell the whole story." Opinion doesn't get at the nuances and caveats. In a lengthy series in the *Tribune*, she dispensed with the "debate" over climate change in one paragraph, then went on to report evidence and what the ominous signs from the scientific community will mean locally.

Once the business community got behind the climate change, covering the story got easier, she said. When her sources began to include investors, pension fund managers, and other business interests, it was a clear signal climate change was indeed happening. Big media—the *NY Times*, *National Geographic*—ran series, and Al Gore's message (in the documentary "An Inconvenient Truth") demonstrated that the world was responding to the issue. "The business community brings increased credibility [to the story]," Fahys said.

Fahys is a product of the energy crisis era and learned about the greenhouse effect and global warming in her high school science courses. "I didn't know [the science] was hotly contested," she laughed. "Global warming got hijacked as a political tool and obscured the issues," she said. In a poll conducted by the *Tribune*, half of Utah's respondents said they believed in global warming, but Fahys saw the results as "faith, not facts." When asked if politicians should do something about reducing energy consumption, two-thirds of the same respondents said yes. And, when asked if conserving energy is helpful to the environment, two-thirds again agreed. The higher positive response on action needed held firm across all variables. Fahys felt simply removing the global warming term brought more people on board the issue.

Fahys sees the same failure to understand the full issue(s)—and politicizing rather than sticking to science facts—in the actions of both of Utah's senators who voted against the naming of a U.S. post office for Rachel Carson. "Opinion keeps journalism alive," she said, "but information and contacts (empowering information) keeps stories from being completely politicized. The majority of politicians distorted the facts about DDT and the solid science in Carson's legacy.

"I follow the logic of a story," she said. "I don't have an agenda, but I do see changes that have to be made…. It's hard to know what to do with the recent bad news on the accelerated rate of global warming." Editors can tire of the stories, especially when readership studies seem to indicate the environment lags behind other issues of interest. "I think they ask the questions wrong," Fahys said. "If they asked people if they care about water, air, pollution, their health, and so on," instead of simple rankings, they'd get a different response.

"There are great opportunities in journalism to do a good job of informing and educating," Fahys believes. She fears people have not gotten the information needed to make decisions. If the people of Utah, for example, decide they want nuclear waste stored in the west desert, "fine, as long as it's an informed decision." In covering the story on nuclear waste storage and disposal in Utah, Fahys admits she's had a hard time deciding what to do about Down-Winders, people suffering from various cancers that they claim have resulted from exposure to the federal government's nuclear test history. "The science isn't there," she says. The health issues are not clear; cancer clusters raise uncertainty questions. "I report people's concerns," she said, "but I also add a paragraph on the lack of supporting science." She says her "instinct is there's something genuinely wrong," but the tools to measure the effects are not yet there. Lobbyists for the nuclear industry are "good at their spin," but she feels their equivocations are inadequate. "My role is to tell people what to think about, not what to think," Fahys repeats. And she's confident "people are smart." If her readers have good information, they'll make good decisions. "I don't have to tell them to stop eating meat," Fahys, a long time vegetarian, says. "Who wants to know what I think?"

When the *Tribune* decided to profile one of the state's most influential people, John Huntsman, Sr., Fahys was called on to cover the environmental side of the story. Huntsman Chemical has plants in Texas and elsewhere, but none in Utah; in Utah, Huntsman has established an expansive cancer research and treatment center. The series, co-reported and written by two of the paper's leading metro and political reporters, sought to investigate rumors heard often on the street and covered in the alternative press, but left unreported in the mainstream media. The gist: Is Huntsman a saint or a killer? In Texas, a $9 million fine had been leveled on the company for pollution, and plant managers faced charges of falsifying environment reports. Locals were also filing lawsuits claiming illness from air pollution. When it became known that Salt Lake City reporters were in Texas to cover the story, a local Texas weekly, owned by an attorney for the Hunstman company, ran stories charging the Utah reporters with paying sources for faulty information, and quoted a supposed Utah businessman as saying "she [Fahys] never got anything right....and [she] would be fired." Fahys, who was leaving for a fellowship in Washington D.C., says she carefully balanced the pro/con in the series, "to an inch. I even balanced the photos," she remembers, and had an unfavorable headline changed on the paper's web page. The series was held up for various reasons, and ran just months before the election for governor, an election eventually won by John Huntsman, Jr. In spite of full-page ads taken out in the *Tribune* denouncing the series and personally attacking and questioning the accuracy of Fahys' reporting (not either of the two other reporters), the public seemed to shrug the whole thing off. However, Huntsman, Sr. cut off all access with *Tribune* reporters. Fahys, not fired but away on a prestigious fellowship, continues to wonder at why the personal attack was so targeted at her, although, the environmental angle was clearly her coverage, and was the most sensitive. "Those full-page attack ads cost $7000 each," she recalls. "I think I earned the paper a big chunk of my salary." There were no regrets from the editors' side, but Fahys says, "I'm battle worn and leery." "I'm the only journalist I know of whose had ads taken out against them, charging me with being fast and loose with the facts," she said. "I don't have a killer instinct, I try to be fair, and the newsroom doesn't seem to care about what's happened to me. My reporting values haven't changed, I still air controversies, but I'm weary of the perception of advocacy."

In a recent story reporting on a land purchase involving The Nature Conservancy in rural Utah, she was again charged with being "unfair" only this time by the environmental community. "Even good friends thought I made TNC look bad," she said, but she felt part of the story—her role in looking out for the ordinary people—exposed how secretive TNC had been and the local mayor's feeling he'd been left in the dark about the numbers involved in multiple offers and the eventual purchase. "TNC dislikes attention to monies being spent and water rights purchases." Fahys said. "But TNC is no sacred cow. Green groups have an agenda just as others do, and the whole story needs to be reported."

People are drawn to people with opinions, bloggers, columnists, and endless talk shows on radio and television. "There's a lot to learn from everyone," Fahys believes, and she writes about what all of those other people think. "A good narrative is really important," Fahys said, "but that's where advocacy can sneak in." She points to John McPhee and Bill Moyers as examples of good journalism. Integrity doesn't mean only liking people who are green, she points out. But she worries about journalists doing the best they can, yet still getting torpedoed, like Dan Rather. "When I make a mistake," she said, "I want a source to call me so I don't make that mistake again." Not run slanderous ads, not cut off access, not make false charges. After the horrific Huntsman experience, she felt vindicated in the end. But the battle scars are getting harder to disguise.

Reliance on Public Relations

While environment reporting specialists rely on their own journalistic skills to gather much of the information they use, they also tap into other sources traditionally used by reporters. For example, public relations people and other environmental communicators can provide "information subsidies," gathering information at their own expense and presenting it to environmental, science, and health reporters for possible use.[29] This reliance on public relations was first quantified by David B. Sachsman in the early 1970s when he found that at least 25 percent and perhaps as much as 50 percent of the environmental news stories published by San Francisco Bay newspapers were influenced by public relations efforts. At that time some 20 percent of the stories were little more than rewritten press releases.[30] Likewise, a study of health reporters at local television stations published in 2004 shows a continuing reliance on public relations and sources for story ideas.[31] Special interests personally contacted these health and medical reporters, thus playing a significant role in setting the agenda for local television news coverage of health. Little actual newsgathering occurred. The author, Andrea H. Tanner of the University of South Carolina, concluded that these beat specialists partake in a "passive news discovery process" rather than conducting enterprise journalism.[32] Tanner also found that health beat reporters (like environmental journalists) spent much of their time covering other stories. Only one-third said they concentrated solely on health reporting. Tanner's 50-some respondents also reported having little or no formal education in health or medicine.[33]

The Dance: The Relationship between
Environmental Communicators and Reporters

Phillip Burgess has the classic profile of a successful environmental communicator: an initial dozen years of experience as a newspaper, radio and TV reporter, plus an additional 25 years as a utility lobbyist and senior environmental communicator for an industry group in Tennessee. He says he needs to call on all that experience in dealing with new communication challenges coming at him from all angles.[34]

More voices have entered environmental debates, due to easy points of entry on the Internet. There are more technological ways for opponents to push out their message, from blogs to Web pages to podcasts to YouTube. Staff cutbacks in the mainstream media mean there are fewer knowledgeable environmental beat reporters and more generalists who may not understand technical information.

Compared to 20 years ago, the reporters currently covering the environment—and the general public—appear to be more green and pro-environment on some issues, at least in the eyes of an industry spokesperson. This pro-environmental trend can make getting across an industry's point of view a real challenge.

"In Congress last year there was a proposal for renewable portfolio standards that would mandate a certain amount of electricity generation coming from renewable resources," said Burgess, communications & government relations director of the Tennessee Valley Public Power Association, Inc. in Chattanooga. "Here in the Tennessee Valley, that is a difficult thing for us to broach. So we were not in favor of that particular part of the energy bill, and we were portrayed by the environmental community as being anti-environment. I can understand that. But on another level, we're not anti-environment. There were just things in that bill that were onerous.[35]

"Twenty years ago, our message would have been received better. Over time, environmental reporters have grown much, much more cynical. If you are not pro-environment, you are against mom and apple pie and the American flag. There may be economic and other factors that force you to be opposed to something that on the surface may look like it is good for the environment. But when you dig down a little deeper, it is not as clear. Sometimes the environmental reporter doesn't get beyond the surface. He doesn't dig down and drill down far enough to see where your [industry] perspective is coming from on how this will impact someone beyond the environment."[36]

About 1,000 miles north of Chattanooga, James Gomes spent 15 years as a lobbyist and communicator as president of the Environmental League of Massachusetts. He faced the same technological changes, the same less-experienced reporters. But as the CEO and primary spokesperson for an advocacy group, he had a different perspective on the changes in the environmental communication industry.[37]

"Is it harder to do environmental communication? No, I think it is easier," said Gomes. "The general public's awareness and knowledge about environmental issues lags a bit behind the specialty people—advocates, experts, academics. That's true in any field. But certainly in the last decade there has been an uptick, in my opinion, and I think polling bears it out, in terms of how much people are aware of issues like climate changes and sustainability in general. So when you have background knowledge there, it makes it easier."[38]

Gomes said the Internet and other technological advances "give us more choices about where we get our information and opinions from. There also is more help available, especially for people more interested in an issue. They are more knowledgeable about it than 10 or 20 years ago."[39]

The differing views between Burgess and Gomes may reflect the different types of environmental communicators (one from industry, the other from an advocacy group), different parts of the country and the different experiences of the two men. But their comments also demonstrate the changes and varied challenges that any newcomer faces when entering the field.

There are commonalities between the environmental reporter and the environmental communicator. They both want to disseminate environmental information to the public. There is a long history of environment journalists starting their careers as reporters, working for several years, and then 2, 5, or 10 years later taking a public relations job or public information officer position with an employer interested in environmental communication. Journalists may decry this trend, lamenting about their colleagues "going to the dark side." They may denigrate PIOs as "flacks" and return their telephone calls with a certain disdain. But there is a dance that develops between the reporter and PIO, one built on the mutual need for one another, and usually a shared desire to use the mass media to convey to an audience accurate information on detailed scientific issues. The reporter also benefits from an "information subsidy," receiving free information that the PIO has spent time and money in collecting and supplying at no direct cost to the reporter.

There are clear differences in the roles. The reporter is interested in multiple perspectives. The reporter is fearful that the public relations person is most interested in a single perspective, that of making his or her client look good or be well positioned in a story or issue. But studies have shown that many major stories on the environment originate not with the journalist, but with a PIO, underscoring the need they have for one another.[40]

The Medium Influences the Message

The nature of the medium may influence how environmental stories are covered by reporters. Journalism and mass communication scholars have found systematic variations among reporters working in different media and on different news beats.[41] In the case of television news, a health reporter's decision to cover a story may depend entirely on the availability of video or "humanization opportunities."[42] Michael R. Greenberg, David B. Sachsman, Peter M. Sandman, and Kandice L. Salomone studied network evening news coverage of environmental risk and found that "risk as calculated by scientists had little to do with the amount of coverage provided by the three networks' evening news broadcasts. Instead, the networks appear to be using the traditional journalistic determinants of news plus the broadcast criterion of visual impact to determine the degree of coverage of risk issues." In addition, the researchers concluded that the networks "are also guided in their coverage by geographical factors (such as cost and convenience) much more than by risk, and apparently sometimes more than by their own broadcast news values."[43]

Size Matters

Research on the health/medical beat found that size matters; some larger markets even employed physicians to report health information.[44] "Specialists in politics…environment and medicine, among other topics, are generally found on the larger newspapers, those with staff—budgets—ample enough to afford them," explain M.L. Stein, Susan Paterno, and R. Christopher Burnett.[45] A number of studies appear to support the conclusion that large newspapers are better (in quality) than small papers.[46] As Leo Bogart concludes, "large papers have the resources to hire and nurture outstanding journalistic talent, to provide the organizational support and the relief from deadline pressures that permit reporters to investigate complex subjects, and to make space available for the full-scale coverage that defies the ordinary limitations of the newshole."[47]

Gatekeepers of Science, Risk, and Technology

The news media serve as gatekeepers and the primary brokers of information on science, risk, hazards, and technology.[48] Communicating with the public by way of science reporters, health reporters, or environmental journalists presumably enhances public understanding and affects the content of mediated messages.[49] Dorothy Nelkin pointed out that medical researchers and other scientists rely on the media to get news of their work to the public, the symbiotic relationship between the media and scientists ultimately shaping what and how much the public knows.[50] According to Nelkin:

> The actual influence of the press…will vary with the selective interest and experience of readers. In esoteric areas of science and technology where readers have little direct information or preexisting knowledge to guide an independent evaluation (e.g., the effect of fluorocarbons on the ozone in the atmosphere), the press, as the major source of information, in effect defines the reality of the situation for them. During the period of maximum press coverage of the ozone controversy, for example, 73.5 percent of the general public had heard about this highly technical issue, previously remote from their experience, for the first time in the press.[51]

The interface of experts and journalists is often complicated by disciplinary barriers and the fragmentation of knowledge within the scientific community.[52] David Suzuki faults narrow training within the sciences and notes, "Unfortunately, the public receives science messages in a disjointed and disconnected way."[53]

The 1995 International Social Survey polled citizens in 20 countries on knowledge of the environment and what affects it, ranking the U.S. public in seventh place.[54] The 2002 report of the Pew Research Center for the People and the Press on what Americans feel about science indicated a very high level of interest: 92 percent reported they were interested and 72 percent said they thought science was beneficial. However, only 30 percent felt they understood the scientific process and only 14 percent felt well informed. Earlier research (in 2001) indicated that people got their general information about science and technology primarily from television (44 percent), newspapers (18 percent), magazines (16 percent), the Internet (9 percent), and books (2 percent). That means 89 percent of science information arrived by way of the media; the remainder came from family, friends, or other sources.[55]

More recently, the National Science Board found that while "more Americans select television as their primary source of science and technology information than any other medium...the Internet ranks second...and its margin over other sources is large and growing."[56] The board found that "more than half of Americans choose the Internet as their main information source [about specific scientific issues]."[57] But "Internet users do not always assume that online science and technology information is accurate."[58] The board reported that "the environment ranks somewhere in the middle among 12 issues."[59] It noted that "in 2007, 43% of Americans expressed strong concern about the environment, up from 35% in 2005."[60]

Pew researchers in 2004 found that nearly half of the 547 national and local print, online, and broadcast journalists surveyed were pessimistic about the quality of current journalism and felt news had become thinner and shallower. Some 80 percent of the sampled reporters from a range of national news outlets complained that media are paying too little attention to complex stories, an obvious category for most science or environment stories, yet they dismissed the suggestion that media overall were too cynical. Print reporters were twice as likely as broadcasters to see themselves in the traditional watchdog role.[61]

Research aimed at demonstrating the processes and effectiveness of environment reporting has been developing since the 1970s.[62] Anders

Hansen edited a compilation of work, primarily from European and Canadian researchers, that offered insights into how environmental journalism in the international arena impacted—and was impacted by—the overall environmental agenda.[63] *Environment Reporting in the 21st Century*, as a sequel to Hansen's efforts and as an extension of the longitudinal research of David H. Weaver and G. Cleveland Wilhoit about American journalists,[64] should prove useful in understanding this specialty beat and those who cover environment issues for public consumption.[65]

Environmental Risk Reporting

There is a need for more and better environmental risk reporting. Greenberg, Sachsman, Sandman, and Salomone found, "In their coverage of environmental risk the networks are guided more by the traditional determinants of news and availability of dramatic visual images than by the scientific risk of the situation involved. They are also guided in their coverage by geographical factors (such as cost and convenience) much more than by risk, and apparently sometimes more than by their own broadcast news values."[66] Sandman, Sachsman, Greenberg, and Gochfeld analyzed the content of environmental stories considered by their newspaper editors to be the very best. The experts "felt very strongly that environmental risk is not covered as much as it should be…that the risk information which needed to be talked about in environmental articles was simply not there."[67] The authors concluded: "Reporters should avoid treating environmental risk as a dichotomy that either 'is' or 'is not.' The important questions for public understanding and public policy are how much risk, under what circumstances, and with what degree of certainty."[68]

A wide range of influences potentially have an impact on environment reporting, including the impact of community structures on local news coverage,[69] the effects of how environmental messages are framed in news stories,[70] and agenda setting for the issue of environmental pollution.[71] Journalists' personal agendas—or risk predispositions—are relevant to the news judgments they make. The current study analyzes the attitudes of those newspaper and television journalists who are assigned to the environment beat, full-time and part-time, and are most likely to cover risk in their reporting.[72]

Do environment reporters exaggerate environmental risks, excessively frightening their readers and viewers? Greenberg, Sachsman, Sandman, and Salomone noted that "journalistic news values focus reporters on events rather than issues, and on the spectacular rather than the chronic" and concluded that "the public's conception of risk is almost certainly distorted by television's focus on catastrophes and its dependence on films."[73]

Commentary: Should Reporters Use Risk as a Determinant of Environmental Coverage?

Should reporters use the scientific concept of degree of risk as a determinant of environmental coverage? Traditionally, journalists define news in terms of timeliness, proximity, human interest, prominence, and consequence (importance).[74] For journalists, risk is part of the news value of consequence. Some scientists argue that reporters should adopt risk as a standard of environmental news. They say that the only journalistic news value that really matters—in scientific terms—is consequence.

Reporters and scientists differ from each other in many ways. They studied different things in school. They adopted disparate goals and even value systems, causing them to view the world differently. For journalists, something is newsworthy if it happens today, nearby, if it is interesting, if it happens to a celebrity, and if it is important. And for many media, if it happens to a celebrity and is interesting, it need not be of any real consequence.

Reporters generally apply the same standards to science reporting that they do to Hollywood or sports reporting. In fact, the two biggest stories on AIDS concerned movie star Rock Hudson and basketball star Magic Johnson. These stories had great journalistic value, but they seemed—to scientists—to be approaching science backwards, in terms of celebrity and human interest.

In the 1980s, when scientists discussed mass media coverage of environmental issues, the discussion was not always complimentary. If scientists from industry, government, and universities could agree on anything, it was that journalists needed help. In 1985, the newly formed National Science Foundation Industry/University Cooperative Center for Research in Hazardous and Toxic Substances (now the Hazardous Substance Management Research Center) at the New Jersey Institute of Technology began funding a project proposed by journalism professors and scientists to teach journalists about risk assessment. The Environmental Risk Reporting Project took place at Rutgers University and the University of Medicine & Dentistry of New Jersey–Robert Wood Johnson Medical School from 1985 to 1990. The project's underlying assumption was that environmental and health journalism would be improved if reporters thought—like scientists—in terms of the degree of risk and if environmental news stories concentrated on the issue of risk.

This five-year effort of the Rutgers group (so-called by Victor Cohn in Reporting on Risk in 1990[75]) was very successful in determining how reporters cover the environment. It was generally successful in teaching journalists how to improve their coverage of the environment. It was even fairly successful in teaching reporters about environmental risk and risk assessment. But its continuing education efforts convinced very few journalists to adopt risk as a basic news value in environmental reporting.

Risk matters to journalists when a situation is very risky and thus of great consequence. Situations of low risk are considered not important and thus not worthy of coverage. Most journalists do not know how to deal with all those degrees of risk between risky and not risky.[76]

The Rutgers group went so far as to make an alternative recommendation regarding improving environmental reporting, one aimed at the sources of news:

> The more productive approach in the long run may be to teach news sources to better understand and deal more effectively with the media.... Environmental news sources who empathize with journalists and are willing to teach reporters about their specific fields can help make mass media coverage of environmental risk as accurate and professional as the American public deserves.[77]

Is Risk a Scientific Standard or a Political Argument?

The journalism professors and scientists who made up the Rutgers group were operating from a basic assumption that an environmental story, and more specifically an environmental risk story (a story that involves an environmental health risk), is a science story. Many of the environmental writers in the 1960s and 1970s were science writers, and it is still common for the environment to be linked to the science beat, along with health and medicine. Science writers generally seem to think that is the way it should be, and many scientists probably agree since they often argue that environmental reporters should have some scientific background.

But the perspective of science is not the only possible or even meaningful way to view issues involving the environment or environmental risk. Today's environmental story is a political, economic, energy, and transportation story as well as a scientific story. It is an urban and suburban story as well as an outdoor story. It attracts backpackers, political investigative reporters, and scientists alike.

From the founding of our first national parks and wilderness areas, the story of the environment has been a political story. When we talk about grazing rights, the introduction of wolves, or the cutting of trees, we have a political story that is also an economic story. But the environment means more to us than just a political, economic, and scientific story. In Landscape and Memory, British-born historian Simon Schama discusses the aesthetic, mythic, philosophical, cultural, and even religious relationship we have with the environment:

> It was an act of Congress in 1864 that established Yosemite Valley as a place of sacred significance for the nation, during the war which marked the moment of Fall in the American Garden. Nor could the wilderness venerate itself. It needed hallowing visitations from New England preachers like Thomas Starr King, photographers like Leander Weed, Eadweard Muybridge, and Carlton Watkins, painters in oil like Bierstadt and Thomas Moran, and painters in prose like John Muir to represent it as the holy park of the West; the site of a new birth; a redemption for the national agony; an American re-creation. The strangely unearthly topography of the place...lent itself perfectly to this vision of a democratic terrestrial paradise.[78]

The environmental movement originally was a conservation movement with a vision very much that of John Muir and the photographs of Ansel Adams. By the early 1960s, however, as Philip Shabecoff writes in *A Fierce Green Fire*, "environmentalism was a disjointed, inchoate impulse; a revolution waiting for a manifesto.... Was the cause love of nature or fear of pollution? Do we need to protect wildlife or is it human beings that are at risk?"[79]

The manifesto for modern environmentalism—and for environmental journalism, for that matter—was written by marine biologist Rachel Carson and published in 1962. In *Silent Spring*, Carson[80] wrote about pollution and the chemicals she called the "elixirs of death," and the "environmental revolution" of the 1960s and 1970s was on its way.[81]

The 1980s saw the rise of the environmental justice movement in small, local groups around the country. Their supporters argued that the nation's poor people and people of color in cities and rural areas suffered more than others from the effects of pollution. "Now the environment story is the urban story," says veteran reporter Paul MacClennan, who started writing a regular environmental column for the *Buffalo News* in 1970.[82]

The environmental justice movement is all about health risk, from lead paint to air and water pollution. At first, some leaders of traditional environmental groups did not seem to appreciate the connection between Rachel Carson's concept of environmental risk and the environmental justice concern for risk, but by the 1990s, most environmental groups had adopted the arguments of the environmental justice movement.

Another "movement" was developing in the 1980s: the "wise use movement." "Wise use" proponents argued that nature could best be preserved through the careful use of natural resources. Farmers, ranchers, loggers, and miners now preached "wise use" when they faced off against traditional conservationists in the western states.

In the 1990s some politicians and corporate leaders voiced their support for a compromise position they called "sustainable development." They argued that industrial development should be encouraged as long as the natural environment was preserved. Although this sounded a lot like wise-use philosophy, the players were different—President Clinton's Council on Sustainable Development rather than wise-use western Republicans. Environmental activists who rejected wise use as an anticonservation argument listened carefully to Vice President Gore's call for sustainable development.

The environmental debate in the 1990s contained a number of conflicting elements that in one way or another were related to the concept of risk. While government agencies continued to set environmental standards based on the government's analysis of existing science, some politicians and industry leaders took the concept of degree of risk one step further, linking risk to cost-benefit analysis. They said that since risk varied by degree, cost should be factored into the setting of environmental standards so long as the benefits were not greatly altered. The automobile industry, for example, argued that existing environmental standards were sufficient and that stricter air pollution standards would be extremely costly while achieving little benefit. Although this was not a new argument in the 1990s, the use of the scientific language of degree of risk to make the cost/environmental-benefit argument appeared to give it a new level of credibility.

Risk was no longer simply a scientific standard. Now it was a political device being used to argue against environmental regulations. Between the Republican congressional victory of 1994 and the reelection of President Clinton in 1996, the language of risk was used by a number of Republican politicians to argue that federal environmental standards should be adjusted to factor in some kind of degree of risk/cost-benefit analysis. Although this probably was not a major issue in Bob Dole's 1996 loss to President Clinton, the Clinton administration took reelection as an environmental victory and proposed a new set of even stricter environmental standards, apparently without consideration of cost.

It is now at least possible to argue that what some viewed as the environmental backlash of the 1990s was partly a result of the adoption of the concept of degree of risk as central to environmental affairs.

In the 1990s, coverage of the environment appeared headed in a number of different directions. Some science-oriented journalists continued to warn their readers of the environmental risks facing the planet. These reporters were in sharp contrast to a new group of writers who defined environmental problems in terms of their degree of risk and then balanced that risk against cost. Some of these journalists seemed to be evaluating the American environment on a mathematical scale in which they judged the quality of the environment to be improving while the cost of the cleanup was rapidly escalating, putting society at large at financial risk. This was the same approach being used by corporate and political interests attempting to rewrite environmental regulations.

The majority of journalists were not focusing on risk. Although many of the news sources that provided environmental information to the media were discussing environmental issues in terms of degree of risk, reporters continued to rely on their own traditional determinants of news. They covered the politics, the economics, the social aspects, and even the racial aspects of environmental stories, in addition to the scientific questions involved. They continued to be event driven and celebrity driven, and they continued to think in terms of today's local news. The television networks also were influenced by the availability of dramatic visual images and by geographical factors such as cost and convenience.[83]

Ten years ago, it seemed that risk was the key to understanding the environment. It appeared that the environmental movement did not place sufficient emphasis on the health risks to people due to pollution, as compared to conservation issues such as endangered species. A concern with risk seemed to be philosophically as well as scientifically correct. Scientists were on the right track, it appeared, when they worried more about environmental issues with significant health risks than they did about those with smaller health risks. Shouldn't every local community think in these same terms? And if so, shouldn't journalists be taught that the environment is about environmental health risk in addition to conservation of nature?

Furthermore, it seemed that this was one area in which all the involved parties could come to agreement. After all, weren't the research efforts at Rutgers being funded by a National Science Foundation Industry/University Cooperative Center that was supported by some thirty companies and large institutions? Here, at least, corporate America was as enlightened as scientific America. The Rutgers group's educational efforts were supported by state and federal government officials, university scientists, and even environmentalists. The team members taught—and really believed—that risk was the most meaningful way to evaluate and report about the environment.

It still is reasonable to feel this way. Scientists continue to value scientific truth and the scientific degree of risk above most things. Perhaps there should be some balance between the cost of cleanup and the chance for some positive results, or even between the need for development and the environmental impact. But it was difficult to prepare for the arguments of the wise-use movement or for those environmental reporters who decided that the environment is cleaning itself up or that nature is so powerful that she cannot really be polluted down to her core. And it was surprising to find people who justified these various points of view by arguing that the environmental risk involved was minimal, if not absent entirely.

The years 1995 and 1996 were very contentious years in environmental affairs. No longer was there much agreement about what the numbers meant either regarding risk or regarding the cost of clean-up. There was, however, one group that remained consistent. The majority of journalists covering environmental affairs never did adopt risk as a basic news value, and so they covered the environment using their traditional standards of timeliness, proximity, human interest, prominence, and consequence (plus cost and convenience and dramatic visual images for network television).[84]

Journalists covered the story in terms of conservative Republican politics versus the environmental movement and the Clinton administration. Their environmental reporting involved many issues (e.g., politics, economics, business, and law) other than science. Reporters basically ignored all those hard-to-understand tables of either risk analysis or cost. While few of them adopted the aesthetic values of the environmental movement, even fewer wrote in terms of wise use or an optimistic environmental future. By hanging on to their own ways of looking at things, the media steered clear of the influence of those involved in environmental affairs. They set their own environmental agendas instead of depending on the value judgments of their sources. The many independent voices of the mass media were maintained.

Environmental politics have calmed down since the election of 1996. Nowadays, politicians on both sides of the fence say they are concerned with the environment. In the 1998 elections, voters across the nation approved almost three-fourths of the state and local environmental initiatives on the ballot.[85]

The economics of the environment remains a major issue, and reporters and editors today generally appear to be conscious of the environmental aspects of many of their most frequently covered stories—from business, land use, and zoning, to energy, transportation, and accidents involving spills.[86]

Most agree that the environmental beat is one of the most difficult to cover because it is a highly specialized science beat and a complicated political, social, and economic story. At the 1998 national conference of the Society of Environmental Journalists, the session on "writing about risk" was well attended, while the program on the economics of emissions trading apparently confused members of the audience.

Small wonder that reporters tend to fall back on the standards for news they learned in journalism school. Timeliness, proximity, human interest, prominence, and consequence have worked well in the past and will continue to determine news coverage in the future. Journalists are not about to adopt degree of risk as a determinant of environmental coverage, and news sources who wish to get their message across would be well advised to tell their stories in journalistic terms rather than in parts per billion.

David B. Sachsman

This commentary was published by Science Communication in 1999.[87]

A Protocol for Ethical Reporting

JoAnn Myer Valenti and Lee Wilkins offered a protocol for ethical reporting of risk to improve public understanding of science and environment issues in the news.[88] Valenti later examined ethical decision making among members of the Society of Environmental Journalists when covering risk and found that extrinsic values such as what's legal and peer evaluation (the opinions of fellow workers) were the major factors in how environment reporters made ethical decisions.[89] When journalists fail to cover risk information completely and accurately, Valenti said, "the consequence is misunderstanding and poor judgments" by readers and viewers.[90]

Other factors also may help explain variations in risk assessment stories. Paul Slovic, Melissa L. Finucane, Ellen Peters, and Donald C. MacGregor stressed the importance of affect, "how we infuse needed 'doses of feeling' into circumstances where lack of experience may otherwise leave us too 'coldly rational.'"[91] Researchers recognized the importance of affect in risk decision making early on. Robert Zajonc argued that affective reactions are often an individual's first reactions.[92] Such reactions occur automatically to guide information processing and judgment. Mary Anne Ferguson, JoAnn Myer Valenti, and Geetu Melwani tested the effectiveness of mediated health risk messages and found significant effects resulting from the receiver's risk-taking predisposition.[93] The attributed source of the message, the perceived target or potential victim of the threat, and the medium of delivery interacted to impact the intended behavioral response. Those who design risk messages as persuasion, such as public relations practitioners, may take into consideration such psychological preconditioning. However, journalists' training to seek out and report events and reactions may offer an exemplary model of how their readers, viewers or listeners ultimately navigate through complex, uncertain, and generally unresolved information. Journalistic training develops a professional "gut instinct" or what Slovic et al. might label the ultimate, risk judgment pooled reaction, based in part on affect and informed by learned reporting skills.[94]

Objectivity and Advocacy

Business advocates have complained that reporters have taken a pro-environment viewpoint on many issues that could affect business, including global warming and the proposed Kyoto treaty;[95] pesticide usage on produce;[96] air pollution standards;[97] the health of the national economy;[98] the need for government regulation;[99] and such issues as overpopulation, species extinction, and air and water pollution.[100] Business-related critics have faulted environment reporters for offering a "pervasive pessimism about the future that has become the hallmark of today's environmental orthodoxy"[101] and for preferring liberal activist sources for environmental information rather than conservative sources.[102] Such claims of anti-business bias are not restricted to environmental reporting. Business leaders have complained for decades that reporters, in general, overemphasize negative news in their business coverage.[103]

Bud Ward, the former editor of *Environment Reporter*, argues that environmental journalists need to work hard at battling the public perception that they are advocates:

> Those journalists longing to be…perceived as being more committed to the 'j' than to the 'e' in the term environmental journalism have their work cut out for them. The remedy lies in the most determined, most independent, and most responsible journalism on issues involving natural resources and the environment. It's not an easy road in today's media climate. It's just the only one that has even the faintest chance of working in the long run.[104]

Other journalists feel it is unfair to single out environment reporters and demand that they have no personal opinions or feelings about the subject they cover. Peter Thompson, an independent radio producer, asks:

> Must a business writer declare that he or she is not a capitalist in order to have credibility? Should a political reporter purport to have no opinion on the virtues of democracy as opposed to dictatorship? Must a crime reporter strive not to care about right and wrong? For someone aspiring to work one of these beats to even suggest that they're indifferent or hostile to the basic concerns of the endeavor would guarantee that they don't get the job. And yet on our beat, we are constantly under pressure,

even from within our ranks, to disavow any concern or values associated with what we cover. What's going on here?[105]

There is little agreement by media scholars on what constitutes bias and how it can and should be measured. An overview of early work in the field is offered by Robert A. Hackett, who challenges such long-held assumptions as the news ought to be balanced, the political orientation of journalists is a major cause of news bias, and that political and ideological partisanship are the most important aspects of bias. He asks whether such a bias paradigm is in decline, then offers alternative approaches. He suggests scholars spend more time examining who is making the claims of bias and what is the impact of those claims on news production. He also called for greater examination of the structure of the news gathering process, including criteria of newsworthiness, technological characteristics of each news medium, and the need to package news in a commercially viable manner. Bias studies appear to be more wide-ranging in their methodology today, when such issues are far more visible with the rise in partisan news outlets and technological advances that allow Internet bloggers to analyze news stories almost in real time.[106]

Setting the Environmental Agenda

In summary, here is a working list of those factors that help set the public agenda concerning environmental issues, along with some comments about each:[107]

- **Government**. Government is the number one actor on the environmental stage and the number one source of public communications about the environment. It is also the *official* source of environmental news. When it is not offset by contradictory sources, it plays a powerful role in influencing the public agenda, unless the mass media pull the rug out from under it by focusing their cameras on dying birds or covering a story in crisis terms.
- **Media**. The mass media have the power to define an environmental story in ways that either place it before the public or keep it off the public agenda. The decisions journalists reach are influenced by their news sources, any conflict among their sources, the presence of expert environmental reporters, the traditional news values, the availability of dramatic pictures, and practical factors such as cost and convenience.
- **Specialized environmental reporters**. These journalists are ready and able to help set the environmental agenda, but there are not enough of them to make a great difference, and they too rely on the traditional standards of news.
- **The traditional news values, dramatic pictures, and practical factors.** Journalism is a profession with its own set of rules and the

news media are businesses that seek to attract large audiences while controlling costs. Their adherence to their own professional standards and necessary business decisions helps them keep control of their own agenda.

- **Dramatic visual impact**. Dramatic pictures and the ability to cover live news events make television a uniquely powerful medium, so powerful that a decision to emphasize the human element of a story can affect the public agenda.

- **Geographical factors such as cost and convenience**. The television networks tend to cover those environmental events that are not too far from the normal locations of their camera crews.

- **Big events**. The environment appears to be an event-driven story. Some environmental events seem to be so big or so important that they become the subject of public discussion as soon as they are known. People seem to pay less attention to chronic environmental issues, where there are no acute events.

- **Accumulation of environmental events**. Somehow negative environmental events seem to accumulate in the minds of journalists and the public, eventually putting the environment on the public agenda.

- **Business**. Industry and industry-related groups have been involved in the "great ecological communications war" since the 1960s.

- **Environmental activists**. When environmentalists are on one side and business is on the other, reporters tend to cover the environment by choosing among the conflicting public statements.

- **Conflicting news sources**. The presence of contradictory statements from various sources, even on local environmental issues, provides reporters with the information they need, and tends to keep the power of agenda-setting in the hands of the press.

- **Universities, institutes, and scientific programs**. These institutions, which are centers of environmental learning, have produced many press releases and public statements since the 1970s, but many journalists apparently consider the environment something other than a scientific story. Journalists are interested in really risky environmental situations. They tend to throw up their hands when scientists try to explain more moderate conditions in terms of the scientific degree of risk.[108]

Environment reporters are gatekeepers who decide whether to separate or link news sources and the public. As such, they play a significant role in the agenda-setting process. We need to know who they are, where they work, how they think, and how they react in order to understand how they do their jobs.

Studying Specialized Environment Reporters

This project is a report of a nationwide series of regional studies of environmental journalists conducted over time. This research examined only specialized environment reporters, those journalists who because of their experience, their expertise, or their willingness, regularly wrote about environmental issues or covered an environment beat. In particular, it involved only those specialized environment reporters who were full-time journalists employed by daily newspapers or television stations.[109]

Environment Reporters in the 21st Century is descriptive research. As such, it attempted to answer a number of basic questions:

Who were the environment reporters in the first five years of the 21st century?

Where did they work? For which media? In which states?

How did they differ from the typical American journalist? How well were they educated? Were they younger or older? Were they more or less experienced? What, if any, were their political leanings?

What did they see as the key elements of environment news? Who were their news sources? What prevented them from doing a better job? Did they view their editors as supportive? What did they think of their jobs and about the way other reporters cover the environment? How did they balance the journalistic goal of objectivity with any personal feelings they had toward protecting the environment?[110]

The context for this study derives from Professors Weaver and Wilhoit, who conducted major studies of the American journalist in 1982, 1992, and 2005.[111] These nationwide surveys provide excellent baseline data and a proven survey instrument. This study of environment reporters in the first five years of the 21st century was designed, in part, to determine how environment journalists compared to Weaver and Wilhoit's baseline data for all journalists. Just as earlier studies of American journalists have provided a record that helps us understand the realities of news professionals, this work offers a layer of findings about those specialists who reported on the environment during a particular slice in time. Such research about journalists, their attitudes about what they do, and why they choose to specialize is useful both to the history of the profession and in order to move beyond anecdotal and stereotypic generalizations.[112]

Notes

1. Earlier versions of elements of this chapter were originally written by the authors and published in:
   David B. Sachsman, James Simon, and JoAnn Myer Valenti, "Risk and the Environment Reporters: A Four-Region Analysis," *Public Understanding of Science* 13 (2004): 399-416.

David B. Sachsman, James Simon, and JoAnn Myer Valenti, "Regional Issues, National Norms: A Four-Region Analysis of U.S. Environment Reporters," *Science Communication* 28 (2006): 93-121.

David B. Sachsman, James Simon, and JoAnn Myer Valenti, "The Environment Reporters of New England," *Science Communication* 23 (2002): 410-41.

David B. Sachsman, James Simon, and JoAnn Myer Valenti, "Environment Reporters and U.S. Journalists: A Comparative Analysis," *Applied Environmental Education and Communication* 7 (2008): 1-19.

David B. Sachsman, James Simon, and JoAnn Myer Valenti, "Wrestling with Objectivity and Fairness: U.S. Environment Reporters and the Business Community," *Applied Environmental Education and Communication* 4 (2005): 363-73.

The final, definitive versions of the papers published in *Public Understanding of Science* and *Science Communication* have been published by SAGE Publications Ltd./SAGE Publications, Inc. All rights reserved.

2.   Hillier Krieghbaum, "The Background and Training of Science Writers," *Journalism Quarterly* 17 (1940): 15-18.

3.   Conrad J. Storad, "Who Are the Metropolitan Daily Newspaper Science Journalists, and How Do They Work?" *Newspaper Research Journal* 6 (1984): 39-48.

4.   Sachsman, Simon, and Valenti, "Regional Issues, National Norms," 94.

5.   Marcel C. LaFollette, *Pragmatic Popularization: Historical Perspectives on Media Presentation of Engineering Research,* paper presentation, American Association for the Advancement of Science, Seattle, WA, February 2004.

6.   David B. Sachsman, "Public Relations Influence on Environmental Coverage (in the San Francisco Bay Area)," (Ph.D. diss., Stanford University, 1973).

Sachsman, Simon, and Valenti, "Regional Issues, National Norms," 94-95.

7.   Sachsman, "Public Relations Influence on Environmental Coverage (in the San Francisco Bay Area)."

8.   Sachsman, Simon, and Valenti, "Regional Issues, National Norms," 95.

9.   David B. Sachsman, "An Early History of Environmental Reporting and Public Relations," *SEJournal* 12 (2002): 1, 14-15.

10.   David Mark Rubin and David Peter Sachs, *Mass Media and the Environment*, Vol. II, report, National Science Foundation Grant GZ-1777, Stanford, CA, September 1971.

11.   John E. Marston, *The Nature of Public Relations* (New York: McGraw-Hill Book Company, Inc., 1963): 207-09.

12.   Russell Wilks, "A Rubber Research Lab Moves into a Small Town," in *Public Relations Ideas in Action*, ed. Allen H. Center (New York: McGraw-Hill Book Company, Inc., 1957): 63-66.

13.   Richard W. Darrow, *Communications in an Environmental Age*, address, 1971 Economic Council of the Forest Products Industry, Phoenix, AZ, January 15, 1971 (New York: Hill and Knowlton, Inc., 1971): 11.

14.   Paul Burton, *Corporate Public Relations* (New York: Reinhold Publishing Corporation, 1966): 207-08.

15.   Walter J. Hickel, "The Making of a Conservationist," *Saturday Review*, October 2, 1971, 65.

16.   Darrow, *Communications in an Environmental Age*, 18.

17.   Sachsman, Simon, and Valenti, "The Environment Reporters of New England," 411.

18.   Jane Delano Brown, Carl Bybee, Stanley Wearden, and Dulcie Straughan, "Invisible Power: Newspaper News Sources and the Limits of Diversity," *Journalism Quarterly* 63 (1986): 45-54.

Herbert Gans, *Deciding What's News* (New York: Random House, 1979).

Michael R. Greenberg, Peter M. Sandman, David. B. Sachsman, and Kandice L. Salomone, "Network Television News Coverage of Environmental Risks," *Environment* 31 (1989): 16-20, 40-44.

Stephen Lacy and David C. Coulson. "Comparative Case Study: Newspaper Source Use on the Environmental Beat," *Newspaper Research Journal* 21 (2000): 13-25.

Sachsman, "Public Relations Influence on Environmental Coverage," 54-60.

Leon V. Sigal, *Reporters and Officials*, (Lexington, MA: D.C. Health, 1973).

Claire E. Taylor, Jung-Sook Lee, and William R. Davie, "Local Press Coverage of Environmental Conflict," *Journalism and Mass Communication Quarterly* 77 (2000): 175-92.

JoAnn Myer Valenti, "Reporting Hantavirus: The Impact of Cultural Diversity in Environmental and Health News," in *Cultural Diversity and the U.S. Media*, eds. Yahya R. Kamalipour and Theresa Carilli, (New York: SUNY Press, 1998): 231-44.

JoAnn Myer Valenti. "Commentary: How Well Do Scientists Communicate to Media?" *Science Communication* 21 (1999): 172-78.

JoAnn Myer Valenti. "A Review of the President's Council on Sustainable Development (U.S.): Building Networks, Throwing Pebbles at a Goliath Media," in *Communicating Sustainability*, ed. Walter Leal Filho, (Bern: Peter Lan Scientific Publishers, 2000): 121-33.

JoAnn Myer Valenti. "Improving the Scientist/Journalists Conversation," *Science and Engineering Ethics* 6 (2000): 543-48.

19.   Ronald P. Lovell, *Reporting Public Affairs: Problems and Solution,* 2nd ed. (Prospect Heights, IL: Waveland, 1993).

20.   Sachsman et al., "Improving Press Coverage of Environmental Risk," 283-96.

21.   Sachsman, Simon, and Valenti, "The Environment Reporters of New England," 411.

22.   Sachsman, "Public Relations Influence on Environmental Coverage."

23.   Bud Ward, "The Environment Beat Bounces Back," *SEJournal* 11 (2001): 1, 12-14.

24.   The Missouri Group, *News Reporting and Writing*, 6th ed, (Boston: Bedford/St. Martin's, 1999).

Ralph S. Izard, Hugh M. Culbertson, and Donald A. Lambert, *Fundamentals of News Writing*, 6th ed., (Dubuque, IA: Kendall/Hunt, 1999).

Sachsman, Simon, and Valenti, "The Environment Reporters of New England," 411-12.

25.   Joseph A. Davis, "Point Source: Environment Beat Sprawls, Grows," *Environment Writer* 13 (2001): 1-2.

JoAnn Myer Valenti, "Ethical Decision Making in Environmental Communication," *Journal of Mass Media Ethics* 13 (1995): 219-31.

Sachsman et al., "Improving Press Coverage of Environmental Risk," 283-96.

Sachsman, "Public Relations Influence on Environmental Coverage."

26.   James Bruggers, "Our Beat is a Different Ball Game," *SEJournal* 8 (1998): 17.

27.   Sachsman, Simon, and Valenti, "The Environment Reporters of New England," 412.

28.   Personal interview with Judy Fahys conducted by JoAnn Myer Valenti on May 15, 2007. Unrelated to the survey.

29.   Oscar Gandy, *Beyond Agenda Setting: Information Subsidies and Public Policy* (Norwood, NJ: Ablex, Publishers, 1982): 8, 30, 64-70.

Patricia A. Curtin, "Reevaluating Public Relations Information Subsidies: Market-Driven Journalism and Agenda-Building Theory and Practice," *Journal of Public Relations Research* 11, 1 (1999): 54.

30.   David B. Sachsman, "Public Relations Influence on Coverage of Environment in San Francisco Area," *Journalism Quarterly* 53.1 (1976): 54-60.

31.   Andrea H. Tanner, "Agenda Building, Source Selection, and Health News at Local Television Stations: A Nationwide Survey of Local Television Health Reporters," *Science Communication* 25 (2004): 350-63.

32.   Ibid.

33.   Sachsman, Simon, and Valenti, "Regional Issues, National Norms," 95.

34.   Phillip Burgess, personal interview conducted by James Simon, September 3, 2008.

35.   Ibid.

36.   Ibid.

37.   James Gomes, personal interview conducted by James Simon, August 14, 2008.

38.   Ibid.

39.   Ibid.

40.   David B. Sachsman, "Public Relations Influence on Coverage of Environment in San Francisco Area," *Journalism Quarterly* 53.1 (1976): 54-60.

41.   Wolfram Peiser, "Setting the Journalist Agenda: Influences from Journalists' Individual Characteristics and from Media Factors," *Journalism and Mass Communication Quarterly* 72 (2000): 271-84.

42.   Tanner, "Agenda Building, Source Selection, and Health News," 350-63.

43.   Michael R. Greenberg, Peter M. Sandman, David B. Sachsman, and Kandice L. Salomone, "Risk, Drama and Geography in Coverage of Environmental Risk by Network TV," *Journalism Quarterly* 66 (1989): 267-76.

Sachsman, Simon, and Valenti, "Risk and the Environment Reporters: A Four-Region Analysis," 400.

44.   Gary Schwitzer, "The Magical Medical Media Tour," *JAMA* 267 (1994): 1969-72.

45.   Mike Stein, Susan Paterno, and R. Christopher Burnett, *Newswriter's Handbook: An Introduction to Journalism* (Ames, IA: Blackwell Publishing, 2006): 237.

46.   Brian Logan and Daniel Sutter, "Newspaper Quality, Pulitzer Prizes, and Newspaper Circulation," *Atlantic Economic Journal* 32 (2004): 100-12.

Philip Meyer and Koang-Hyub Kim, "Quantifying Newspaper Quality: 'I Know It When I See It,'" paper presentation, Newspaper Division, Association for Education in Journalism and Mass Communication, Kansas City, MO, July 2003.

George Gladney, "Newspaper Excellence: How Editors of Small & Large Papers Judge Quality," *Newspaper Research Journal* 11 (1990): 58-72.

47.   Leo Bogart, "Reflections on Content Quality in Newspapers." *Newspaper Research Journal* 25 (2004): 40-53.

Sachsman, Simon, and Valenti, "Regional Issues, National Norms," 96-97.

48.   Susanna Hornig, "Science Stories: Risk, Power and Perceived Emphasis," *Journalism Quarterly* 67 (1990): 767-76.

Eleanor Singer and Phyllis Endrey, "Reporting Hazards: Their Benefits and Costs," *Journal of Communication* 37 (1987): 10-27.

Paul Slovic, "Perceptions of Risk," *Science* 236 (1987): 280-85.

49.   JoAnn M. Valenti, "Improving the Scientist/Journalists Conversation," *Science and Engineering Ethics* 6 (2000): 543-48.

50.   Dorothy Nelkin, *Selling Science: How the Press Covers Science and Technology* (New York: Freeman, 1995).

51. Dorothy Nelkin, *Selling Science* (New York: W. H. Freeman, 1987), 77.
     Sachsman, Simon, and Valenti, "Regional Issues, National Norms," 96.
52. Fotis C. Kafatos and Thomas Eisner, "Unification in the Century of Biology," *Science* 303 (2004): 1257.
53. David Suzuki, "A Look at World Parks," *Science* 301 (2003): 1289.
     Sachsman, Simon, and Valenti, "Regional Issues, National Norms," 96.
54. "Environmental Knowledge Gap," *Science* 268 (1995): 647.
55. Pew Research Center for the People and the Press, *The State of the News Media 2002: An Annual Report on American Journalism* (Washington, DC: 2002), http://www.stateofthenewsmedia.org/journalist_survey.html. [no longer available at this address]
56. National Science Board. *Science and Engineering Indicators 2008. Science and Engineering Indicators* Two volumes: Volume 1, NSB 08-01; Volume 2, NSB 08-01A, (Arlington, VA: National Science Foundation: 2008): 7-3, 7-4.
57. Ibid.
58. Ibid.
59. Ibid.
60. Ibid.
61. Pew Research Center, *The State of the News Media 2002.*
     Sachsman, Simon, and Valenti, "Regional Issues, National Norms," 96.
62. Tony Atwater, Michael B. Salwen, and Ronald B. Anderson. "Media Agenda Setting with Environment Issues," *Journalism Quarterly* 62 (1985): 393-97.
     James G. Cantrill, "Communication and Our Environment: Categorizing Research in Environmental Advocacy," *Journal of Applied Communication Research* 21 (1993): 14-15, 66-95.
     Victor Cohn, *Reporting on Risk* (Washington, DC: Media Institute, 1990).
     Sharon M. Friedman, "Two Decades of the Environmental Beat," *Gannett Center Journal* 4 (1990): 17.
     Greenberg et al., "Network Television News Coverage of Environmental Risks," *Environment* 31 (1989): 16-20, 40-44.
     David B. Sachsman, "Public Relations Influence on Coverage of Environment in San Francisco Area," *Journalism Quarterly* 53 (1976): 54-60.
     Claire E. Taylor, Jung-Sook Lee, and William R. Davie, "Local Press Coverage of Environmental Conflict," *Journalism and Mass Communication Quarterly* 77 (2000): 175-92.
     JoAnn M. Valenti, *Ethical Decision Making in Environmental Journalism,* paper presentation, Association for Education in Journalism and Mass Communication, Washington, DC, 1995.
     JoAnn M. Valenti, "Ethical Decision Making in Environmental Communication," *Journal of Mass Media Ethics* 13 (1998): 219-31.
63. Anders Hansen, ed, *The Mass Media and Environmental Issues* (London: Leicester University Press, 1993).
64. David H. Weaver, and G. Cleveland Wilhoit, *The American Journalist in the 1990s: U.S. News People At the End of an Era* (Mahwah, N.J.: Lawrence Erlbaum, 1996).
     Weaver et al., *The American Journalist in the 21st Century: U.S. News People At the Dawn of a New Millennium* (Mahwah, NJ: Lawrence Erlbaum, 2007).
65. Sachsman, Simon, and Valenti, "Regional Issues, National Norms," 96-97.
66. Greenberg, et al., "Risk, Drama and Geography in Coverage of Environmental Risk by Network TV," *Journalism Quarterly* 66 (1989): 267-76.
67. Greenberg et al., "Network Evening News Coverage of Environment Risk," *Risk Analysis* 9 (1989): 125.

68.   Peter M. Sandman, David. B. Sachsman, Michael R. Greenberg, and Michael Gochfeld, *Environmental Risk and the Press* (New Brunswick, NJ: Transaction Books, 1987), 101.
    Sachsman, Simon, and Valenti, "Risk and the Environment Reporters: A Four-Region Analysis," 400.
69.   Robert J. Griffin and Sharon Dunwoody, "Impacts of Information Subsidies and Community Structure on Local Press Coverage and Environmental Contamination," *Journalism and Mass Communication Quarterly* 66 (1995): 275.
70.   Joel J. Davis, "The Effects of Message Framing on Response to Environmental Communications," *Journalism and Mass Communication Quarterly* 72 (1995): 285-99.
71.   Christine R. Ader, "A Longitudinal Study of Agenda Setting for the Issue of Environmental Pollution," *Journalism and Mass Communication Quarterly* 72 (1995): 300-11.
72.   Sachsman, Simon, and Valenti, "Risk and the Environment Reporters: A Four-Region Analysis," 400.
73.   Greenberg et al., "Network Television News Coverage of Environmental Risks," *Environment* 31 (1989): 16-20, 40-44.
    Sachsman, Simon, and Valenti, "Risk and the Environment Reporters: A Four-Region Analysis," 400.
74.   Curtis MacDougall, *Interpretative Reporting,* 7th ed. (New York: MacMillan, 1977), 56.
75.   Victor Cohn, *Reporting on Risk,* (Washington, DC: Media Institute, 1990), 61. "Dr. Michael R. Greenberg, Professor of Urban Planning and Public Health; Dr. Peter M. Sandman, Professor of Environmental Journalism and Director, Environmental Communication Research Program, Rutgers University; and Dr. David B. Sachsman, Dean, School of Communications, California State University at Fullerton. For convenience I have referred to them in several instances as 'the Rutgers group' or 'the Rutgers professors,' since Sachsman is a former New Jerseyite. They are authors of two highly recommended manuals."
76.   Sandman et al., *Environmental Risk and the Press*, 99-100.
77.   Sachsman et al., "Improving Press Coverage of Environmental Risk," 295-96.
78.   Simon Schama, *Landscape and Memory* (New York: Alfred A. Knopf, 1995), 7.
79.   Philip Shabecoff, *A Fierce Green Fire* (New York: Hill and Wang, 1993), 106-107.
80.   Rachel Carson, *Silent Spring* (Boston: Houghton Mifflin, 1962, 1987).
81.   Shabecoff, *A Fierce Green Fire*, 107.
82.   David B. Sachsman, "Environmental Beat is Challenging, Changing," *Chattanooga Free Press*, October 18, 1998, 5(B).
83.   Greenberg et al., "Risk, Drama and Geography in Coverage of Environmental Risk by Network TV," *Journalism Quarterly* 66 (1989): 267-76.
84.   Ibid.
85.   "Voters and the Environment," editorial, *New York Times,* November 9, 1998, 28A.
86.   Sachsman, "Environmental Beat is Challenging, Changing," *Chattanooga Free Press*, October 18, 1998, 5B.
87.   David B. Sachsman, "Commentary: Should Reporters Use Risk as a Determinant of Environmental Coverage?" *Science Communication* 21.1 (1999): 88-95.
88.   JoAnn M. Valenti and Lee Wilkins, "An Ethical Risk Communication Protocol for Science and Mass Communication," *Public Understanding of Science* 18 (1995): 177-94.

89. JoAnn M. Valenti, "Ethical Decision Making in Environmental Communication," *Journal of Mass Media Ethics* 13 (1998): 219-31.

90. Ibid., 229.
    Sachsman, Simon, and Valenti, "Risk and the Environment Reporters: A Four-Region Analysis," 400-01.

91. Paul Slovic, Melissa L. Finucane, Ellen Peters, and Donald C. MacGregor, "The Affect Heuristic," in *Heuristics and Biases: The Psychology of Intuitive Judgment*, eds. Thomas Gilovich, Dale Griffin, and Daniel Kahneman (New York: Cambridge University Press, 2002): 39-420.

92. Robert B. Zajonc, "Feeling and Thinking: Preferences Need No Inferences," *American Psychologist* 35 (1980): 151-75.

93. Mary Anne Ferguson, JoAnn Myer Valenti and Geetu Melwani, "Communicating with Risk Takers: A Public Relations Perspective," *Public Relations Research Annual* l3 (1991): 195-224.

94. Paul Slovic, Melissa L. Finucane, Ellen Peters, and Donald C. MacGregor, "Risk as Analysis and Risk as Feelings: Some Thoughts about Affect, Reason, Risk, and Rationality," paper presentation, Annual Meeting of the Society for Risk Analysis, New Orleans, LA, December, 1991.
    Sachsman, Simon, and Valenti, "Risk and the Environment Reporters: A Four-Region Analysis," 401.

95. Media Research Center, Free Market Project (2001, May 7). "Clamoring for Kyoto: The Network's One-Sided Coverage of Global Warming," May 7, 2001. December 20, 2004. http://sercure.mediaresearch.org/specialreports/fmp/2001/globalwarming.html [No longer available at this address]

96. Free Market Project, Media Research Center, "Media Aid Environmental Hit Job on ABC Reporter," *MediaNomics* 8 (2000).

97. L. Brent Bozell, III. "Flat Earth Environmental Reporting." Syndicated Column, *Creators Syndicate*, July 1997. December 20, 2004. http://www.mediaresearch. org/BozellColumns/newscolumn/1997/coll9970710.asp. [No longer available at this address]

98. "How Media Bias Colors the News," *Investor's Business Daily*. Lexis Nexis, October 25, 2004. December 16, 2004. http://web.lexisnexis.com/universe/document?_m=499e136769c770d6&_md5=36ee9fcba09d7bab4533aac925684416. [No longer available at this address]

99. S. Robert Lichter, Stanley Rothman and Linda S. Lichter, *The Media Elite* (Bethesda, MD: Adler & Adler, 1986).

100. Stephen F. Hayward, "Mixed Atmospheres: Good and Bad Environmental Reporting Swirl Together," *The American Enterprise* (July/August, 2003): 36-38.

101. Ibid., 36.
    See also: Bjørn Lomborg, *The Skeptical Environmentalist: Measuring the Real State of the World* (Cambridge University Press, 2001).
    Julian L. Simon, "Resources, Population, Environment: An Oversupply of False Bad News." *Science*, New Series, 208 (Jun. 27, 1980): 1431-1437.

102. S.Robert Lichter, Linda S. Lichter and Stanley Rothman, *Watching America* (New York: Prentice Hall, 1991).

103. Lisa Barchie, *Business and the Media* (Columbia, MO: Freedom of Information Center FOI-463, 1982).
    Robert K. Goidel and Ronald E. Langley, "Media Coverage of the Economy and Aggregate Economic Evaluations: Uncovering Evidence of Indirect Media Effects," *Political Research Quarterly* 48.2 (1995).

Raphael, L. Tokunaga, and C. Wai, "Who is the Real Target?: Media Response to Controversial Investigative Reporting on Corporations," *Journalism Studies* 5.2 (2004).

Sachsman, Simon, and Valenti, "Wrestling with Objectivity and Fairness: U.S. Environment Reporters and the Business Community," 363.

104.   Bud Ward, "Just Thinking." *Environment Writer* November, 2004. December 20, 2004. http://www.environmentwriter.org/resources/think/1104_think.htm.

Sachsman, Simon, and Valenti, "Wrestling with Objectivity and Fairness: U.S. Environment Reporters and the Business Community," 364.

105.   Peter Thompson, "A Business Writer Can be a Capitalist, so…," Excerpt from "Are We Fooling Ourselves," *SEJournal* 12.4 (Spring 2003): 23.

106.   Robert A. Hackett, "Decline of a Paradigm? Bias and Objectivity in News Media Studies," *Critical Studies in Mass Communication* 1.3 (1984): 229-59.

Sachsman, Simon, and Valenti, "Wrestling with Objectivity and Fairness: U.S. Environment Reporters and the Business Community," 364.

107.   David B. Sachsman, *Who Sets the Environmental Agenda?* Paper presentation, International Congress on Hazardous Waste: Impact on Human and Ecological Health, 1995.

108.   Ibid., 14-16.

109.   Sachsman, Simon, and Valenti, "The Environment Reporters of New England," 412.

110.   Sachsman, Simon, and Valenti, "The Environment Reporters of New England," 412-13.

111.   Weaver et al., *The American Journalist in the 21st Century: U.S. News People At the Dawn of a New Millennium.*

112.   Sachsman, Simon, and Valenti, "The Environment Reporters of New England," 413.

2

Studying Specialized
Environment Reporters[1]

This book reports the findings of a nationwide series of regional studies of environment reporters conducted during the first five years of the
21st century. This research examined specialized environment reporters,
those journalists who because of their expertise, their experience, or their
willingness, regularly wrote about environmental issues or covered an
environment beat. In particular, this research involved those specialized
environment reporters who were full-time journalists employed by daily
newspapers or television stations in 2000-2005.[2]

This effort was inspired, in part, by the work done for more than
two decades by research teams headed by David H. Weaver of Indiana
University. The teams conducted comprehensive national studies of U.S.
journalists every 10 years.[3] The statistical profiles, each drawn from a
sample of more than 1,000 working journalists, offer rich data showing
how journalists have changed in terms of demographics, attitudes, and
work routines. While the samples were large enough to allow the researchers to generalize about subgroups such as newspaper and television
reporters, the samples could not offer insights into specialized subgroups
such as beat reporters.[4]

From 2000 to 2005, the authors of this book sought to remedy the lack
of baseline data about the subgroup of reporters who cover environmental
issues. These journalists provide a vital link between scientists and other
experts studying environmental issues and the general public, who want
to know about the natural world in which they live.[5] Previously, there
had been no major project that looked at the personal characteristics of
environment reporters, their attitudes, and their work routines. This study
sought to fill that gap, both by reporting on those characteristics and
then comparing them, whenever possible, to the national data generated

by the Weaver group. This research provides the baseline data needed for the systematic study of American journalists and specialized reporters.[6] Like most studies based on interview data, it provides information regarding a particular slice in time, information that can be compared with findings in the future.

Our first proposition is that environmental journalists are similar to U.S. journalists in many individual and work-related characteristics, perhaps due in part to the similar backgrounds and basic professional training of most reporters. Likewise, we believe that differences between environment reporters and U.S. journalists in general may relate to variations in their education. Finally, we propose that the larger the newspaper, the more likely it will be to employ one or more specialized environment reporters, suggesting that bigger is better for specialized reporting. As recently as 2006, the *Los Angeles Times* employed "more than two dozen" reporters and editors who specialized in "coverage of science, technology, medicine, or the environment,"[7] and, like the *New York Times*, was a poster child for the concept of bigger is better. While this may no longer be true, since newspapers large and small have been cutting their budgets in recent years, generally speaking, large newspapers appear to have the most specialized reporters. The question here is whether the same concept holds true for the more typical "large" newspaper, with a circulation of more than 60,000.[8]

The American Journalist and the Environment Reporter

The first major national survey of American journalists was done by John W. C. Johnstone and associates at the University of Illinois at Chicago. The 1971 survey was published in 1976 as *The News People: A Sociological Portrait of American Journalists and Their Work* by the University of Illinois Press.[9] David H. Weaver and G. Cleveland Wilhoit continued this landmark project in 1982-83 and 1992. Their work was published as *The American Journalist: A Portrait of U.S. News People and Their Work* in 1986 and as *The American Journalist in the 1990s: U.S. News People at the End of an Era* in 1996. In 2002, Weaver, Randal A. Beam, Bonnie J. Brownlee, Paul S. Voakes, and Wilhoit conducted the most recent survey, which was published as *The American Journalist in the 21st Century: U.S. News People at the Dawn of a New Millennium.*[10]

The 2002 survey, consisting of 97 questions, was completed by 1,149 American journalists working for daily and weekly newspapers, radio and television, news magazines, and wire services, "plus additional separate samples of 315 minority and on-line journalists."[11] "The maximum sampling error at the 95% level of confidence for this main probability sample is plus or minus 3 percentage points."[12] It provides extensive data, including the basic characteristics of U.S. journalists, their education, their media use, their politics, their job satisfaction, and their perceptions of the workplace. The results of the current survey showed some differences from previous findings, including the fact that the average journalist in 2002 was older than in the previous decade. But, overall, the authors concluded, "The picture of U.S. journalists in 2002" is "one marked more by stability than change."[13] According to the survey, the typical American journalist was Caucasian, male, married, and "just over forty."[14] He was a graduate of a public university who was satisfied with his current employment working for a daily newspaper owned by a large corporation. He either majored in journalism or communication (57.7 percent), English (14.9 percent), or a wide variety of other subjects. The physical and biological sciences (including agriculture) were near the bottom of the list with only 2.9 percent.[15]

One might think that reporters assigned to covering a specialized beat like the environment would be more experienced and better educated in their subject areas than the average U.S. journalists described by Weaver. After all, explain M. L. Stein, Susan Paterno, and R. Christopher Burnett, "[S]pecialized journalism is becoming increasingly important to the media and is a goal of many journalists."[16] In the 1960s and 1970s, environment reporting often was a province of the science beat.[17] Twenty years later, when the Society of Environmental Journalists was created, environment reporters came with a variety of different backgrounds, and environmental stories often were also government stories, science stories, health stories, and even business stories.[18] Today, environment reporting tends to be "the chronicling [of] the endless tug of war in politics, economics, and environmental advocacy," says former *Atlanta Constitution* staff reporter and nature writer McKay Jenkins.[19] But science remains fundamental to the environment beat, and so one would hope that environment reporters would differ from other journalists, many of whom apparently spent their college years avoiding science and math.[20] Journalism professor Bernard A. Morris questions whether a traditional journalism school education qualifies reporters to write about health and science, arguing that while "new graduates are prepared to cover simple stories that reflect their undergraduate training," they may not be prepared for coverage of more complex issues.[21] Morris believes that many journalists "take courses in the natural sciences and physical sciences," pointing to "specialized journalism programs sponsored by various foundations at universities across the country."[22] But he concludes that "much more work needs to be done both within journalism and outside."[23]

Science writers had been studied as early as the 1930s.[24] But while modern environment reporters had been described and discussed since the 1970s,[25] there was no thorough data-based statistical analysis of these specialized professionals. More was known about the sources they used[26] than about their demographics or feelings. What was missing was precisely the kind of baseline data and description provided by Weaver and Wilhoit for U.S. journalists in general.[27]

What factors do journalists consider when they are writing environmental stories? How often do they say they use a risk assessment angle compared to other issues? Do environmental journalists differ due to regional differences? From their earliest days in journalism school, reporters are taught which values make a story newsworthy. While the lists of news values may vary, most include timeliness, proximity, prominence, consequence, and human interest. "Nothing is so dead as yesterday's newspaper…or the radio and television newscast of an hour ago," quotes Curtis D. MacDougall in *Interpretative Reporting*.[28] And many newspaper editors consider their essential mission to be local journalism, asking their reporters to find the local angle in national and even international stories.[29]

Scientists and the journalists who cover them often disagree on the framing of stories. The AIDS epidemic became a hot, front-page story when it was revealed that movie star Rock Hudson had contracted the disease. And it reached a larger and younger audience when basketball star Magic Johnson announced that he had tested positive for the HIV antibody. Some scientists were surprised that it took a combination of prominence and human interest to put such an important story on the front page. For scientists, consequence (or importance) is the only news value that really matters, while for journalists it is simply one factor among many.[30]

Many scientists spend much of their careers analyzing risk, but they often must rely on environment reporters to communicate their findings to the general public through newspapers and TV stories. These scientists might benefit from better understanding environment reporters. Do environment reporters consider the risk assessment angle when writing their stories? Are environment reporters concerned that they may be exaggerating environmental risks, excessively frightening their readers and viewers?[31]

Research Questions

Environment Reporters in the 21st Century is descriptive research. This project studied the attitudes, opinions, and demographics of environmental journalists in the United States. It analyzed baseline data collected in a nationwide series of regional studies of newspaper and TV environment reporters. The authors proceeded region by region, not necessarily expecting regional differences, but rather regional similarities that would point to the existence of national standards for environmental journalism. The presence of similarities of responses among regions may be the sign of such national trends, while the presence of regional differences needs to be explained.[32]

This research sought to answer a number of research questions:

Who were the environment reporters in the first five years of the 21st century? Where did they work during the period examined? For which media? In which states? Do newspapers employ more environmental specialists than television stations? Do bigger newspapers have more environment reporters than smaller papers?[33]

Did these environmental journalists differ due to regional differences? How did they differ from the typical American journalist? Were they younger or older? Were they more or less experienced? What, if any, were their political leanings? How were they educated? Are environment reporters journalists first, perhaps due in part to the basic professional education and training received by most journalists? Can differences between environment reporters and other journalists be linked to variations in their education or factors that affected their choice of study?

From what sources do environment reporters get their information? Do environmental journalists in different regions rely on similar news sources?[34]

What do environmental specialists see as the key elements of environment news? How often do environment reporters say they use a risk assessment angle in their stories compared to other issues? Do correlations exist between the use of particular news sources, story frames, or work routines and the use of a risk assessment angle?[35]

What prevents environment reporters from doing a better job? Do they view their editors as supportive? What did they think of their jobs (at the time they were interviewed) and about the way other reporters cover the environment? Do environment reporters believe that environmental journalists generally have overblown environmental risks, unduly alarming the public? Do they think an environmental problem is generally a better news story than an environmental success, and do they feel that environmental journalists generally concentrate far too much on problems and pollution, rather than writing stories to help the public understand research or complex issues?[36]

Should environment reporters work with community leaders to solve environmental problems? How do they balance the journalistic goal of objectivity with any personal feelings they have toward protecting the environment? Are objectivity and advocacy polar opposites that never overlap or are they separate dimensions that can overlap on some issues and in some circumstances?

Method

The lack of previous large-scale demographic studies of environment reporters may be due to a stumbling block in such research: there is no definitive list of these reporters. Many belong to the Society of Environmental Journalists; many do not. Some cover the environment as a beat, on a full-time basis. Other self-identified environment reporters spend most of their time covering a variety of issues and switch to the environment when there is breaking news on the topic.[37]

This study used a variety of existing sources to identify environment reporters, including commercial directories of newspapers and television stations that list reporters in various specialties. The researchers contacted newspapers and television stations, asking to speak to the environment reporter, an editor, or to anyone else who identified themselves as currently working to "cover the environment on a regular basis as part of your reporting duties." All potential reporters were called. They were interviewed if they met one of two criteria listed in a screening question: they covered the environment as a beat; or they covered a variety of issues, including the environment, but wrote about the environment on a regular basis. The interviewers telephoned every U.S. daily newspaper listed in *Editor & Publisher Yearbook* and every television station that had a news director listed in *Broadcasting & Cable Yearbook* (thus trying to exclude from the count all those stations that employed no reporters at all).[38]

The researchers asked environment reporters to identify others at their news organization or at other news outlets who might qualify to be interviewed. The interviewers cast a wide net, seeking to gather information both on specialized beat reporters and those who cover the environment as one of many tasks completed on a given day.[39] The interviewers consisted of the authors, graduate students, and some advanced undergraduates. Consistency and reliability were assured through training, pre-testing, and the use of a fully scripted questionnaire. The complete questionnaire was pre-tested successfully on five current and former environment reporters and editors. The interviewers followed the script and noted the responses on a printed survey form. Later, the data were entered into an SPSS spreadsheet program for analysis. Very few of the interviews were conducted with reporters who were recommended only by an earlier interviewee. In the South, for example, no reporters who were interviewed were recommended only by an interviewee. Each respondent was interviewed by telephone for about 40 minutes. The results of this study are based on these self-reports of the respondents, not on a content analysis of their work. We studied the reporters, not their stories.[40] The reporters were promised confidentiality. Thus, their names are not listed.

The study focused on one region of the country at a time, dividing the nation into seven regions rather than the four regions and nine divisions used by the U.S. Census.[41] The study began in 2000 in New England, where the researchers identified 55 environment reporters. Each of these reporters completed a 40-minute telephone survey interview, resulting in a 100 percent response rate. Interviewers worked their way through the other regions, interviewing 91 of 91 reporters (100 percent) in the Mountain West in 2001; 151 of 158 reporters (95.6 percent) in the South in 2002-03; 116 of 127 reporters (91.3 percent) in the Pacific West in 2002 and 2004-05; 53 of 53 reporters (100 percent) in the Mid Atlantic region in 2003-04; 101 of 117 reporters (86.3 percent) in the Mid Central region in 2004-05; and 85 of 85 reporters (100 percent) in the West Central region in 2004-05. In all, the researchers interviewed 577 of 603 newspaper reporters (95.7 percent) and 75 of 83 television reporters (90.4 percent). There was no evidence that responses varied based on when reporters were interviewed.[42]

Overall, the researchers interviewed 652 of the 686 environment reporters identified, or 95.0 percent. Since the researchers successfully interviewed all but five percent of the subjects they found and since there was no evidence that responses differed due to the year interviewed, it is not unreasonable to treat this research as if it were a national census, rather than a series of regional studies. The results allow the project to report with unusual detail—and without a sampling error—which journalists were environment reporters, where these reporters worked, their personal and job-related characteristics, and how they compared to and differed from U.S. journalists in general.[43]

Does this mean that there were only 686 specialized environment reporters working for daily newspapers and television stations in the United States in 2000-2005? While the study tried to be inclusive (counting, for example, reporters who had just started covering the environment on a regular basis and had not yet done many stories), judgment calls were made that excluded a number of others. And no study conducted over a five-year period by a variety of interviewers can be certain that every callback has been made.

The study excluded those full-time television weather reporters in small markets who also occasionally handled an environment story such as storm damage. It also left out former environment reporters who had recently taken on another assignment. That this category is even mentioned may be a sign of the times. The researchers know a number of journalists who have left the environment beat in recent years for a variety of reasons. In future research, these reporters should be studied to find out why they left the beat. This study focused on current, active, full-time reporters who covered the environment.[44]

In a similar vein, the project left out a number of reporters who were on leave for medical and professional reasons at the time of the interviews. Since the researchers could not determine whether these reporters would have qualified for inclusion in the study, they have not been counted.[45]

The *Christian Science Monitor*, headquartered in Boston and now an online-only newspaper, required special handling due to its national audience. The *Monitor* then employed three environment reporters who only worked part-time for the newspaper. They were excluded due to the study's focus on reporters who work full-time for their media. The paper did have a full-time environment reporter, but that person was stationed in the Rocky Mountain states (as of May 2000) and therefore the reporter's views were not necessarily representative of journalists covering the environment in New England. As a result, the *Monitor* was excluded from the study of New England.[46]

Another special case involved a reporter who worked half time for two affiliated newspapers; he was counted as a reporter for each newspaper in the geographic and circulation breakdowns, but he was counted only once as part of the overall numbers of environment reporters in the region and he was interviewed only once. A different reporter covered the environment in a state other than the home state of the newspaper. This reporter was counted in his home state for questions relating to him personally, but was counted as part of the newspaper's overall count of environment writers in the geographic and circulation breakdowns.[47]

Environment Reporters in the 21st Century is divided into three parts. Chapter 1 presented the history of the environment beat and a review of the literature regarding environment reporting in America. This chapter, Chapter 2, introduces the study conducted by the authors from 2000 to 2005, explaining in detail the methodology involved.

Part II presents the findings of this research. Chapter 3 provides the demographics of environment reporters and compares them to U.S. journalists in general. It also describes where environmental journalists were employed during the time period studied. Chapter 4 provides a window into the attitudes of environment reporters towards their jobs, their employers, and their audiences, while Chapter 5 describes how these reporters cover the environment, which news angles they include in their stories, which sources they use, and whether they are satisfied with the work done by their colleagues. Chapter 6 shows the conflict that exists among environment reporters between those who believe that journalists should never be advocates for the environment or work with the community to solve environmental problems and those who believe they should sometimes be environmental advocates or civic journalists. This fundamental conflict among reporters appears to be more complex than previously acknowledged.

Part III, The Craft: Telling the Environment Story, provides in depth accounts of environment reporters at work, based on the experiences of a number of journalists interviewed after the original study. Were the early years of the 21st century a golden age of environmental reporting, given the cutbacks already occurring? The final chapter in the book, Environment Reporters in a Time of Change, puts this research in historical perspective, viewing it in terms of the economic decline of the newspaper business and of local television news.

Notes

1.   Earlier versions of elements of this chapter were originally written by the authors and published in:

David B. Sachsman, James Simon, and JoAnn Myer Valenti, "Risk and the Environment Reporters: A Four-Region Analysis," *Public Understanding of Science* 13 (2004): 399-416.

David B. Sachsman, James Simon, and JoAnn Myer Valenti, "Regional Issues, National Norms: A Four-Region Analysis of U.S. Environment Reporters," *Science Communication* 28 (2006): 93-121.

David B. Sachsman, James Simon, and JoAnn Myer Valenti, "The Environment Reporters of New England," *Science Communication* 23 (2002): 410-41.

David B. Sachsman, James Simon, and JoAnn Myer Valenti, "Environment

Reporters and U.S. Journalists: A Comparative Analysis," *Applied Environmental Education and Communication* 7 (2008): 1-19.

The final, definitive versions of the papers published in *Public Understanding of Science* and *Science Communication* have been published by SAGE Publications Ltd./SAGE Publications, Inc. All rights reserved.

2.   Sachsman, Simon, Valenti, "The Environment Reporters of New England," 412.

3.   David H. Weaver et al., *The American Journalist in the 21st Century: U.S. News People at the Dawn of a New Millennium* (Mahwah, N.J.: Lawrence Erlbaum, 2007).

David H. Weaver and G. Cleveland Wilhoit, *The American Journalist: A Portrait of U.S. News People and Their Work* (Bloomington: Indiana University Press, 1986).

————, *The American Journalist in the 1990s: U.S. News People at the End of an Era* (Mahwah, NJ: Lawrence Erlbaum, 1996).

4.   Sachsman, Simon, Valenti, "Environment Reporters and U.S. Journalists," 1.

5.   Tony Atwater, Michael B. Salwen, and Ronald B. Anderson, "Media Agenda Setting with Environment Issues," *Journalism Quarterly* 62 (1985): 393-97.

Paul Rogers, "Complexity in Environment Reporting is Critical to Public Decision Making: '...The Craft is Now Firmly Entrenched as a Key Beat in American Journalism,'" *Nieman Reports* 56 (winter 2002): 32.

6.   Sachsman, Simon, Valenti, "Environment Reporters and U.S. Journalists: A Comparative Analysis," 1-2.

7.   Robert Lee Hotz, "Large Newspapers" In *A Field Guide for Science Writers,* eds. Deborah Blum, Mary Knudson, and Robin Marantz Henig (New York: Oxford University Press, 2006), 57.

8.   Sachsman, Simon, Valenti, "Environment Reporters and U.S. Journalists: A Comparative Analysis," 1-2.

9.   John W. C. Johnstone, Edward J. Slawski, and William W. Bowman, *The News People: A Sociological Portrait of American Journalists and Their Work.* (Urbana: University of Illinois Press, 1976).

10.   David H. Weaver, Randal A. Beam, Bonnie J. Brownlee, Paul S. Voakes, and G. Cleveland Wilhoit, *The American Journalist in the 21st Century: U.S. News People at the Dawn of a New Millennium.* (Mahwah, N.J.: Lawrence Erlbaum, 2007).

Sachsman, Simon, Valenti, "Environment Reporters and U.S. Journalists: A Comparative Analysis," 2.

11.   Weaver et al., *The American Journalist in the 21st Century*, 255.

12.   Ibid., 259.

13.   Ibid., 239.

14.   Ibid., 1.

15.   Sachsman, Simon, Valenti, "Environment Reporters and U.S. Journalists," 2.

16.   Meyer L. Stein, Susan F. Parterno, and R. Christopher Burnett, *Newswriter's Handbook: An Introduction to Journalism,* 2nd ed. (Ames, IA: Blackwell Publishing, 2006), 237.

17.   David B. Sachsman, "Public Relations Influence on Environmental Coverage (in the San Francisco Bay Area)" (Ph.D. diss., Stanford University, 1973).

Conrad J. Storad, "Who Are the Metropolitan Daily Newspaper Science Journalists, and How Do They Work?" *Newspaper Research Journal* 6.1 (1984). 39-48.

18.   Bud Ward, "The Environment Beat Bounces Back," *SEJournal* 11 (Spring 2001): 1.

19. Deborah Bloom, Mary Knudson, and Robin M. Henig, eds., *A Field Guide for Science Writers*, 2nd ed. (New York: Oxford University Press, 2006), 229.

20. David B. Sachsman, "Linking the Scientist and the Journalist." In *HazPro '85*. ed. Richard A. Young (Northbrook, IL: Pudvan Publishing Company, 1985), 196-202.

21. Bernard R. Morris, "Are Journalists Qualified to Write About Health and Science?" *Journal of the Mississippi Academy of Sciences* 44.4 (1999): 188.

22. Ibid., 189.

23. Ibid., 189.

Sachsman, Simon, Valenti, "Environment Reporters and U.S. Journalists," 2-3.

24. Hillier Krieghbaum, "The Background and Training of Science Writers," *Journalism Quarterly* 17 (1940).

25. Tony Atwater, Michael B. Salwen, and Ronald B. Anderson, "Media Agenda Setting with Environment Issues," *Journalism Quarterly* 62 (1985).

James G. Cantrill, "Communication and Our Environment: Categorizing Research in Environmental Advocacy," *Journal of Applied Communication Research* 21 (1993).

Victor Cohn, *Reporting on Risk* (Washington, DC: Media Institute, 1990).

Sharon M. Friedman, "Two Decades of the Environmental Beat," *Gannett Center Journal* 4 (1990).

————. "The Third Decade of Environmental Journalism: A Qualitative Review." Paper presented at the Association for Education in Journalism and Mass Communication Conference, Kansas City, MO, August 1, 2003.

Michael R. Greenberg, Peter M. Sandman, David B. Sachsman, and Kandice L. Salomone, "Network Television News Coverage of Environmental Risks," *Environment* 31 (March 1989): 16-20, 40-44.

Anders Hansen, ed. *The Mass Media and Environmental Issues* (London: Leicester University Press, 1993).

David B. Sachsman, "Public Relations Influence on Environmental Coverage (in the San Francisco Bay Area)" (Ph.D. diss., Stanford University, 1973).

————, "Public Relations Influence on Coverage of Environment in San Francisco Area," *Journalism Quarterly* 53 (Spring 1976): 54-60.

————, "The Mass Media 'Discover' the Environment: Influences on Environmental Reporting in the First Twenty Years," in *The Symbolic Earth: Discourse and Our Creation of the Environment*, ed. J. G. Cantrill and C. L. Oravec. (Lexington, K.Y.: The University Press of Kentucky, 1996), 241-56.

Claire E. Taylor, Jung-Sook Lee, and William R. Davie, "Local Press Coverage of Environmental Conflict," *Journalism and Mass Communication Quarterly* 77 (Spring 2000): 175-92.

JoAnn Myer Valenti, "Reporting Hantavirus: The Impact of Cultural Diversity in Environmental and Health News," in *Cultural Diversity and the U.S. Media*, edited by Yahya Kamalipour and Theresa Carilli, 231-44. New York: SUNY Press, 1998.

JoAnn Myer Valenti, and Lee Wilkins, "An Ethical Risk Communication Protocol for Science and Mass Communication," *Public Understanding of Science* 18 (1995).

26. Michael R. Greenberg, Peter M. Sandman, David B. Sachsman, and Kandice L. Salomone, "Network Television News Coverage of Environmental Risks," *Environment* 31 (March 1989): 16-20, 40-44.

Stephen Lacy and David C. Coulson, "Comparative Case Study: Newspaper

Source Use on the Environmental Beat," *Newspaper Research Journal* 21 (winter 2000): 13-25.

David B. Sachsman, "Public Relations Influence on Environmental Coverage (in the San Francisco Bay Area)" (Ph.D. diss., Stanford University, 1973).

Conrad Smith, "News Sources and Power Elites in Coverage of the *Exxon Valdez* Oil Spill," *Journalism Quarterly* 70 (summer 1993): 393-403.

Claire E. Taylor, Jung-Sook Lee, and William R. Davie, "Local Press Coverage of Environmental Conflict," *Journalism and Mass Communication Quarterly* 77 (spring 2000).

JoAnn Myer Valenti, "Reporting Hantavirus: The Impact of Cultural Diversity in Environmental and Health News," in *Cultural Diversity and the U.S. Media*, ed. Yahya Kamalipour and Theresa Carilli (New York: SUNY Press, 1998), 231-44.

————. "Commentary: How Well Do Scientists Communicate to Media?" *Science Communication* 21 (1999): 172-78.

JoAnn Myer Valenti, "A Review of the President's Council on Sustainable Development (U.S.): Building Networks, Throwing Pebbles at a Goliath Media," in *Communicating Sustainability*, ed. Walter Leal Filho (Bern: Peter Lan Scientific Publishers, 2000), 121-33.

————. "Improving the Scientist/Journalists Conversation." *Science and Engineering Ethics* 6 (2000): 543-48.

27.   Sachsman, Simon, Valenti, "Environment Reporters and U.S. Journalists," 3.
28.   Curtis D. MacDougall, *Interpretative Reporting* (New York: Macmillan, 1982): 114.
29.   Sachsman, Simon, Valenti, "Risk and the Environment Reporters," 399.
30.   Ibid., 399-400.
31.   Ibid., 400-01.
32.   Ibid., 401.
33.   Ibid.
34.   Ibid.
35.   Ibid.
36.   Ibid., 401-02.
37.   Sachsman, Simon, Valenti, "Environment Reporters and U.S. Journalists," 3.
38.   Ibid., 3.
39.   Ibid.
40.   Sachsman, Simon, Valenti, "Risk and the Environment Reporters," 402.
41.   The states in New England were Connecticut, Maine, Massachusetts, New Hampshire, Rhode Island, and Vermont; those in the Mountain West were Arizona, Colorado, Idaho, Montana, Nevada, New Mexico, Utah, and Wyoming. Those in the Pacific West were the Pacific Northwestern states of Alaska, Oregon, and Washington, and California and Hawaii; and those in the South were Alabama, Arkansas, Florida, Georgia, Kentucky, Louisiana, Mississippi, North Carolina, South Carolina, Tennessee, and Virginia. The Mid Atlantic region included Delaware, the District of Columbia, Maryland, New Jersey, New York, Pennsylvania; the Mid Central consisted of Illinois, Indiana, Michigan, Ohio, West Virginia, and Wisconsin; while the West Central included Iowa, Kansas, Minnesota, Missouri, Nebraska, North Dakota, Oklahoma, South Dakota, Texas.
42.   Sachsman, Simon, Valenti, "Environment Reporters and U.S. Journalists," 4.

In fact, the similarities of the responses from different regions at different times argues that differences in time period had little if any influence on reporter responses.

43.   Ibid.
44.   Sachsman, Simon, Valenti, "The Environment Reporters of New England,"
        414.
45.   Ibid.
46.   Ibid., 415.
47.   Ibid.

Part II

The Environment Reporters of the 21st Century

3

The Environment Reporters[1]

Editor Jim Smith sat at his desk and sighed. His newspaper, *The Connecticut Post* (circulation 75,000 daily, 85,000 Sunday) was facing potential layoffs in the newsroom, and he was sorting out how important each reporting function was to the paper. "I know that readers care about the environment," he said. "All the research shows they care. And journalists care. All the surveys I participate in show a high degree of interest in environmental coverage, so that helps. But it's in competition with everything else, [even though] to me it's high up on the list."[2]

Smith, 60, ticked off all the environmental stories that routinely make his front page: "River pollution, global warming, endangered species, animals, plants, and water. And if you are in an area like we are, where there are a lot of rivers and the Long Island Sound, you have got to [cover]…what is in front of the readers' very eyes. Streams, lakes, salt water—that's why the environmental beat is there. But staffs are shrinking. What beats do you lose?"[3] (As the book was going to press, Smith was replaced as editor of the *Post* amidst the sweeping staff reductions that rocked many daily newspapers across the country.)

Where Are the Environment Reporters?

Across the country, newspaper editors and TV station managers often are divided as to whether the environment is an essential beat. Daily newspapers are far more likely than television stations to have an environment reporter. This study found that during the first five years of the 21st century 534 out of 1,462 daily newspapers (36.5 percent) in the United States had at least one reporter who covered the environment on a regular basis. This was a much higher percentage than that for television stations, where the study found 86 stations with environment

Table 3.1

News Organizations with Environment Reporters*

Region	Newspapers			Television Stations		
	Total Daily News-papers	Newspapers with Environment Reporters	% Papers with Env. Reporters	TV Stations with News Directors	TV Stations with Environment Reporters	% Stations with Env. Reporters
		Papers/Reporters			Stations/Reporters	
New England	82	42** with 51	51.2%	33	4 with 4	12.1%
Mountain West	110	55 with 81	50.0%	81	10 with 10	12.3%
South	310	124 with 131	40.0%	194	23** with 27	11.9%
Pacific West	147	93** with 114	63.3%	96	15** with 13	15.6%
Mid Atlantic	169	48** with 53	28.4%	89	0 with 0	0.0%
Mid Central	310	101 with 103	32.6%	138	15** with 14	10.9%
West Central	334	71** with 70***	21.3%	228	19** with 15	8.3%
Total	1,462	534 with 603	36.5%	859	86 with 83	10.0%

Q: Do you cover the environment on a regular basis as part of your reporting duties?

*The number of news organizations with environment reporters differs from the number of environment reporters because some news organizations have more than one environment reporter, while others share an environment reporter.

** In New England, two newspapers shared one reporter; in the Pacific West, four papers shared one, three shared one, and three shared one. In the Mid Atlantic states, two papers shared one, while in the West Central region, four interrelated newspapers employed a total of three reporters (with one reporter's work being published in four papers, one reporter's work being published in two papers, and the third reporter's work being published in only one paper). In the South, two television stations each had two reporters and one station had four, while two stations shared one reporter; in the Pacific West, three stations shared one reporter; in the Mid Central, two stations shared one; and in the West Central four stations shared one and two stations shared one.

*** One newspaper had an environment reporter who was previously counted and interviewed when he worked in a different region. The reporter's inter-view was counted only once while both newspapers were given credit for the presence of an environment reporter.

Table 3.2

Newspapers with Environment Reporters by Circulation

Number of Environment Reporters	Less than 14,000	14,000-29,999	30,000-59,999	More than 60,000	Total Newspapers	Total Reporters	Interviewed Reporters
0	613	210	66	39	928	-	-
1	149	119	96	112	476	466.25*†	445.25*
2	6	11	5	20	42	78.75 *	77.75*
3	1	0	2	6	9	27	25
4	0	0	0	4	4	16	16
5	0	0	1	2	3	15	13
Total	769	340	170	183	1,462	603	577

Total of 534 out of 1,462 (36.5%) newspapers had 603 reporters

* The reason the number of reporters is given in fractions is because some newspapers shared environment reporters. If two newspapers shared one environment reporter, the reporter was split .50 and .50. The sharing of environment reporters also accounts for the fact that there were fewer total reporters than there were newspapers with one environment reporter and the fact that the number of environment reporters at newspapers with two environment reporters does not add up to double the number of those newspapers.

† One newspaper had an environment reporter who was previously counted and interviewed when he worked in a different region. The reporter was counted only once while both newspapers were given credit for the presence of an environment reporter.

reporters compared to the 859 TV stations with a news director listed in *Broadcasting & Cable Yearbook*, or 10.0 percent.[4]

Some news organizations, almost all larger newspapers, had more than one person covering the environment. Some newspapers belonging to a chain shared reporters. The 534 newspapers with environmental journalists actually employed a total of 603 environment reporters. This included 42 newspapers with two environment reporters, nine newspapers with three, four newspapers with four, and three newspapers with five environment reporters, while 18 newspapers shared eight reporters. Meanwhile 86 television stations employed a total of 83 environment reporters, including three stations with a total of eight environment reporters and 13 stations sharing five environmental journalists (see Table 3.1).[5]

The circulation size of the newspapers was strongly related to the number of environment reporters. Of the newspapers with fewer than 14,000 daily circulation, 20.3 percent employed an environment reporter. As circulation increased, so did the likelihood of a newspaper having an environment reporter. Looking at newspapers with more than 60,000 in circulation, 78.7 percent had at least one environment reporter; 17.5 percent had two or more (see Table 3.2). The bigger the newspaper, the more specialists, suggesting that bigger is better for specialized environmental reporting.[6]

In television, the size of the market may have played a role in determining the presence of an environment reporter at ABC, NBC, and CBS-affiliated VHF stations with news directors listed in *Broadcasting & Cable Yearbook*. Thirteen percent of these network-affiliated stations in the top 20 television markets had an environment reporter (six reporters at 46 stations), compared to 10.0 percent for all TV stations identified as having environment reporters.[7]

Regional differences also appear to play a role in determining which newspapers feature environment reporters, as well as how many such journalists are employed. The percentage of newspapers with environment reporters was much higher in the Pacific West (63.3 percent), New England (51.2 percent), and the Mountain West (50.0 percent) than the national average of 36.5 percent. Furthermore, in these three regions, the number of environment reporters was considerably higher than the number of newspapers with environment reporters, meaning many newspapers had more than one environment reporter. Some regional differences appear to be related to newspaper circulation. The West Central region, which had the lowest percentage of newspapers with environment reporters (21.3 percent), had the highest number of very small circulation newspapers (231 out of 334 or 69.2 percent of the total). Regional differences were less pronounced for television stations than newspapers, with five of the seven regions fairly close to the national average of 10.0 percent. The Pacific West had the highest percentage of TV stations with environment reporters (15.6 percent), as well as the highest percentage of newspapers with such a reporter.[8]

Who are the Environment Reporters?

Across the newsroom at *The Connecticut Post*, reporter MariAn Gail Brown was working the telephone, trying to wrap up a story on crime so she could get back to environmental health stories. Brown, 43, has been a professional journalist for 22 years. She has a coveted job at The *Post*, working as an investigative reporter on the State Desk, where she is usually given major stories to cover. But like many reporters in this study who cover the environment on a regular basis, she has to juggle non-environment stories, too. She estimates only about one-third of her time is spent on environment stories, and the percentage is that high because she has become expert at broadening the audience for her stories.

"With some people in the news room, if I suggest a West Nile encephalitis story, they absolutely groan," she said, referring to the mosquito-borne illness. "But if you can get at the impact, why is something important, 'why should I care,' what difference it makes, then you can sell it better. It's a matter of how compelling an argument can you make.... You also need to know the pet areas of editors. My last editor liked health stories, so I wrote more about mad cow disease, is our blood supply infected, and that gave me more freedom to do such stories.... My editor now likes FOI [Freedom of Information] issues and taking on the government. And while you still need to have a good project story on the environment, you can get his attention by filing FOI requests to get things, documents from government agencies.... You need to push the hot buttons of editors. Even with an environment story, you often can show how a program can save money, or show government inefficiency," said Brown in an interview conducted separately from this study's anonymous national survey of reporters.[9]

Brown is an example of how the reporters who cover the environment on a regular basis are pulled from all corners of the newsroom. In 2000-2005, when the reporters in the study were asked their official job title, fewer than a third (29.0 percent) of the titles included the word "environment." In addition, a handful of science reporters (1.9 percent of the total), health reporters (0.8 percent), and a mixture of natural resource, agriculture, and outdoors reporters (5.6 percent) said they

Table 3.3
Job Titles of "Environment Reporters"

Job Titles	New England (2000)	Mountain West (2001)	South (2002-2003)	Pacific West (2002, 2004-2005)	Mid Atlantic (2003-2004)	Mid Central (2004-2005)	West Central (2004-2005)	National (2000-2005)
Environment Reporter, Writer; All Environment Combos	10 18.2%	28 30.8%	60 39.7%	29 25.4%	16 31.4%	24 23.8%	21 24.7%	188 29.0%
All Natural Resources, Agricultural, Outdoor except Environment	0 0%	8 8.8%	13 8.6%	9 7.9%	1 2.0%	2 2.0%	3 3.5%	36 5.6%
All Science except Environment	5 9.1%	1 1.1%	2 1.3%	2 1.8%	0 0.0%	1 1.0%	1 1.2%	12 1.9%
All Health except Environment	2 3.6%	0 0.0%	0 0.0%	1 0.9%	1 2.0%	0 0.0%	1 1.2%	5 0.8%
Reporter, General Assignment, Staff Writer	30 54.5%	45 49.5%	74 49.0%	55 48.2%	29 56.9%	51 50.5%	36 42.4%	320 49.4%
Specialized Reporters— Business, Politics, Sports	6 10.9%	5 5.5%	0 0.0%	9 7.9%	3 5.9%	1 1.0%	0 0.0%	24 3.7%
Specialized Editor, Manager—City Editor, Assignment Editor	2 3.6%	4 4.4%	2 1.3%	9 7.9%	1 2.0%	22 21.8%	23 27.1%	63 9.7%
Total	55 100.0%	91 100.0%	151 100.0%	114* 100.0%	51* 100.0%	101 100.0%	85 100.0%	648* 100.0%

Q: What is your exact job title at (Name of Organization)?

* The total *n* varies due to some participants not answering the question.

Table 3.4
Percentage of Time Spent Covering "Environment" Stories

Region	0-33%	34-66%	67-100%	Total	n
New England (2000)	58.2%	23.6%	18.2%	100%	55
Mountain West (2001)	37.4%	31.9%	30.7%	100%	91
South (2002-03)	51.7%	18.5%	29.8%	100%	151
Pacific West (2002, 2004-05)	35.3%	23.3%	41.4%	100%	116
Mid Atlantic (2003-04)	49.1%	17.0%	33.9%	100%	53
Mid Central (2004-05)	69.3%	15.8%	14.9%	100%	101
West Central (2004-05)	64.7%	22.4%	12.9%	100%	85
Total	52.2%	21.8%	26.0%	100%	652

Q: Looking back on the past year, about what percentage of your time has been spent on reporting environmental stories (however you want to define them)? _____%

*mean computed against ungrouped "percentage of time" variable covered environment stories. In contrast, almost half (49.4 percent) held the title of reporter, general assignment reporter, or staff writer. Another 13.4 percent were beat reporters in other areas (e.g., business, politics, and sports) or worked as both an editor and as a reporter. Many said they were assigned environment stories whenever a local story broke that needed coverage, then used any free time for enterprise stories involving the environment (see Table 3.3).

These job titles also varied across the country. In the South, 39.7 percent of reporters had the word "environment" in their job title, compared to a low of 18.2 percent in New England. Science reporters who covered the environment were most prevalent in New England; those reporters labeled natural resources, agricultural, or outdoors writers were more likely to be found in the Mountain West and the South.[10]

While some of these environment reporters covered the issue full-time, most divided their time, as can be inferred from their job titles. The reporters were asked to estimate how much of their work time they spent, in the previous 12 months, on environment stories. While 26.0 percent said they spent more than two-thirds of their time on environment stories, on average these reporters spent 43.0 percent (mean) of their workweek in the previous year on environmental reporting. More than half of the reporters (52.2 percent) spent less than 34 percent of their time on these stories. Again, in the Pacific West and Mountain West, there was more of an emphasis on environment stories. These two regions were the only areas where the average reporter spent 50 percent or more of his or her time on the environment (see Table 3.4).[11]

In summary, the first part of this study indicates that most newspapers and television stations do not have a reporter covering the environment on a regular basis. Newspapers with larger circulations and those in the Pacific West, New England, and the Mountain West were more likely to have an environment reporter than smaller newspapers or those in other regions. And newspapers were much more likely to have a specialist than television stations, even those TV stations in large markets. Reporters who cover the environment on a regular basis have a wide variety of job titles, reflecting the fact that some cover the beat full-time while others juggle environmental issues with other issues of the day.[12]

Comparing Environment Reporters and U.S. Journalists in General

This study compared environment reporters with U.S. journalists across three dimensions. The first, shown in Table 3.5 and Table 3.6, includes personal characteristics such as age, ethnicity, gender, religion, and education. Table 3.7 looks at media usage patterns such as which newspapers and magazines were read by reporters and how often reporters watched television news. The third dimension detailed in the next chapter presents job characteristics such as perceived level of autonomy and the amount of editing that reporters experience.[13]

Personal Characteristics

Age and Experience

Weaver et al. (2007) describe a graying of the journalism workforce "as the baby boomers move through the decades."[14] The aging of the workforce can be seen in Table 3.5, where the percentage of U.S. journalists shifted from ages 25-34 and 35-44 in the 1992 study to a sharp increase of reporters aged 45-54 in 2002.

There was a striking similarity in the age groupings of the environment reporters and the U.S. journalists in 2002. Most reporters were spread fairly evenly across the three age groups ranging from age 25 to 54; there was a lower percentage of reporters in the 18-24 age group and in the age 55 and higher group.[15]

The aging of the workforce also was reflected in the years of experience. Female environment reporters averaged 11.8 years experience, slightly less than female U.S. journalists (13.0 years). Male environment reporters averaged 16.2 years of experience, compared to 18 years for the U.S. journalists. The slightly lower experience level for both male and female environment reporters (compared to U.S. journalists in general in 2002) is surprising, given that beat assignments, such as covering the environment, are considered prestigious in many newsrooms and often go to more experienced journalists. However, there may really be no difference since the national sample survey's "maximum sampling error at the 95% level of confidence" was "plus or minus 3 percentage points."[16]

Religion

The environment reporters were more likely than U.S. journalists to be Protestant, while the U.S. journalists had higher percentages of Catholic and Jewish reporters. A slightly higher percentage of U.S. journalists (36.0 percent) than environment reporters (30.0 percent) said they considered religion to be very important to them, while the percentages saying religion was somewhat important were almost identical.[17]

Ethnicity and Gender

While both groups were overwhelmingly white, the percentage of white environment reporters was higher (96.6 percent to 91.6 percent). The percentage of males was double that of females in both groups.[18]

Political Affiliation

Although environmental journalists are often typecast as liberal and pro-Democratic Party in their orientation, the study found the percentage of environment reporters identifying themselves as Democrats (32.6) was a bit lower than U.S. journalists in 2002 (35.9) and much lower than U.S. journalists in 1992 (44.1). The environment reporters had far more Independents (51.8 percent to 32.5 percent), while U.S. journalists in 2002 had almost twice as many Republicans as did the environment reporters (18.0 percent to 9.3 percent) (see Table 3.5).[19]

Table 3.5
Personal Characteristics of Environment Reporters vs. U.S. Journalists

Personal Characteristics	Environment Reporters (2000-05)	U.S. Journalists (2002)*	U.S. Journalists (1992)**
Age			
18-24	4.5%	4.4%	4.1%
25-34	28.0%	29.3%	37.2%
35-44	28.9%	27.9%	36.7%
45-54	30.6%	28.2%	13.9%
55+	8.0%	10.1%	8.1%
Total	100.0%	99.9%***	100.0%
n	647[a]		
Years in journalism (mean)			
Male	16.2 years	18.0 years	15.0 years
Female	11.8 years	13.0 years	12.0 years
All****	14.9 years	N/A	N/A
Religion			
Protestant	52.6%	46.2%	54.4%
Catholic	28.6%	32.7%	29.9%
Jewish	3.5%	6.2%	5.4%
Other/None	15.3%	14.8%	10.2%
Total	100.0%	99.9%***	99.9%***
n	633[b]		
Importance of religion			
Very important	30.0%	36.0%	38.0%
Somewhat important	35.6%	36.0%	34.0%
Not very important	20.9%	N/A	N/A
Not at all important	13.6%	N/A	N/A
Total	100.1%***	N/A	N/A
n	627[c]		

Table 3.5
(continued from previous page)

Ethnicity			
White/Other	96.6%	91.6%	92.5%
African American	0.9%	3.7%	3.7%
Hispanic	1.4%	3.3%	2.2%
Asian	0.8%	1.0%	1.0%
Native American	0.3%	0.4%	0.6%
Total	100.0%	100.0%	100.0%
n	640[d]		
Gender			
Male	70.7%	67.0%	66.0%
Female	29.3%	33.0%	34.0%
Total	100.0%	100.0%	100.0%
n	648[e]		
Political Affiliation			
Democrat	32.6%	35.9%	44.1%
Republican	9.3%	18.0%	16.4%
Independent	51.8%	32.5%	34.4%
Other	6.3%	13.6%	5.1%
Total	100.0%	100.0%	100.0%
n	604[f]		
Income			
Less than $35,000	47.8%	N/A	N/A
$35,000 to $60,000	40.2%	N/A	N/A
More than $60,000	12.0%	N/A	N/A
Total	100.0%	N/A	N/A
n	609[g]		

Results reported in percentage unless otherwise noted.

U.S. journalists' median income in 2002, $43,588

* Weaver et al. (2007), pp. 6-22, and 97-99. "The maximum sampling error at the 95% level of confidence for this main probability sample is plus or minus 3 percentage points," pp. 259.[20]

** Weaver and Wilhoit (1996), pp. 6-21 and 92-96. "The sampling error margin at the 95% level of confidence for this main probability sample of 1,156 was plus or minus three percentage points," pp. 251.[21]

*** Totals do not equal 100% due to rounding.

*** Mean computed against ungrouped "years in journalism" variable.

[a] Total does not include reporters who responded no answer (5).

[b] Total does not include reporters who responded no answer (6) or refused to answer (13).

[c] Total does not include reporters who responded don't know (2), no answer (6), or refused to answer (17).

[d] Total does not include reporters who responded no answer (5) or refused to answer (7).

[e] Total does not include reporters who responded no answer (3) or refused to answer (1).

[f] Total does not include reporters who responded don't know (3), no answer (12), or refused to answer (33).

[g] Total does not include reporters who responded don't know (4), no answer (20), or refused to answer (19).

Income

Given the average 14.9 years experience of environment reporters, their reported salary level was very low. Some 47.8 percent said they earned less than $35,000 a year; another 40.2 percent said they earned from $35,000 to $60,000, while the remaining 12.0 percent earned more than $60,000 a year. The U.S. journalists earned a median $43,588 in 2002; no breakdown by income group was published.[22]

Education

The levels of education completed by environment reporters and U.S. journalists in the 2002 survey were very similar. However, there were meaningful differences in terms of undergraduate majors and minors, and probably graduate degrees as well. While the most popular major among both groups was journalism/communication, 23.3 percent of the environment reporters who graduated from college (and answered the question) majored in one or another of the sciences compared to only 2.9 percent of the journalists in general. Furthermore, 38.7 percent of the environment reporters who were college graduates (and answered the question) said they minored in one or another of the sciences. Of the 114 environment reporters who received master's or other advanced degrees, 87 specified the academic area and of these16 received master's in the sciences. Since a bachelor's degree in the sciences generally is a prerequisite for a graduate degree, one can assume that there were very few science master's among the U.S. journalists in general (see Table 3.6).[23]

Despite all of this education, more than a third of the environment reporters agreed that most environmental journalists are not well enough educated to cover news about environmental issues, and about three-quarters of the reporters felt they needed additional training. What kinds of training? Training in the natural sciences, the environment, and journalism led the list (see Table 3.6).

Summary: Personal Characteristics

The older workforce employed in journalism by 2002 may have reduced the greater age and experience level one might expect from beat reporters like those covering the environment. In their personal characteristics, similarities outweighed differences. Neither group had the overwhelmingly pro-Democratic party registration that exists in the popular mind. Many of the environment reporters were better educated

Table 3.6
Personal Characteristics of Environment Reporters vs. U.S. Journalists

Personal Characteristics	Environment Reporters (2000-05)	U.S. Journalists (2002)*	U.S. Journalists (1992)**
1. Level of school completed			
H.S. or less	0.6%	1.8%	4.3%
Some college	6.2%	8.9%	13.6%
College graduate	68.1%	68.0%	64.5%
Some graduate training	7.6%	4.7%	6.2%
Master's degree or more	17.6%	16.6%	11.4%
Total	100.1%***	100.0%	100.0%
N	648[a]	1148	1147
2. Undergraduate majors			
(of college graduates responding)			
Journalism/Communication	44.9%	57.7%	56.3%
Journalism/Communication plus another field	5.1 %		
Subtotal: Journalism + Comm.	50.0%	57.7%	56.3%
Science	23.3%	2.9%****	2.2%****
All other fields	25.7%	39.2%	41.4%
No major	1.0%	N/A	N/A
Total	100.0%	99.8%	99.9%
N	572[b]	N/A	N/A
3. Undergraduate minor			
(of college graduates)			
Journalism/Communication	4.4%	N/A	N/A
Science	38.7%	N/A	N/A
Other	14.9%	N/A	N/A
No minor	41.9%	N/A	N/A
Total***	99.9%	N/A	N/A
N	542[c]	N/A	N/A
4. Graduate subjects of study			
Journalism/Communication	50.6%	N/A	N/A
Science	18.4%	N/A	N/A
Ph.D./law/MD	3.4%	N/A	N/A
Other	27.6%	N/A	N/A
Total	100.0%	N/A	N/A
N	87 (of 114)[d]	N/A	N/A
5. Have you had short courses, sabbaticals, workshops since becoming a journalist? (% yes shown)	73.8%	64.0%	58.0%
6. Most environmental journalists are not well enough educated to cover news about environmental issues. Do you…			
Strongly agree	4.4%	N/A	N/A
Agree	32.5%	N/A	N/A
Disagree	55.8%	N/A	N/A
Strongly disagree	7.3%	N/A	N/A
Total	100.0%	N/A	N/A
N	520[e]		
7. Do you feel you need additional training in journalism or other subjects? (% yes shown)	76.5% †	77.0%	61.6%
What area:			
Natural science	13.3% (87)	N/A	N/A
Environment	9.7% (63)	N/A	N/A
Journalism/Communication	9.7% (63)	34.2%	11.4%
Computers/new technology/multimedia	3.8% (25)	12.4%	N/A
English, literature, writing	3.2% (21)	<1.5%	4.7%
Law	1.5% (10)	5.2%	2.2%
Political science/government	1.4% (9)	2.1%	4.9%
Business	1.1% (7)	2.1%	7.2%
Economics	1.1% (7)	<1.5%	2.9%

History	0.9% (6)	<1.5%	3.8%
Photography	0.3% (2)	4.1%	1.6%
Modern languages	0.3% (2)	6.2%	2.6%
News analysis, clinics, seminars	0.2% (1)	8.2%	9.8%
Shorthand	0.0% (0)	<1.5%	0.3%
General (e.g. "any course," "all subjects")	4.4% (29)	NA	NA
Specific answers not otherwise listed (e.g. philosophy)	4.0% (26)	NA	NA
No Answer; non-responsive	21.8% (142)	NA	NA
Not seeking additional training	23.5% (152)	23.0%	38.4%
Total	100.0%	100.0%††	100.0%
N	646[f]	1149	1148

Q: What is the highest grade of school, or level of education, you have completed? (Ask open ended; circle best category); 1) no school or kindergarten, 2) grades 1-11, 3) completed high school, 4) 1-3 years of college, 5) graduated from college, 6) some graduate work, no degree, 7) master's degree, 8) doctorate, law or medical degree, 9) vocational or technical school beyond.

Q: What was your undergraduate major? 1) Journalism, 2) Journalism and other major (Specify Other_____), 3) Other major(s)—What was it? (Specify Other_____), 4) Did not have a major…

Q: What was your undergraduate minor, if any? 1) Journalism, 2) Journalism and other minor (Specify Other_____), 3) Other minor(s)—What was it? (Specify Other_____), 4) Did not have a minor…

Q: What field were you in graduate or professional school? Field_____

Q: Have you had any short courses, sabbaticals, workshops or fellowships since becoming a journalist? 1) Yes, 2) No

Q: Most environmental journalists are not well enough educated to cover news about environmental issues. Do you…

Q: Do you feel you need additional training in journalism or other subjects? 1) Yes, 2) No

* Weaver et al. (2007), pp. 31-53.
** Weaver and Wilhoit (1996), pp. 29-47.
*** Totals do not equal 100% due to rounding.
**** The figures for Science majors among U.S. journalists in 2002 include 2.8 % "physical and biological sciences" plus 0.1% "agriculture" and for 1992, 2.1% "physical and biological sciences" plus 0.1% "agriculture."
† In cases of multiple responses and multiple-word responses (e.g., environmental journalism), first response or first word coded.
†† In Weaver et al. (2007), subjects mentioned by fewer than 1.5% of the respondents are listed here as <1.5%. Weaver et al. (2007) lists the total percentage as 100%.

[a] Total does not include reporters who responded no answer (3) or refused to answer (1).
[b] Total does not include reporters who responded don't know (1), no answer (22), or refused to answer (13), and the 44 who either did not attend or did not graduate from college.
[c] Total does not include reporters who responded don't know (13), no answer (52), or refused to answer (1), and the 44 who either did not attend or did not graduate from college.
[d] Of the 114 reporters who said they held master's or other advanced degrees, the total reported does not include those who responded no answer (27).
[e] Total does not include reporters who responded no opinion (65), don't know (61), no answer (2), and refused to answer (4).
[f] Total does not include reporters who responded don't know (1), no answer (3), and refused to answer (2).

Table 3.7
Media Usage Patterns of Environment Reporters vs. U.S. Journalists

Media Usage Patterns	Environment Reporters (2000-05)	U.S. Journalists (2002)*	U.S. Journalists (1992)**
Magazines Used			
Newsweek	24.2%	31.2%	32.2%
Time	20.6%	27.9%	28.5%
National Geographic	15.5%	<1%	8.9%
The New Yorker	15.2%	16.1%	8.7%
Atlantic Monthly	8.0%	4.3%	5.2%
Sports Illustrated	6.3%	16.0%	16.5%
U.S. News	5.5%	5.0%	9.2%
Harper's	5.4%	3.0%	4.2%
Smithsonian	4.4%	2.4%	4.4%
Environment Magazine	4.4%	N/A	N/A
Outside	3.8%	N/A	N/A
Rolling Stone	3.4%	5.7%	6.9%
NY Times Sunday Magazine	2.6%	N/A	N/A
Columbia Journalism Review	2.5%	N/A	N/A
The Economist	2.5%	3.7%	N/A
Vanity Fair	2.3%	6.4%	N/A
Newspapers Used			
New York Times	46.5%	38.1%	26.1%
Washington Post	15.3%	20.0%	11.1%
Wall Street Journal	14.3%	22.9%	23.4%
USA Today	11.8%	19.2%	21.9%
Los Angeles Times	9.2%	7.4%	5.4%
Boston Globe	4.9%	3.5%	3.5%
Chicago Tribune	4.8%	7.3%	4.6%
San Francisco Chronicle	3.7%	2.2%	4.4%
Denver Post	3.5%	2.8%	3.0%
Oregonian	2.9%	1.9%	N/A
Atlanta Journal Constitution	2.6%	3.9%	2.7%
Dallas Morning News	2.3%	2.7%	2.2%
Rocky Mountain News	2.0%	2.0%	2.0%
Hartford Courant	1.5%	N/A	1.5%
Chicago Sun Times	1.2%	2.1%	1.4%
# of days watching network news			
0	50.9%	40.4%	34.0%
1	13.1%	13.7%	15.5%
2	9.7%	12.4%	12.1%
3	7.4%	11.9%	11.6%
4	4.8%	4.6%	7.3%
5	6.3%	10.1%	10.3%
6	0.8%	2.6%	3.3%
7	6.9%	4.3%	5.8%
# of days watching cable news			
0	30.4%	16.6%	N/A
1	12.0%	10.0%	N/A
2	9.7%	9.0%	N/A
3	6.0%	11.1%	N/A
4	6.0%	7.5%	N/A
5	10.0%	18.7%	N/A
6	3.1%	3.8%	N/A
7	22.7%	23.2%	N/A

*Weaver et al. (2007), pp. 23-29.
**Weaver and Wilhoit (1996), pp. 21-26.

Table 3.8
Environment Reporters, Reasons for Going into Journalism

	# of people
1) Writing	216
2) Making a Difference, Helping people and Providing a Service	110
3) Inform, Communicate, and Educate the Truth	105
4) Like/Enjoy it	71
5) Interesting	68
6) Wanting to Learn	39
6) Story Telling	39
7) Curiosity	37
8) Fell into it	30
8) Variety/Change	30
9) Exciting/Fun	29
10) School	28
11) Good fit/Good at it	24
12) Needed a job	23
13) Research	22
14) Freedom and Autonomy	21
15) Follow and Debate Public Issues	19
16) Always wanted to	17
17) Challenge	12
17) Don't Know	12
18) Being involved in the public	8
19) Tradition	7
19) Rewarding	7
20) Good pay	5
20) To do well	5

Q: In looking back, why did you become a journalist?
Multiple responses coded from individual respondents. Responses with more than five mentions are presented.

in the sciences than U.S. journalists in general. Fifty percent of the environment reporters majored in journalism/communication, but many of these minored in a science, and nearly a quarter majored in one of the sciences.[24]

Media Usage Patterns

The environment reporters and U.S. journalists in general shared preferences in the newspapers and magazines they read and the amount of time they spent watching television news. The top four magazines read on a regular basis by environment reporters and U.S. journalists in

2002 were almost the same: *Newsweek, Time, National Geographic,* and *The New Yorker* for environment reporters, versus *Newsweek, Time, The New Yorker,* and *Sports Illustrated* for U.S. journalists. Not surprisingly, the environment reporters were more likely to read magazines devoted to the natural world, such as *National Geographic, Smithsonian, E: The Environment Magazine,* and *Outside* (see Table 3.7).

The top four newspapers were the same for both groups and reflected the national orientation of all four papers: *The New York Times, The Washington Post, The Wall Street Journal,* and *USA Today.* The prominence of *The New York Times* to both groups is worthy of note. *The Times* was read on a regular basis by almost twice as many U.S. journalists as the second most popular newspaper, *The Washington Post.* Among environment reporters, *The Times* was read more than three times as often as the runner-up, again *The Washington Post.*

The two groups also were similar in not watching conventional evening television network news broadcasts, perhaps in part because they are still working or returning home from work in the early evening. Instead, they were more likely to watch cable TV news, taking advantage of its 24/7 availability. For example, 50.9 percent of environment reporters and 40.4 percent of U.S. journalists (in 2002) said they did not watch any network news broadcasts in an average week. In contrast, 30.4 percent of environment reporters and 16.6 percent of U.S. journalists watched no cable TV news, while 22.7 percent of environment reporters and 23.2 percent of U.S. journalists watched cable news every day.[25]

Choosing Journalism as a Career

The environment reporters offered a long list of reasons why they decided to go into the field. Topping the list was the ability to write for a living; 216 of the 652 environment reporters volunteered that answer, plus 39 said they loved their story-telling function and 22 enjoyed the research that went into the job. (Multiple responses are included, so percentages do not equal 100 percent. See Table 3.8)

The second major reason for entering the field was an altruistic one: making a difference, helping people and providing a service, cited by 110 reporters. In a similar vein, 105 reporters cited the ability to inform, communicate, and educate people on the truth. Nineteen mentioned their function of helping people follow and participate in debating public issues, while eight reporters said they enjoyed being involved with the public. Three said they simply wanted to do well.

A third dimension was the sheer enjoyment of performing the journalist role. Seventy-one reporters said they entered the field simply because they liked it or enjoyed it. Another 68 found it interesting, 39 said it enabled them to learn more, 37 said it enabled them to pursue their sense of curiosity. Thirty reporters said they liked the variety and change that came with the job while 29 said they found it to be exciting and fun.

The responses by environment reporters were similar in most respects to the U.S. journalists surveyed in 2002. Their responses fell into four major categories delineated by Weaver et al.: "the intrinsic appeal of the tasks that journalists perform; the desire to be in a profession that has an important social or political role; the journalist's early experiences with or connection to the profession; the belief that the work would be varied and exciting."[26]

Discussion

Research in mass communication requires the systematic accumulation of baseline data. There is a critical need for baseline information from which to develop theoretical work in the future. This need for baseline data is particularly true for comparative journalism research, especially in terms of changes or trends within and between journalistic beats. This study provides such essential baseline data regarding environment reporters, and compares this information to existing studies of U.S. journalists in general. This research tells us where the environment reporters worked, who they were, and how they compared to other American journalists from 2000 to 2005.[27]

Daily newspapers are far more likely than television stations to have an environment reporter and newspapers with larger circulations are most likely to have environment reporters and to have more than one environment reporter. Daily newspapers in the Pacific West, New England, and the Mountain West were more likely to have environment reporters than those in other regions.[28] The West Central region, which had the highest number of very small circulation newspapers, had the lowest percentage of newspapers with environment reporters.

Reporters who cover the environment on a regular basis have a wide variety of job titles, reflecting the fact that some cover the beat most of the time while others juggle environmental issues with other issues of the day. Reporters spent, on average, 43.0 percent of their time on environmental stories; the percentage of time rose to 50.0 percent and higher for those in the two most western regions. The environment reporters were journalists first; nearly half were simply called reporters, general assignment reporters, or staff writers.[29]

The older workforce employed in journalism by 2002 may have reduced the greater age and experience level one might expect from beat reporters like those covering the environment. In their personal characteristics, the similarities between environment reporters and U.S. journalists were remarkable. The two groups were particularly similar in age, years in journalism, and gender. And there were more similarities than differences in religion, importance of religion, ethnicity, political affiliation, and education. But while the most popular major among both groups was journalism/communication, many of the students who would go on to become environment reporters did not fit the common stereotype of journalism majors as students who tended to avoid the sciences. The differences between journalists and scientists sometimes are attributed to the assumption that they studied different subjects in college. Although almost all scientists were science majors and half of the environment reporters were journalism or communication majors, many of the environment reporters studied the sciences extensively in college, minoring or even majoring in one or another of the sciences, and 16 of the 114 environment reporters with advanced degrees hold a master's in the sciences.[30]

The environment reporters and U.S. journalists in general shared preferences in the newspapers and magazines they read and the amount of time they spent watching television news. The top four newspapers were the same for both groups and reflected the national orientation of all four papers.[31]

Overall, the dominant finding of this chapter is that environment reporters working at daily newspapers and television stations share many individual characteristics and media usage patterns with U.S. journalists in general. The environment reporters went into journalism for non-scientific reasons such as the ability to write, make a difference, and inform and educate people—reasons similar to those of U.S. journalists in general. Environment reporters are journalists first, perhaps due in part to their similar backgrounds and to the basic professional training received by most journalists. The differences that exist between some environment reporters and U.S. journalists in general may be related to differences that do exist in their college education.[32]

This leads to an idea that, if correct, is even more basic: *Journalists are journalists first*, linked to their colleagues in the newsroom by their similar backgrounds and the professional training and experience common to most reporters. Such a theory of journalism education is worth pursuing because, if provable, it explains the similarities that exist among

American journalists regardless of their age, ethnicity, gender, or politics. And it may also provide an explanation for the conflicts that exist between reporters and their sources, whose education and training differ.

The findings that newspapers employ more specialized reporters than TV stations and that the bigger the newspaper, the more specialists, point to another idea, that bigger is better for specialized reporting. This big newspaper theory of specialized reporting is not always true, given regional differences, etc., but it appears often enough to be worth pursuing, especially at a time when the fate of some big newspapers is threatened by corporate readjustments. If bigger really is better, then perhaps big newspapers should be sustained, despite their cost of operation.

Those high costs, and resulting staff layoffs, have caused soul-searching by many reporters. In an effort to make herself more knowledgeable and marketable, Brown earned her law degree in 2006. She wonders about the future of environment beat reporters as the mainstream media reduce staff.

"Newspapers are cutting back everywhere. You constantly hear, 'Do more with less. Do more with less. Do more with less.' That filters down, even to people with specialty beats who have to do other things at times. Specialists do have more freedom to do more project stories, but with cutbacks it is hard to devote as much time to the beat."[33]

As she mentally runs through her environment stories in the past few months—from a rise of coyotes in suburban Connecticut to global warming's effect on the region's traditional fall foliage—she becomes animated and talks about strategies for getting readers enthused about her work. She reflects the many reasons environment reporters choose journalism. The ability to write. Make a difference. Inform and educate people.

"Some people hear the word environment and are turned off. But they have been turned off since high school—they didn't get it then and they don't get it now. They groaned in earth science, tried to be invisible in chemistry, and in physics they tried to avoid the class if they [could]," she said. "I play up the larger impact, when you can go beyond" the audience's initial reluctance. "People are kind of, like, 'Oh, an environment story.' But if they are literally touching, feeling, start[ing] to discover things, they'll read and enjoy the story even if they never pick up *Science* magazine or *Nature*."[34]

Notes

1. An earlier version of elements of this chapter was originally written by the authors
    and published in:
    David B. Sachsman, James Simon, and JoAnn Myer Valenti, "Environment
    Reporters and U.S. Journalists: A Comparative Analysis," *Applied Environmental
    Education and Communication* 7 (2008): 1-19.
2. Jim Smith, personal interview conducted by James Simon, April 3, 2007. Unrelated
    to the survey.
3. Ibid.
4. Sachsman, Simon, and Valenti, "Environment Reporters and U.S. Journalists,"
    4.
5. Ibid., 4.
6. Ibid., 5.
7. Ibid.
8. Ibid.
9. MariAn Gail Brown, personal interview conducted by James Simon, March 29,
    2007. Unrelated to the survey.
10. Sachsman, Simon, and Valenti, "Environment Reporters and U.S. Journalists,"
    6.
11. Ibid., 6.
12. Ibid., 6-7.
13. Ibid., 7.
14. David H. Weaver, Randal A. Beam, Bonnie J. Brownlee, Paul S. Voakes, and G.
    Cleveland Wilhoit, *The American Journalist in the 21st Century: U.S. News People
    at the Dawn of a New Millennium* (Mahwah, N.J.: Lawrence Erlbaum, 2007), 6.
15. Sachsman, Simon, and Valenti, "Environment Reporters and U.S. Journalists,"
    10-11.
16. Weaver et al., *The American Journalist*, 259.
    Sachsman, Simon, and Valenti, "Environment Reporters and U.S. Journalists,"
    11.
17. Ibid.
18. Ibid.
19. Ibid.
20. Ibid., 8.
21. Ibid.
22. Ibid., 11.
23. Ibid.
24. Ibid., 11-12.
25. Ibid., 12.
26. Weaver et al. *The American Journalist*, 56.
27. Sachsman, Simon, and Valenti, "Environment Reporters and U.S. Journalists,"
    17.
28. Ibid.
29. Ibid.
30. Ibid.
31. Ibid., 17-18.
32. Ibid., 18.
33. MariAn Gail Brown, personal interview with James Simon, March 29, 2007.
34. Ibid.

4

The Work Environment[1]

Even after spending 17 years covering environmental issues for the *Louisville Courier-Journal*, Jim Bruggers says he has no problem finding stories that his readers feel are important. "You are exploring and writing about concerns that go to the food we eat, the air we breathe, the water we drink, the places we go to recreate. The landscapes that sustain us, the mountains with their natural beauty. All of these things. To a lot of people they are very important issues. It really is a beat that touches people's lives."[2]

Bruggers, a former president of the national Society of Environmental Journalists, said many of his peers enjoy the freedom and autonomy they generally have in covering the beat and deciding which stories make it to the public agenda. Shining the media spotlight on an issue and having an impact is also important to many environment reporters, he said in an interview conducted separately from this study's anonymous national survey of reporters. "Reporters want to feel they have something to contribute to the newsroom and their communities. They want respect, and giving someone a greater level of autonomy is a way of showing respect," he said. "And being able to make a difference is a classic reason why at least the last generation of journalists went into the field."[3]

But the field has changed. Barriers loom, such as staffing cutbacks and greater difficulty in getting time to do an extended series of stories. "Information is coming at me faster," Bruggers said, "and I try to stay up with national trends, but it's hard to decide which angle to pick and not pick."

Then there are technological changes, such as the daily blog postings he does for his readers. "Every hour I spend on the blog, I am not investigating things," he said. "But it seems to have increased the profile of the

Table 4.1
Job Satisfaction of Environment Reporters and U.S. Journalists in General

Job Satisfaction	Environment Reporters (2000-05)	U.S. Journalists 2002*	U.S. Journalists 1992**
Very Satisfied	201 31.2%	33.3%	27.0%
Satisfied	348 54.0%	50.6%	50.0%
Somewhat Dissatisfied	81 12.6%	14.4%	20.0%
Very Dissatisfied	14 2.2%	1.7%	3.0%
Total	644*** 100%	1149 100%	1156 100%

Q: All things considered, how satisfied are you with your present job?
Would you say...

* Weaver et al. (2006), pp. 107.
** Weaver and Wilhoit (1996), pp. 100.
*** The total N may vary due to some participants not answering the question.

paper even though I don't get as many hits as, say, the Kentucky Derby," Bruggers said. "The blog allows me to touch on more issues, and I hope it's also reaching Internet readers who may not read the newspaper."

Bruggers' comments reflected many of the workaday concerns mentioned by environment reporters. These journalists report high job satisfaction, but concern about barriers to reporting like time constraints. They relish the high level of autonomy most enjoy and the chance to help people. But some worry that environment stories are less important to their editors or audience members than they are to the reporters themselves.

The Environment Reporters and Job Satisfaction

Reporters who choose to cover specialized stories like the environment might be expected to report higher levels of job satisfaction than U.S. journalists in general.[4] While this study found high levels of job satisfaction among environment reporters in every region and during every period of time, from 2000 to 2005, these levels were very similar to those found for U.S. journalists in 2002. Some 85.2 percent of environment reporters said they were very satisfied or satisfied with their jobs, compared to 83.9 percent of U.S. journalists (see Table 4.1).[5] The level of job satisfaction among journalists was relatively high in this period, compared to 1992, when 77 percent of U.S. journalists said they were satisfied, and it very well may be lower today, given the current economic difficulties of newspapers and television stations. But during the period in question, the job satisfaction levels of environment reporters in all regions and in every year from 2000 to 2005 were remarkably similar, a clear indication that the year in which environment reporters were interviewed did not affect their responses.

Job Satisfaction by Characteristics of Environment Reporters

This study then broke down job satisfaction by the personal and job characteristics of environment reporters. In doing so, it appears that job satisfaction had a somewhat negative relationship with amount of education. Environment reporters with less than a college degree were more likely to be satisfied than those with more education.[6] The four environment reporters with a high school degree or less reported being fairly satisfied or very satisfied. Thirty-seven of the 39 environment reporters with some college (94.9 percent) said they were fairly satisfied or very satisfied. This satisfaction level dropped to 84.7 percent for the 438 college graduates and 80.9 percent for the 47 with some graduate school. However, this satisfaction level picked back up for the 109 reporters with a graduate degree (84.4 percent satisfied) and the three with doctorates (100 percent satisfied).

There also seemed to be slight differences in job satisfaction related to religious affiliation. But *importance* of religion did relate to job satisfaction; the more important religion was to environment reporters, the more likely the reporters were to say they were satisfied in their jobs. Environment reporters and U.S. journalists (2002) who were white were very likely to be satisfied with their jobs. And these percentages were almost identical: 85.9 percent and 84.5 percent respectively. However, the six African-American environment reporters were much more satisfied (100.0 percent) than their U.S. journalist counterparts (77.0 percent). Hispanic environment reporters were less satisfied (66.7 percent) than Hispanic U.S. journalists (78.0 percent). Asian-American reporters in both categories were equally satisfied (80.0 percent to 80.9 percent). Men were more satisfied than women both among environment reporters and U.S. journalists, with very similar numbers. Likewise, comparing job satisfaction by age among both categories of reporters showed similar results (see Table 4.2).[7]

Table 4.2
Job Satisfaction by Individual Characteristics of Environment Reporters
(Percentages represent those reporters saying they were "very satisfied"
or "fairly satisfied" with their jobs)

	Environment Reporters (2000-05)	U.S. Journalists (2002)*
OVERALL	85.2%	83.9%
1. Personal characteristics		
Age		
18-24	89.7%	90.7%
25-34	83.4%	79.8%
35-44	87.7%	85.0%
45-54	83.7%	85.5%
55+	84.6%	87.1%
Education		
HS or less	100.0%	N/A
Some college	94.9%	N/A
College grad	84.7%	N/A
Some graduate school	80.9%	N/A
MA or more	84.8%	N/A
Religion		
Protestant	84.5%	N/A
Catholic	85.4%	N/A
Jewish	90.9%	N/A
Other	88.1%	N/A
None	83.0%	N/A
Importance of Religion		
Very important	87.0%	N/A
Somewhat important	86.1%	N/A
Not very important	84.5%	N/A
Not at all important	80.7%	N/A
Ethnicity		
1. White	85.9%	84.5%
Non-white	70.3%	N/A
2. White	85.9%	84.5%
African American	100.0%	77.0%
Hispanic	66.7%	78.0%
Asian-American	80.0%	80.9%
Native American	50.0%	89.7%**
Gender		
Men	87.1%	86.6%
Women	80.4%	78.7%
Political Affiliation		
Democrat	83.2%	N/A
Republican	91.1%	N/A
Independent	85.0%	N/A
Other	81.6%	N/A

Table 4.2
(continued from previous page)

	Environment Reporters (2000-05)	U.S. Journalists (2002)*
Income		
Less than $35,000	81.2%	N/A
$35,000 to $60,000	90.5%	N/A
More than $60,000	82.2%	N/A
Marital status		
Married	87.5%	N/A
Unmarried	82.2%	N/A
2. Job characteristics		
Region		
New England (2000)	85.5%	N/A
Mountain West (2001)	85.6%	N/A
South (2002-03)	86.7%	N/A
Pacific West (2002, 2004-05)	85.3%	N/A
Mid Atlantic (2003-04)	82.7%	N/A
Mid Central (2004-05)	85.7%	N/A
West Central (2004-05)	83.1%	N/A
Job titles		
All environment titles	89.8%	N/A
Other titles	83.3%	
Medium		
Newspaper reporter	84.5%	N/A
TV reporter	90.7%	83.4%
Percent of time covering environment		
1-33%	82.4%	N/A
34-66%	85.0%	N/A
67%+	90.8%	N/A
Years in journalism		
1-10	84.7%	N/A
11-20	84.3%	N/A
21+	86.7%	N/A
Years covering environment		
1-10	87.0%	N/A
11-20	85.0%	N/A
21+	84.0%	N/A
How good a job does your own news organization do in enhancing the public's understanding of environmental issues?		
Outstanding	95.2%	95.9%
Very good	90.5%	89.8%
Good	86.6%	77.6%
Only fair	72.9%	N/A
Poor	40.0%	N/A

Table 4.2
(continued from previous page)

	Environment Reporters (2000-05)	U.S. Journalists (2002)*
How much freedom do you usually have in selecting the stories you work on?		
Almost complete freedom	89.3%	N/A
A great deal of freedom	89.7%	N/A
Some freedom	61.7%	N/A
Not much freedom	42.9%	N/A
None at all	0.0%	N/A
How much freedom do you usually have in deciding which aspects of a story should be emphasized?		
Almost complete freedom	88.7%	N/A
A great deal of freedom	86.9%	N/A
Some freedom	71.4%	N/A
Not much freedom	0.0%	N/A
None at all	0.0%	N/A
If you have a good idea which you think important and should be followed up, how often are you able to get the subject covered?		
Almost complete freedom	91.4%	N/A
A great deal of freedom	87.3%	N/A
Some freedom	70.8%	N/A
Not much freedom	50.0%	N/A
None at all	0.0%	N/A
How much editing do your stories get from others at (your organization)?		
A great deal	80.0%	N/A
A considerable amount	89.5%	N/A
Some	87.4%	N/A
Little	82.6%	N/A
None at all	76.2%	N/A

Percentages represent those reporters saying they were "very satisfied" or "fairly satisfied" with their jobs.
Q: All things considered, how satisfied are you with your present job? Would you say 1) very satisfied, 2) fairly satisfied, 3) somewhat dissatisfied, or 4) very dissatisfied

* Weaver et al. (2007), pp. 108-11 and 190.
** Includes American Indians, Alaska Natives, Pacific Islanders or Others.

Job satisfaction also related highly with job-related characteristics. Television reporters covering the environment were more likely, on average, to report higher levels of job satisfaction than newspaper reporters. Those with an official title including the word "environment" were more likely to be satisfied. The percentage of time covering the environment related strongly with job satisfaction; reporters spending at least two thirds of their time on the environment were more likely to be satisfied than those spending less time.

The study found relationships between job satisfaction and various measures of autonomy. Environment reporters were more likely to be satisfied with their job if they felt their news organizations did a good job of enhancing the public's understanding, if they had freedom in selecting stories and deciding what aspects to emphasize, and if they were free to follow up on a story. The tendency of some reporters to complain about too much editing—and too little editing—is reflected by the results of this study. Reporters who said they received a considerable amount of editing, some editing, or little editing were more likely to be satisfied with their jobs than those whose stories received no editing—or received a great deal of editing (see Table 4.2).[8]

The study also asked environment reporters why they were satisfied or dissatisfied with their jobs. We focused on 20 reasons that were mentioned by at least ten reporters. Eighteen of the 20 were positive, reflecting the general level of satisfaction. Journalists said they were satisfied for such reasons as the level of autonomy they enjoyed in their job (mentioned by 142 of the 652 reporters), the freedom they enjoyed (80 mentions), and the management support they enjoyed (80 mentions). The only specific reasons for dissatisfaction mentioned (by at least five reporters) were salary (mentioned by 23) and time constraints (16 mentions) (see Table 4.3).

Reporters who choose to cover specialized stories like the environment might be expected to report higher levels of job satisfaction than U.S. journalists in general. While this study found high levels of job satisfaction among environment reporters, the levels were similar to those found for U.S. journalists.[9]

Judging Jobs in Journalism

We also asked about the importance of nine factors in evaluating jobs in the journalism field. The reporters gave a rating to each factor ranging from 1 (very important) to 5 (not important at all) (see Table 4.4).

The results are consistent with the indicators of job satisfaction and the reasons, discussed in Chapter 3, why these reporters went into the

Table 4.3
Reasons Why Environment Reporters were Satisfied/Dissatisfied with Jobs

Reasons they were satisfied	# of reporters
1) Autonomy	142
2) Freedom	80
3) Great Environment and Management Support	80
4) Pay and Benefits	67
5) Enjoyment of the Job	64
6) Editorial Support	43
7) Chance to Influence and Help People	32
8) Inform and Educate the Public	28
9) Location	26
10) Flexibility and Time	25
12) Interesting	21
13) Challenging	18
14) Variety	18
15) Enjoy Writing	17
17) Like to Learn Aspect	15
18) Good Beat	14
19) Job Security	12
20) Make a Difference	11
Reasons they were dissatisfied	
11) Bad Pay	23
16) Lack of Time/Constraints	16

Q: What are the most important reasons you say you are (satisfied/dissatisfied) with your present job?

Note: Up to three responses coded for each respondent. Of the 652 reporters, 448 offered an initial response, 360 offered a second response, and 229 offered a third response. This list consists of all responses of ten or more reporters.

journalism field in the first place. Autonomy, mentioned as the top reason for job satisfaction (see Table 4.3 above), received the highest mean score (1.68, 1 = very important, 2 = important) as a factor in judging the value of a journalism job. The chance to help people (mean = 1.80), the editorial policies (1.85), and job security (1.99) rounded out the four highest scored reasons. At the bottom of the list was "the chance to get ahead in the organization," which had a mean score of 2.64 (2 = important, 3 = neither important nor unimportant).

The results were consistent across the regions of the country and thus consistent across time, from 2000 to 2005. Autonomy topped the list in each individual region, garnering the highest percentage of people who said it was important or very important. The chance to get ahead was least important among all the factors in all eight regions (see Table 4.5).

Autonomy in the Newsroom

Specialized reporting slots such as covering the environment may be thought to offer the reporter more autonomy in story selection and more independence in the handling of stories. Nevertheless, the percentage of environment specialists who said they had "almost complete" autonomy in the newsroom was less than their colleagues among U.S. journalists. For example, when asked whether "they are almost always able to get a story covered that they think should be covered," 52 percent of the U.S. journalists in 2002 responded they had "almost complete" ability to get a story covered, compared to 36.1 percent of the environment writers (see Table 4.6).

The trend continued across related questions. Forty percent of U.S. journalists said they had almost complete freedom in selecting the stories they work on, compared to 33.1 percent of the environment reporters. Forty-two percent of U.S. journalists said they had "almost complete freedom in deciding which aspects of a news story should be emphasized," compared to 38.2 percent of environment reporters. When asked about "the amount of editing your stories get from others at your organization," 16 percent of U.S. journalists reported receiving no editing, while only 3.4 percent of environment reporters said they received "none at all" (see Table 4.6).

However, when one measures autonomy by combining those who said they had "almost complete" freedom with those who said they had a "great deal" of freedom, the numbers are more complex. Regarding the amount of freedom men and women had in selecting stories, the percentage of newspaper environment reporters who said they had "almost complete" or a "great deal" of freedom was greater than their male and female counterparts among U.S. journalists in general. In television, on the other hand, only female environment reporters said they had more freedom than their counterparts (see Table 4.7).

Barriers to Reporting on Environment Stories

Autonomy in journalism is often thought of as freedom from editorial rule, since griping about editors is an age-old tradition in the field.

Table 4.4

Judging Jobs in Journalism

(Raw numbers and percentages represent the actual number of respondents in each category.)

Environment Reporters...	Very Important	Important	Neither	Not Important	Not Important at all	Total	Mean*
The amount of autonomy you have	276 42.5%	325 50.0%	30 4.6%	19 2.9%	0 0.0%	650[a] 100.0%	1.68
The chance to help people	234 36.0%	335 51.5%	57 8.8%	23 3.5%	1 0.2%	650[b] 100.0%	1.80
The editorial policies	269 41.5%	268 41.4%	56 8.6%	51 7.9%	4 0.6%	648[c] 100.0%	1.85
Job security	149 22.9%	409 62.9%	48 7.4%	38 5.8%	6 0.9%	650[d] 99.9%**	1.99
The chance to develop a specialty	162 24.8%	362 55.5%	80 12.3%	47 7.2%	1 0.2%	652 100.0%	2.02
The chance to influence public affairs	138 21.4%	335 51.9%	105 16.3%	55 8.5%	13 2.0%	646[e] 100.1%**	2.18
Fringe benefits	76 11.7%	427 66.0%	76 11.7%	60 9.3%	8 1.2%	647[f] 99.9%**	2.22
The pay	72 11.1%	431 66.2%	81 12.4%	55 8.4%	12 1.8%	651[g] 99.9%**	2.24
The chance to get ahead	55 8.4%	292 44.9%	149 22.9%	141 21.7%	14 2.2%	651[h] 100.1%**	2.64

Now I'd like to find out how important a number of things are to you in judging jobs in your field, not just your job.

Q: The amount of autonomy you have? Is it...
Q: The chance to help people? Is it...
Q: Is the editorial policies of the organization? Is it...
Q: Job security? Is it...
Q: The chance to develop a specialty? Is it...
Q: The chance to influence public affairs? Is it...
Q: Fringe benefits? Are they...
Q: For instance, how much difference does the pay make in how you rate a job in your field—pay is...
Q: The chance to get ahead in the organization? Is it...

* Job factors are ranked by mean score, lowest to highest. Index ranged from: very important=1 to not important at all =5.
** Percentage does not total 100 because of rounding.
[a] Total does not include reporters who responded don't know (1) or no answer (1).
[b] Total does not include reporters who responded don't know (1) or refused to answer (1).
[c] Total does not include reporters who responded don't know (1), no answer (1), or refused to answer (2).
[d] Total does not include reporters who responded no answer (2).
[e] Total does not include reporters who responded don't know (1), no answer (3), or refused to answer (2).
[f] Total does not include reporters who responded no answer (2) or refused to answer (3).
[g] Total does not include reporters who refused to answer (1).
[h] Total does not include reporters who refused to answer (1).

Table 4.5
Judging Jobs in Journalism, by Region
(Raw numbers and percentages represent the portion of respondents who said the issue is very important or important.)

Environment Reporters...	New England (2000)	Mountain West (2001)	South (2002)	Pacific West (2002, 2004-2005)	Mid Atlantic (2003-2004)	Mid Central 2004-2005)	West Central (2004-2005)	National*
The amount of autonomy you have	54 98.2%	87 96.7%	138 91.4%	102 88.7%	50 94.3%	92 91.1%	78 91.8%	601/650 92.5%
The chance to help people	48 87.3%	77 84.6%	134 89.3%	94 81.0%	48 90.6%	94 93.1%	74 88.1%	569/650 87.5%
The editorial policies	48 87.3%	79 86.8%	115 76.2%	95 83.3%	46 86.8%	85 85.0%	69 82.1%	537/648 82.9%
Job security	48 87.3%	75 83.3%	131 86.8%	102 87.9%	49 92.5%	88 87.1%	65 77.4%	558/650 85.8%
The chance to develop a specialty	49 89.1%	78 85.7%	125 82.8%	88 75.9%	44 83.0%	69 68.3%	71 83.5%	524/652 80.4%
The chance to influence public affairs	44 80.0%	65 72.2%	108 72.0%	81 71.1%	43 81.1%	70 70.0%	62 73.8%	473/646 73.2%
Fringe Benefits	50 90.9%	74 81.3%	115 77.7%	77 66.4%	41 77.4%	79 79.8%	67 78.8%	503/647 77.7%
The pay	49 89.1%	71 78.0%	121 80.0%	91 78.4%	39 73.6%	73 73.0%	59 69.4%	503/651 77.3%
The chance to get ahead	36 65.5%	47 51.6%	85 56.7%	50 43.1%	30 56.6%	55 54.5%	44 51.8%	347/651 53.3%

Now I'd like to find out how important a number of things are to you in judging jobs in your field, not just your job.

Q: The amount of autonomy you have? Is it...
Q: The chance to help people? Is it...
Q: Is the editorial policies of the organization? Is it...
Q: Job security? Is it...
Q: The chance to develop a specialty? Is it...
Q: The chance to influence public affairs? Is it...
Q: Fringe benefits? Are they...
Q: For instance, how much difference does the pay make in how you rate a job in your field—pay is...
Q: The chance to get ahead in the organization? Is it...

* In the National categories, the first number is the total of respondents in that category who said very important or important. The second number is the number of reporters who said very important, important, neither, not important, or not important at all (but does not include those responding no opinion, don't know, no answer, or refused to answer). The percentage is the percentage of respondents in each category who said the issue is very important or important when judging jobs in journalism. Each evaluation is rank ordered nationally by mean, rather than by the percent answering very important or important.

Table 4.6
Job Characteristics of Environment Reporters vs. U.S. Journalists:
Autonomy in the Newsroom

Job Characteristics	Environment Reporters (2000-05)	U.S. Journalists (2002)*	U.S Journalists (1992)**
They are almost always able to get a story covered that they think should be covered			
Almost complete	36.1%	52.0%	55.0%
Great deal	45.6%	N/A	N/A
Some	16.4%	N/A	N/A
Not much	1.8%	N/A	N/A
Not at all	0.0%	N/A	N/A
Total	99.9%***	N/A	N/A
They have almost complete freedom in selecting the stories they work on			
Almost complete	33.1%	40.0%	44.0%
Great deal	53.2%	N/A	N/A
Some	12.5%	N/A	N/A
Not much	1.1%	N/A	N/A
Not at all	0.2%	N/A	N/A
Total	100.1%***	N/A	N/A
They have almost complete freedom in deciding which aspects of a news story should be emphasized			
Almost complete	38.2%	42.0%	51.0%
Great deal	50.5%	N/A	N/A
Some	10.8%	N/A	N/A
Not much	0.6%	N/A	N/A
Not at all	0.0%	N/A	N/A
Total	100.1%***	N/A	N/A
The amount of editing your stories gets from others at your organization			
Great deal	3.1%	N/A	N/A
Considerable amount	11.7%	N/A	N/A
Some	44.8%	N/A	N/A
Little	36.9%	N/A	N/A
None at all	3.4%	16.0%	23.0%
Total	99.9%***	N/A	N/A

*Weaver et al. (2007), pp. 73-75.

**Weaver and Wilhoit (1996), pp. 62-65.

***Totals do not equal 100% due to rounding.

Table 4.7
Amount of Freedom Men and Women had in Being Able to Select Stories

Amount of freedom in selecting the stories they work on:	Environment Reporters (2000-05)				U.S. Journalists (2002)*			
	Print		Broadcast		Print		Broadcast	
	Men $n = 399$	Women $n = 173$	Men $n = 58$	Women $n = 16$	Men $n = 580$	Women $n = 291$	Men $n = 184$	Women $n = 84$
Almost complete	31.8%	35.3%	41.4%	12.5%	35.0%	39.9%	39.7%	31.0%
Great deal	56.1%	50.9%	34.5%	68.8%	45.2%	38.8%	41.3%	35.7%
Some freedom	11.3%	12.7%	20.7%	12.5%	17.9%	16.2%	17.4%	31.0%
Not much	0.8%	1.2%	3.4%	0.0%	0.0%	0.0%	0.0%	0.0%
None at all	0.0%	0.0%	0.0%	6.3%	1.9%	5.2%	1.6%	2.4%

Q: How much freedom do you usually have in selecting the stories you work on? Would you say…

*Weaver et al. (2007), p. 187.

This study tested the proposition that reporters say editors are a barrier to environment reporting. Reporters were asked about 17 potential barriers, including editors, time constraints, competition in the local media market, and pressure from advertisers. Reporters ranked each of them on a scale ranging from 1 (always a barrier) to 5 (never a barrier).

This study found that everyday, practical journalistic process concerns such as time constraints were far more likely to be rated as always or often a barrier (see Table 4.8). The problem of time constraints led the list with a mean of 2.46 (2 = often a barrier, 3 = sometimes). The second most common barrier was financial, travel or other resource constraints (mean = 3.09). The expected problem of editors or supervisors ranked ninth of the 17; 25.9 percent of the respondents said editors were a barrier at least sometimes. Other factors such as a reporter's colleagues, advertisers, competition in the local media market, and university sources of information were seen as rarely (in terms of their means) posing barriers to reporting on environmental stories. A regional breakdown showed time constraints were a universal barrier; at least 88.7 percent of the environment reporters in every region said they were always, often, or sometimes a barrier to their work (see Table 4.9).

Reporters' Perceptions of Editors and the Audience

While editors were not singled out as a barrier to environment reporting, did reporters think they were supportive of the efforts to cover the environment? How did reporters feel about readers and viewers who consume news stories? The study used a three-part series of questions designed to showcase differences in the ways reporters view themselves, their editors, and their readers or viewers in terms of environmental coverage.

Not surprisingly, most environment reporters felt environmental stories were important and worthy of play. Some 98.8 percent of reporters said such stories were important or very important (see Table 4.10). But the results did not vary much for editors or the public. Some 85.6 percent of environment reporters felt their editors viewed environmental stories as important or very important, and 82.4 percent of environment reporters felt the public viewed these stories as important and worthy of play. The results were consistent across regions and thus consistent across time, from 2000 to 2005 (see Table 4.11).

The study also sought to gauge reporter views of the audience in other questions. Asked whether "the audience has little interest in environment stories," only 10.6 percent of environment reporters agreed (see Table 4.12). This is one place in the survey where regional differences

Table 4.8
Potential Barriers to Environmental Reporting
(Raw numbers and percentages represent the actual number of respondents
in each category.)

Environment Reporters...	Always	Often	Sometimes	Rarely	Never	Total	Mean*
Time constraints	88 13.6%	236 36.4%	285 43.9%	20 3.1%	20 3.1%	649[a] 100.1%**	2.46
Financial, travel or other resource constraints	33 5.1%	149 23.1%	289 44.8%	74 11.5%	100 15.5%	645[b] 100.0%	3.09
Size news hole	27 4.2%	113 17.5%	286 44.4%	128 19.9%	90 14.0%	644[c] 100.0%	3.22
Audiences lack of technical knowledge on env. issues	18 2.8%	123 19.3%	282 44.3%	108 17.0%	106 16.6%	637[d] 100.0%	3.25
Your lack of technical knowledge on env. issues	9 1.4%	28 4.3%	334 51.9%	163 25.3%	110 17.1%	644[e] 100.0%	3.52
Government sources	4 0.6%	53 8.1%	322 49.4%	114 17.5%	159 24.4%	652 100.0%	3.57
Need to give stories a "human face"	17 2.6%	73 11.3%	244 37.8%	150 23.2%	162 25.1%	646[f] 100.0%	3.57
Legal concerns	16 2.5%	29 4.5%	163 25.3%	207 32.2%	228 35.5%	643[g] 100.0%	3.94
Your editors or supervisors	6 0.9%	17 2.6%	145 22.4%	183 28.2%	297 45.8%	648[h] 99.9%**	4.15
Ethical concerns	8 1.3%	20 3.2%	111 17.9%	195 31.5%	285 46.0%	619[i] 99.9%**	4.18
Other business or corporate interests	1 0.2%	28 4.4%	137 21.5%	118 18.5%	354 55.5%	638[j] 100.1%**	4.25
Environmental activists	0 0%	11 1.7%	123 19.0%	150 23.1%	364 56.2%	648[k] 100.0%	4.34
University sources	1 0.2%	5 0.8%	100 15.6%	172 26.9%	361 56.5%	639[l] 100.0%	4.39
Your publisher, station manager or owner	1 0.2%	14 2.2%	83 13.0%	161 25.2%	381 59.5%	640[m] 100.1%**	4.42
The competition in local news market	0 0%	13 2.0%	74 11.5%	109 17.0%	446 69.5%	642[n] 100.0%	4.54
Advertisers	0 0%	12 1.9%	69 10.9%	98 15.5%	453 71.7%	632[o] 100.0%	4.57
Your colleagues	0 0%	6 0.9%	30 4.6%	128 19.8%	482 74.6%	646[p] 99.9%**	4.68

I'd like to find out whether certain people, problems and institutions are a <u>barrier</u> in reporting on environmental stories. For example,

Q: Time constraints. Would you say they are...

Q: Financial, travel, or other resource constraints. Would you say they are...

Q: The size of the news hole. Would you say the size of the news hole is...

Q: The audience's lack of technical knowledge on environmental issues. Would you say that is...

Q: Your lack of technical knowledge on environmental issues. Would you say that is...

Q: The need to give stories "a human face." Would you say that is...

Q: Government sources. Would you say they are...

Q: Legal concerns. Would you say they are...

Q: Your editors or supervisors. Would you say they are...

Q: Ethical concerns. Would you say they are...

Q: Other business or corporate interests. Would you say they are...

Q: Environmental activists. Would you say they are...

Q: University sources. Would you say they are...

Q: Your publisher, station manager or owner. Would you say they are...

Q: The competition in local news markets. Would you say they are...

Q: Advertisers. Would you say they are...

Q: Your colleagues. Would you say they are...

* Barriers are ranked by mean score, lowest to highest. Index ranged from: Always = 1.0 to Never = 5.0.

** Percentage does not total 100 because of rounding.

[a] Total does not include reporters who responded don't know (3).

[b] Total does not include reporters who responded don't know (1), no answer (5), or refused to answer (1).

[c] Total does not include reporters who responded don't know (3), no answer (4), or refused to answer (1).

[d] Total does not include reporters who responded don't know (10), no answer (4), or refused to answer (1).

[e] Total does not include reporters who responded don't know (4) or no answer (4).

[f] Total does not include reporters who responded no answer (5) or refused to answer (1).

[g] Total does not include reporters who responded don't know (4) or no answer (5).

[h] Total does not include reporters who responded don't know (2) or no answer (2).

[i] Total does not include reporters who responded don't know (17), no answer (11), or refused to answer (5).

[j] Total does not include reporters who responded don't know (7), no answer (3), or refused to answer (4).

[k] Total does not include reporters who responded don't know (2), no answer (1), or refused to answer (1).

[l] Total does not include reporters who responded don't know (7), no answer (5), or refused to answer (1).

[m] Total does not include reporters who responded don't know (7) or no answer (5)

[n] Total does not include reporters who responded don't know (5) or no answer (5).

[o] Total does not include reporters who responded don't know (12), no answer (7), or refused to answer (1).

[p] Total does not include reporters who responded don't know (3) or no answer (3).

Table 4.9
Potential Barriers to Environmental Reporting, by Region
(Raw numbers and percentages represent the portion of respondents who said the issue is always, often, or sometimes a barrier.)

Environment Reporters…	New England (2000)	Mountain West (2001)	South (2002)	Pacific West (2002, 2004-2005)	Mid Atlantic (2003-2004)	Mid Central (2004-2005)	West Central (2004-2005)	National*
Time constraints	50 92.6%	88 96.7%	138 91.4%	113 97.4%	47 88.7%	92 92.9%	81 95.3%	609/649 93.8%
Financial, travel or other resource constraints	35 64.8%	69 75.8%	119 78.8%	90 77.6%	31 58.5%	68 70.8%	59 70.2%	471/645 73.0%
Size news hole	38 69.1%	61 67.0%	96 64.4%	70 60.3%	33 63.5%	70 71.4%	58 69.9%	426/644 66.1%
Audience's lack of technical knowledge on env. issues	25 48.1%	56 61.5%	102 68.5%	64 57.1%	32 61.5%	81 81.8%	63 76.8%	423/637 66.4%
Your lack of technical knowledge on env. issues	30 55.6%	55 60.4%	78 52.3%	69 60.0%	33 62.3%	53 54.6%	53 62.4%	371/644 57.6%
Government sources	29 52.7%	54 59.3%	85 56.3%	69 59.5%	39 73.6%	56 55.4%	47 55.3%	379/652 58.1%
Need to give stories a "human face"	24 43.6%	47 51.6%	79 52.3%	68 58.5%	28 52.8%	48 50.0%	40 47.6%	334/646 51.7%
Legal concerns	17 31.5%	21 23.3%	59 39.1%	21 18.6%	21 40.1%	37 37.4%	32 38.1%	208/643 32.3%
Your editors or supervisors	23 41.8%	23 25.3%	41 27.2%	30 25.9%	17 32.7%	19 19.2%	15 17.9%	168/648 25.9%
Ethical concerns	7 13.0%	25 28.7%	36 24.7%	21 18.9%	9 17.3%	18 20.0%	23 29.1%	139/619 22.5%
Other business or corporate interests	12 21.8%	28 31.1%	39 26.7%	24 21.1%	12 22.6%	27 27.3%	24 29.6%	166/638 26.0%
Environmental activists	17 31.5%	21 23.1%	34 22.5%	22 19.0%	7 13.5%	19 19.0%	14 16.7%	134/648 20.7%
University sources	4 7.3%	20 23.0%	27 18.1%	19 16.8%	8 15.4%	18 18.4%	10 11.8%	106/639 16.6%
Your publisher, station manager or owner	10 18.2%	18 20.2%	27 17.9%	14 12.2%	12 24.5%	10 10.2%	7 8.4%	98/640 15.3%
The competition in local news market	6 11.1%	13 14.4%	15 9.9%	17 14.8%	11 22.4%	15 15.2%	10 11.9%	87/642 13.6%
Advertisers	6 11.1%	12 14.0%	15 10.1%	11 9.6%	5 9.8%	17 17.3%	15 18.5%	81/632 12.8%
Your colleagues	3 5.6%	6 6.6%	8 5.3%	8 6.9%	3 5.8%	4 4.0%	4 4.9%	36/646 5.6%

I'd like to find out whether certain people, problems and institutions are a <u>barrier</u> in reporting on environmental stories. For example,

Q: Time constraints. Would you say they are…

Q: Financial, travel, or other resource constraints. Would you say they are…

Q: The size of the news hole. Would you say the size of the news hole is…

Q: The audience's lack of technical knowledge on environmental issues. Would you say that is…
Q: Your lack of technical knowledge on environmental issues. Would you say that is…
Q: The need to give stories "a human face." Would you say that is…
Q: Government sources. Would you say they are…
Q: Legal concerns. Would you say they are…
Q: Your editors or supervisors. Would you say they are…
Q: Ethical concerns. Would you say they are…
Q: Other business or corporate interests. Would you say they are…
Q: Environmental activists. Would you say they are…
Q: University sources. Would you say they are…
Q: Your publisher, station manager or owner. Would you say they are…
Q: The competition in local news markets. Would you say they are…
Q: Advertisers. Would you say they are…
Q: Your colleagues. Would you say they are…

* In the National categories, the first number is the total of respondents in that category who said always, often, or sometimes. The second number is the number of reporters who answered always, often, sometimes, rarely, or never (but does not include those responding no opinion, don't know, no answer, or refused to answer). The percentage is the percentage of respondents in each category who said the issue is always, often, or sometimes a barrier to environmental reporting. Each potential barrier is rank ordered nationally by mean, rather than by the percent answering always, often, or sometimes

Table 4.10
Reporters' Perceptions of Importance of Environmental Stories
to their Editors, their Readers, and Themselves

(Raw numbers and percentages represent the actual number of respondents in each category.)

Perceptions of Importance	Very Important	Important	Neither	Not Important	Not Important at all	Total	Mean*
The Reporter	439 67.6%	202 31.1%	8 1.2%	0 0.0%	0 0.0%	649[a] 99.9%**	1.34
The Editor	207 32.4%	339 53.1%	78 12.2%	14 2.2%	0 0.0%	638[b] 99.9%**	1.84
The Public	170 26.6%	356 55.8%	93 14.6%	18 2.8%	1 0.2%	638[c] 100.0%	1.94

Q: To what extent do you think environmental stories are important and worthy of prominent play? In general, do you see them as…
Q: How about your editors? To what extent do your editors feel environmental stories are important and worthy of prominent play? In general, do they see them as…
Q: How about the public? To what extent does the public feel environmental stories are important and worthy of prominent play? In general, do they see them as…

* Perceptions are ranked by mean score, lowest to highest. Index ranged from: Very Important = 1.0 to Not Important at all = 5.0.
** Percentage does not total 100 because of rounding.
a Total does not include reporters who responded don't know (1) or refused to answer (2).
b Total does not include reporters who responded don't know (6) or no answer (8).
c Total does not include reporters who responded don't know (10) or no answer (4).

Table 4.11
Reporters' Perceptions of Importance of Environmental Stories to Themselves, their Editors, and the Public, by Region
(Raw numbers and percentages represent the portion of respondents who said the issue is very important or important.)

Perceptions of Importance	New England (2000)	Mountain West (2001)	South (2002)	Pacific West (2002, 2004-2005)	Mid Atlantic (2003-2004)	Mid Central 2004-2005)	West Central (2004-2005)	National*
The Reporter	55 100.0%	90 100.0%	148 98.0%	115 100.0%	51 98.0%	97 96.0%	85 100.0%	641/649 98.8%
The Editor	43 78.2%	79 86.8%	128 85.3%	104 89.7%	42 82.4%	77 82.8%	73 89.0%	546/638 85.6%
The Public	45 83.3%	76 85.4%	120 81.1%	107 93.0%	41 77.4%	70 73.7%	67 79.8%	526/638 82.4%

Q: To what extent do you think environmental stories are important and worthy of prominent play? In general, do you see them as…
Q: How about your editors? To what extent do your editors feel environmental stories are important and worthy of prominent play? In general, do they see them as…
Q: How about the public? To what extent does the public feel environmental stories are important and worthy of prominent play? In general, do they see them as…

*In the National categories, the first number is the total of respondents in that category who said very important or important. The second number is the number of reporters who said very important, important, neither, not important, or not important at all (but does not include those responding no opinion, don't know, no answer, or refused to answer). The percentage is the percentage of respondents in each category who said the importance of environmental stories is very important or important.

emerged. Reporters in the West Central states (17.1 percent), the Mid Central (11.3 percent), and the South (11.0 percent) were more likely to think readers and viewers had little interest in environment stories, compared to 5.6 percent of reporters in New England, 8.0 percent in the Mid Atlantic states, 8.9 percent in the Pacific West, and 9.9 percent in the Mountain West (see Table 4.13).

On another audience dimension, 54.9 percent of environment reporters agreed that audience members prefer breaking news about environmental issues to an analysis of those issues. Here, too, there were noticeable regional differences in the reporters' assessment of audience desires. While 72.9 percent of Mid Atlantic reporters felt the audience preferred breaking news to analytical stories, reporters were far less likely to agree with that assessment in the Pacific West (41.1 percent), New England (44.4 percent), and the Mountain West (45.0 percent).

Table 4.12
Reporters' Perceptions of Audience Interest
(Raw numbers and percentages represent the actual number of respondents in each category.)

Environment Reporters…	Strongly Agree	Agree	Disagree	Strongly Disagree	Total	Mean*
Audience prefers breaking news to analysis of environmental issues	47 8.3%	265 46.7%	241 42.4%	15 2.6%	568[a] 100.0%	2.39
Audience has little interest in environmental stories	3 0.5%	64 10.1%	441 69.8%	124 19.6%	632[b] 100.0%	3.09

Q: (Readers, viewers) are more interested in the day's breaking news about environmental issues than in analysis of those environmental issues. Do you…

Q: The majority of (readers, viewers) have little interest in (reading about, viewing) problems such as the environment. Do you…

* Sources that they talk to are ranked by mean score, lowest to highest. Index ranged from: Strongly agree = 1.0 to Strongly disagree = 4.0.

a Total does not include reporters who responded no opinion (44), don't know (39), or refused to answer (1).

b Total does not include reporters who responded no opinion (16), or don't know (4).

Table 4.13
Reporters' Perceptions of Audience Interest, by Region
(Raw numbers and percentages represent actual number of respondents in each category who strongly agreed or agreed with the statement)

Environment Reporters…	New England	Mountain West	South	Pacific West	Mid Atlantic	Mid Central	West Central	National*
Audience prefers breaking news to analysis of environmental issues	20 44.4%	36 45.0%	78 58.6%	39 41.1%	35 72.9%	56 59.6%	48 65.8%	312/568 54.9%
Audience has little interest in environment stories	3 5.6%	9 9.9%	16 11.0%	10 8.9%	4 8.0%	11 11.3%	14 17.1%	67/632 10.6%

Q: (Readers, viewers) are more interested in the day's breaking news about environmental issues than in analysis of those environmental issues. Do you…

Q: The majority of (readers, viewers) have little interest in (reading about, viewing) problems such as the environment. Do you…

*In the National categories, the first number is the total of respondents in that category who answered strongly agree or agree. The second number is the number of reporters who answered strongly agree, agree, neither, disagree, or strongly disagree (but does not include those responding no opinion, don't know, no answer, or refused to answer). The percentage is the percentage of respondents in each category who said they strongly agree or agree with the statement. Each perspective on coverage or audience interest is rank ordered nationally by mean, rather than by the percent answering strongly agree.

Bruggers said the most challenging and intellectually stimulating part of the job is how it cuts across the newsroom. "One day I may be a cops reporter because someone in town has been arrested for black-market sale of regulated chemicals like Freon.... The next day I may cover the governor or state legislature as a political reporter. Then the next day a business may get into trouble, and I am a business reporter. It really cuts across all the other beats and is incredibly diverse. The potential stories are never boring. It's always something different, a broad range of issues."

Bruggers is saying that environment stories frame themselves depending on whether they are about business, politics, etc. Most environment reporters agree, stating that they cover environmental stories from many different angles. The reporters' use of news angles or frames is discussed in detail in the next chapter.

Notes

1.   Earlier versions of elements of this chapter were originally written by the authors and published in:
        David B. Sachsman, James Simon, and JoAnn Myer Valenti, "Environment Reporters and U.S. Journalists: A Comparative Analysis," *Applied Environmental Education and Communication* 7 (2008): 1-19.
2.   Jim Bruggers, personal interview conducted by James Simon, May 7, 2007. Unrelated to the survey.
3.   Ibid.
4.   Sachsman, Simon, Valenti, "Environment Reporters and U.S. Journalists," 14.
5.   Ibid.
6.   Ibid.
7.   Ibid.
8.   Ibid. 14, 17.
9.   Ibid. 18.

5

Covering the Environment[1]

Mike Dunne was one of America's excellent environment reporters.
This chapter is dedicated to Dunne, who passed away shortly after he
contributed to this book.

Whether he was writing about the aftermath of Hurricane Katrina
or Louisiana's vanishing wetlands, environment reporter Mike Dunne
sounded like a professional juggler when he described how he weighed
which sources to quote and what kind of framework to use in presenting
a story. "I might need the state regulator's voice and an environmental
group, or a business and then the academic/scientist," Dunne said, running through the sources he routinely used as a special projects reporter
for *The Advocate* in Baton Rouge, Louisiana.[2]

"Balance is always important—getting both or all sides of a story.
That does not mean I give each side the same number of paragraphs
or words or inches but I get their point of view into the story. And, of
course, some folks communicate better than others and often I go to the
folks I know can communicate. An expert who can't make his study or
knowledge of the topic understandable makes it harder work for me. So,
if I have a choice of two, I will often pick and focus more on the one
who does communicate."

Dunne used that kind of balancing act to help win numerous reporting
awards on the state, regional, and national levels, including the Scripps-
Howard Edward Meeman Award given for the best environmental writing
in the nation.

"You want to connect with the reader, up top, early on. Environmental
stories are great for that because it is about the environment—it affects
everybody. It's a political story. It's an economic story. It's a human
interest story. It's a nature story. It covers everything; that's what I love

Table 5.1

Additional News Angles or Frames Included in Environmental Stories

(Raw numbers and percentages represent the actual number of respondents in each category.)

Environment Reporters...	Always	Often	Sometimes	Rarely	Never	Total	Mean*
Government angle	83 12.8%	409 63.0%	136 21.0%	16 2.5%	5 0.8%	649[a] 100.1%**	2.15
Human interest angle	103 15.8%	302 46.4%	222 34.1%	22 3.4%	2 0.3%	651[b] 100.0%	2.26
Business or economic angle	74 11.4%	315 48.5%	218 33.6%	37 5.7%	5 0.8%	649[c] 100.0%	2.36
Pollution angle	60 9.3%	281 43.4%	277 42.8%	25 3.9%	4 0.6%	647[d] 100.0%	2.43
Nature or wilderness angle	32 4.9%	303 46.7%	253 39.0%	55 8.5%	6 0.9%	649[e] 100.0%	2.54
Science or technology angle	31 4.8%	219 33.6%	315 48.4%	81 12.4%	5 0.8%	651[f] 100.0%	2.71
Political angle	49 7.5%	217 33.4%	266 40.9%	106 16.3%	12 1.8%	650[g] 99.9%**	2.72
Health angle	27 4.2%	209 32.2%	329 50.6%	76 11.7%	9 1.4%	650[h] 100.1%**	2.74
Risk assessment angle	16 2.5%	123 19.4%	307 48.3%	175 27.6%	14 2.2%	635[i] 100.0%	3.08

Q: Sometimes environmental stories deal only with the environment. Sometimes they also deal with other issues.

Looking back on the stories you have done, how often would you say they also <u>involve a business or economic angle</u>. Would you say your environmental stories...

Q: A government angle. Would you say your environmental stories...

Q: A political angle. Would you say your environmental stories...

Q: A human interest angle. Would you say your environmental stories...

Q: A pollution angle. Would you say your environmental stories...

Q: A nature or wilderness angle. Would you say your environmental stories...

Q: A science or technology angle. Would you say your environmental stories...

Q: A health angle. Would you say your environmental stories...

Q: A risk assessment angle. Would you say your environmental stories...

* Story angles are ranked by mean score, lowest to highest. Index ranged from: Always = 1.0 to Never = 5.0.

** Percentage does not total 100 because of rounding.

[a] Total does not include reporters who responded don't know (1) or no answer (2).

[b] Total does not include reporters who responded no answer (1).

[c] Total does not include reporters who responded no answer (2) or refused to answer (1).

[d] Total does not include reporters who responded don't know (3) or no answer (2).

[e] Total does not include reporters who responded no answer (1) or refused to answer (2).

[f] Total does not include reporters who responded no answer (1).

[g] Total does not include reporters who responded don't know (1) or no answer (1).

[h] Total does not include reporters who responded no answer (2)

[i] Total does not include reporters who responded don't know (6), no answer (9), or refused to answer (2).

about it," he said in an interview conducted separately from this study's anonymous national survey of reporters.[3]

Dunne also loved the challenge of taking the technical jargon of his sources and presenting it to the audience in terms that could be understood. "If I don't do a good job of translating the technical into the everyday, then I've failed my job. People love those kinds of stories....I get a lot of response from science stories that help explain what hurricanes do, or why the coast does what it does, and why the coast disappears. I get a better response out of that than the government stories," he said.

News Angles in Environmental Stories

Dunne's balancing act in using varied sources and varied frameworks for stories mirrored the decisions faced by environment reporters throughout the country, including the 652 interviewed for this study.

Sometimes environmental stories deal only with the environment. Sometimes they also deal with other issues. The study asked reporters how often they used nine potential story frameworks or angles. The reporters ranked each from a score of 1 (always) to 5 (never).

The mean scores for eight of the nine angles ranged between often (score of 2) and sometimes (score of 3) (see Table 5.1). A government angle was the highest ranked and most frequently used (mean = 2.15), followed by a human interest angle (2.26), business or economic (2.36), pollution (2.43), nature or wilderness (2.54), science or technology (2.71), political (2.72), health (2.74), and risk assessment angle (3.08).

Table 5.2 shows the heavy use of almost all of the angles by combining the percentage of reporters who said they always, often, or sometimes used a given angle. Nationally, the top five angles were used by at least 90 percent of the environment reporters. Three others were used by at least 80 percent of reporters. The least used was a risk assessment angle, and even there 70.2 percent of reporters nationwide said they used it sometimes, often, or always.

News Sources Used in Environmental Reporting

Environment reporters have a wide variety of sources they can use for information, and this study asked a number of questions about these sources. First, the reporters were asked how often they used 29 types of sources, ranging from federal agencies to state and local government offices, environment groups and environmentalists, to business groups, plus academics. They rated them using a five point scale running from 1 = always used as a source to 5 = never used.

Table 5.2
Additional News Angles or Frames Included in Environmental Stories, by Region

(Raw numbers and percentages represent the respondents who said stories always, often, or sometimes involve the angle. Nationally, each news angle is rank ordered by mean, rather than by the percent answering always, often, or sometimes. Regionally, the rank orders by mean are listed in parentheses.)

Environment Reporters...	New England (2000)*	Mountain West (2001)*	South (2002-2003)*	Pacific West (2002, 2004-2005)*	Mid Atlantic (2003-2004)*	Mid Central (2004-2005)*	West Central (2004-2005)*	National**
Government angle	54 98.1% (1)	91 100.0% (1)	147 97.3% (1)	115 99.1% (1)	51 96.2% (2)	92 92.0% (2)	78 94.0% (2)	628/649 96.8% (1)
Human interest angle	54 98.8% (2)	89 97.8% (4)	143 92.3% (2)	111 95.7% (4)	50 94.3% (3)	98 98.0% (1)	82 96.5% (1)	627/651 96.3% (2)
Business or economic angle	49 90.7% (3)	88 96.7% (2)	141 94.0% (4)	110 94.8% (2)	48 90.6% (4)	92 92.0% (4)	79 92.9% (3)	607/649 93.5% (3)
Pollution angle	54 98.1% (4)	81 90.0% (7)	147 97.4% (3)	112 96.6% (6)	50 96.2% (1)	94 95.0% (3)	80 95.2% (4)	618/647 95.5% (4)
Nature or wilderness angle	53 96.4% (5)	89 97.8% (3)	132 88.6% (5)	110 94.8% (5)	44 83.0% (5)	86 86.0% (6)	74 87.1% (7)	588/649 90.6% (5)
Science or technology angle	49 89.0% (6)	81 89.0% (6)	131 86.8% (6)	100 86.2% (7)	45 84.9% (6)	85 85.0% (7)	74 87.1% (6)	565/651 86.6% (6)
Political angle	46 83.6% (7)	82 90.1% (5)	122 80.8% (8)	107 92.2% (3)	40 75.5% (8)	65 65.0% (9)	70 83.3% (8)	532/650 81.8% (7)
Health angle	53 96.4% (8)	71 78.0% (8)	130 86.1% (7)	99 85.3% (8)	46 86.8% (7)	88 88.9% (5)	78 91.8% (5)	565/650 86.9% (8)
Risk assessment angle	38 71.7% (9)	62 70.0% (9)	105 71.4% (9)	72 64.3% (9)	35 66.0% (9)	70 71.4% (8)	64 77.1% (9)	446/635 70.2% (9)

Q: Sometimes environmental stories deal only with the environment. Sometimes they also deal with other issues.

Looking back on the stories you have done, how often would you say they also involve a business or economic angle. Would you say your environmental stories...

Q: A government angle. Would you say your environmental stories...

Q: A political angle. Would you say your environmental stories...

Q: A human interest angle. Would you say your environmental stories...

Q: A pollution angle. Would you say your environmental stories...

Q: A nature or wilderness angle. Would you say your environmental stories...

Q: A science or technology angle. Would you say your environmental stories...

Q: A health angle. Would you say your environmental stories...

Q: A risk assessment angle. Would you say your environmental stories...

* In the regional categories, the first number is the total of respondents in that category who said always, often, or sometimes. The percentage is the percentage of respondents in each category who said their stories always, often, or sometimes involve the angle. The third number, given in parentheses, is the rank order of each story angle by mean, rather than by the percentage answering always, often, or sometimes.

** In the national categories, the first number is the total of respondents in that category who said always, often, or sometimes. The second number is the number of reporters who answered always, often, sometimes, rarely, or never (but does not include those responding no opinion, don't know, no answer, or refused to answer). The percentage is the percentage of respondents in each category who said their stories always, often, or sometimes involve the angle. Each news angle is rank ordered nationally by mean, rather than by the percent answering always, often, or sometimes.

Table 5.3 uses mean scores to rank order all 29 sources. There were many state agencies and local government offices in the top half of the list, with the state department of environmental quality ranking number one. Local environmental groups and local individuals active on the environment were very popular sources. Although they only represented two of the 29 sources, they were ranked second and third in frequency of use by the reporters. Only one question was asked about academic researchers; they were the fifth most used source. But out of the top 15 sources, there is only one federal agency: the U.S. Environmental Protection Agency. Environment reporters generally are far more likely to use sources closer to home than those that are distant. While federal agencies may seem to dominate the headlines, the majority of them were ranked in the lower half of the list of 29 sources.

The results are at odds with the popular concept of liberal environmental reporters tilting toward environmental advocacy groups as sources to the detriment of competing business interests. (The issue of whether environment reporters are balanced in their coverage of business also is explored later in this chapter and, at length, in Chapter 6, "Wrestling with Objectivity and Fairness.")

This study included four nationally known environmental groups by name—Sierra Club, Audubon Society, Natural Resources Defense Council, and Greenpeace. All four were ranked in the bottom half of the 29 sources; in fact, Greenpeace was the single least used source. In contrast, local manufacturers and developers and other business leaders were ranked seventh, and the Chamber of Commerce was ranked eighteenth. The Chemical Manufacturers Association, on the other hand, was ranked third from the bottom of the list.

Since this study was conducted regionally, the researchers were able to compare the sources used by environment reporters in each region. In almost every case, the regional figures for the use of sources were consistent with the national figures given in Table 5.3. The regional results were so consistent with the national results that there are only a handful of outliers: New England environment reporters used the Audubon

Table 5.3
Ranking of Environment Reporter Sources, by Mean Score
(1 = always used as source; 5 = never used)

Rank Order	Source	Type of Source	Mean
1.	State Department of Env. Quality	State Government Agencies	2.25
2.	Local Environmental groups	Local Env. Groups / Individuals	2.30
3.	Individual Citizens active on the Env.	Local Env. Groups / Individuals	2.33
4.	State Department of Natural Resources	State Government Agencies	2.37
5.	Academic officials, professors, researchers	Academics	2.48
6.	State Department of Health	State Government Agencies	2.66
7.	Local manufacturers, developers, or business leaders	Business-Related Organizations	2.71
8.	State legislative offices	State Government Agencies	2.72
9.	Environmental Protection Agency	Federal Agencies	2.77
10.	Health Department	Local Env. Groups / Individuals	2.78
11.	Mayor or top municipal official	Local Env. Groups / Individuals	2.86
12.	Local city or town council offices	Local Env. Groups / Individuals	2.92
13.	County administrators	Local Env. Groups / Individuals	2.93
14.	Governor's office	State Government Agencies	3.05
15.	Department of Transportation	State Government Agencies	3.11
16.	Department of Food and Agriculture	State Government Agencies	3.20
17.	Centers for Disease Control and Prevention	Federal Agencies	3.27
18.	Chamber of Commerce	Business-Related Organizations	3.30
19.	Sierra Club	Local Env. Groups / Individuals	3.33
20.	Audubon Society	Local Env. Groups / Individuals	3.49
21.	Department of Energy	Federal Agencies	3.55
22.	Department of Transportation	Federal Agencies	3.61
23.	Natural Resources Defense Council	Local Env. Groups / Individuals	3.81
24.	Food and Drug Administration	Federal Agencies	3.89
25.	National Science Foundation	Federal Agencies	3.98
26.	Agency for Toxic Substances and Disease Registry	Federal Agencies	4.03
27.	Chemical Manufacturers Association	Business-Related Organizations	4.06
28.	National Health and Safety Administration	Federal Agencies	4.11
29.	Greenpeace	Local Env. Groups / Individuals	4.36

Q: Now I am going to read you a list of potential <u>sources</u> that you might use on environmental stories. Please tell me if you always use the source in your reporting, often use it, sometimes use it, rarely use it or never use it.

Federal:
Q: For example, the federal Environmental Protection Agency. Would you say that you...
Q: The Centers for Disease Control and Prevention. Would you say that you...
Q: The Department of Energy. Would you say that you...
Q: The Department of Transportation. Would you say that you...
Q: The Food and Drug Administration. Would you say that you...
Q: National Science Foundation. Would you say that you...
Q: Agency for Toxic Substances and Disease Registry. Would you say that you...
Q: National Health and Safety Council. Would you say that you...

State:
Q: Your Department of Environmental Quality (or Environmental Management). Would you say that you...
Q: Your Dept. of Natural Resources. Would you say that you...
Q: Your state Department of Health (or Public Health). Would you say that you...
Q: Legislative offices. Would you say that you...
Q: The governor's office. Would you say that you...
Q: Your state Dept. of Transportation. Would you say that you...
Q: Your state Department of Food and Agriculture. Would you say that you...

Local:
Q: Local departments of health. Would you say that you...
Q: The mayor or top municipal official in local cities and towns. Would you say that you...
Q: Local City or town council offices. Would you say that you...
Q: County administrators. Would you say that you...

Environmental Organizations:
Q: Local environmental groups. Would you say that you ...
Q: And how about individual, local citizens who are active on the environment? Would you say that you...
Q: Sierra Club. Would you say that you...
Q: Audubon Society. Would you say that you...
Q: Natural Resources Defense Council. Would you say that you...
Q: Greenpeace. Would you say that you...

Business:
Q: Local manufacturers, developers or other business leaders. Would you say that you...
Q: The Chamber of Commerce. (local or national if they ask) Would you say that you...
Q: The Chemical Manufacturers Association. Would you say that you ...

Academic:
Q: Academic officials, professors and researchers at colleges and universities. Would you say that you...

Table 5.4
Most Used and Least Used Sources, by Region
(Percentages represent the portion of respondents who said they use the source always, often, or sometimes.)

Environment Reporters…	Top 3	Bottom 3
New England	1. State Department of Environmental Quality (100.0%) 2. Individual Citizens (100.0%) 3. Local Environmental Groups (100.0%)	27. Chemical Manufacturers Association (20.0%) 28. National Health and Safety Council (18.2%) 29. Greenpeace (10.9%)
Mountain West	1. Local Environmental Groups (100.0%) 2. State Department of Environmental Quality (96.7%) 3. Individual Citizens (96.6%)	27. National Health and Safety Council (18.7%) 28. Food and Drug Administration (17.6%) 29. Greenpeace (10.9%)
South	1. State Department of Environmental Quality (94.6%) 2. Local Environmental Groups (93.4%) 3. Individual Citizens (93.2%)	27. National Health and Safety Council (29.3%) 28. National Science Foundation (26.0%) 29. Greenpeace (13.2%)
Pacific West	1. Local Environmental Groups (98.3%) 2. Individual Citizens (93.7%) 3. State Department of Environmental Quality (93.0%)	27. Food and Drug Administration (24.1%) 28. National Health and Safety Council (24.1%) 29. Greenpeace (11.2%)
Mid Atlantic	1. Individual Citizens (92.5%) 2. Local Environmental Groups (92.3%) 3. State Department of Natural Resources (91.7%)	27. National Science Foundation (26.4%) 28. National Health and Safety Council (22.6%) 29. Greenpeace (17.0%)
Mid Central	1. State Department of Natural Resources (98.0%) 2. Local Department of Health (94.9%) 3. Individual Citizens (94.9%)	27. Chemical Manufacturers Association (25.5%) 28. Agency for Toxic Substances and Disease Registry (24.0%) 29. Greenpeace (15.3%)
West Central	1. State Department of Environmental Quality (95.2%) 2. Academic Officials, Professors, Researchers (94.1%) 3. Local Environmental Groups (92.9%)	27. National Health and Safety Council (30.6%) 28. Chemical Manufacturers Association (21.2%) 29. Greenpeace (7.1%)

Society as a source more often than reporters in any other region, and used manufacturers, developers, and local business leaders, and county administrators less often. Mountain West reporters used the federal Department of Energy more often than environment reporters in any other region, and used the Centers for Disease Control less often than reporters in any other region. West Central reporters used the U.S. Environmental Protection Agency less frequently than environment reporters in any other region. Consistency among regions is illustrated in Table 5.4, which shows the three most used and the three least used sources, by region. The complete data for the use of sources by environment reporters can be found in Appendix B.

Another way to analyze the use of sources is to focus on what type of source a reporter talks to, regardless of the agency or office. Using a five-point scale, ranging from 1 = always to 5 = never, the reporters were asked to indicate how often they talked to public information officers, scientists, and administrators. While there is sometimes a knee-

Table 5.5
Use and Value of Public Information, Scientific, and Administrative Sources

(Raw numbers and percentages represent the actual number of respondents in each category.)

Environment Reporters...	Always	Often	Sometimes	Rarely	Never	Total	Mean*
1. *Who do you talk to?*							
Public Information Officers	71 11.0%	388 59.9%	157 24.2%	30 4.6%	2 0.3%	648[a] 100.0%	2.23
Scientists	33 5.1%	333 51.2%	221 34.0%	56 8.6%	7 1.1%	650[b] 100.0%	2.49
Administrators	16 2.5%	289 44.5%	283 43.5%	56 8.6%	6 0.9%	650[c] 100.0%	2.61

2. *Whose time do you value?*	Very high value	Fairly high value	Some value	Little value	No value	Total	Mean**
Scientists	304 47.3%	277 43.1%	56 8.7%	2 0.3%	4 0.6%	643[d] 100.0%	1.64
Administrators	96 14.9%	259 40.2%	245 38.0%	43 6.7%	2 0.3%	645[e] 100.1%***	2.37
Public Information Officers	27 4.2%	182 28.3%	370 57.6%	58 9.0%	5 0.8%	642[f] 99.9%***	2.74

Ok, now I'd like to know who you talk to when you call these public and private organizations for information on environmental stories.

Q: For example, how about public information officers.
Q: How about scientists? In your environmental reporting, would you say you talk to scientists...
Q: How about administrators of the government agency or private group. In your environmental reporting, would you say you talk to administrators...

Finally, we want to know whether you value the time you spend with each of these sources.

Q: How about the public information officers. Would you say the time you spend with them on a story has...
Q: How about scientists. Would you say the time you spend with them on a story has...
Q: How about administrators. Would you say the time you spend with them on a story has...

* Sources that they talk to are ranked by mean score, lowest to highest. Index ranged from: Always = 1.0 to Never = 5.0.
** Sources that they value are ranked by mean score, lowest to highest. Index ranged from: Very high value = 1.0 to No value = 5.0.
***Percentage does not total 100 because of rounding.
[a] Total does not include reporters who responded no answer (3) or don't know (1).
[b] Total does not include reporters who responded no answer (2).
[c] Total does not include reporters who responded no answer (2).
[d] Total does not include reporters who responded no answer (6) or don't know (3)
[e] Total does not include reporters who responded no answer (5) or don't know (2).
[f] Total does not include reporters who responded no answer (7) or don't know (3).

jerk contempt on the part of reporters toward public relations people, the study indicates that public information officers (PIOs) were talked to more often (mean = 2.23) than scientists (2.49) and administrators (2.61). All three mean scores were very close; all were between a score of 2 (often) and 3 (sometimes). The higher use of PIOs reflects the journalistic reality that they often serve as gatekeepers; the reporters cannot reach the scientists or top administrators until they first talk to the PIOs (see Table 5.5).

The reporters were asked to go beyond simple usage and to rate how much value they placed on time spent with public information officers, scientists, and administrators; scores ranged from very high value (1) to no value (5). The results were quite different. Scientists topped the list with a mean score of 1.64, followed by administrators (2.37), and PIOs (2.74).

Table 5.6 shows the results were consistent across regions. It also shows that when one combines the top three scores for the use of sources (talk to source always, often, sometimes) and value (very highly value, highly value, some value), the differences among the PIOs, scientists, and administrators seem to narrow. Overall, more than 90 percent of reporters indicated they either used or valued all three sources (using them, perhaps, for different needs).

Mike Dunne said he looked for an ideal set of sources and an effective framework in bringing a story idea to life:

"Personally, I want to talk with the people who have the direct knowledge. So, I am looking for public information officers who can hook me up with those people; facilitate and interview rather than having a 'spokesperson' do it. Unfortunately, this is getting harder and harder to do as agencies and universities and other groups ban people from speaking directly with the media unless it has been cleared, and often listen in on, by the PIOs. I want to talk directly to the scientists and administrators and the PIO as a last resort. There is a lot of difference between interviewing the people with the knowledge and someone who has talked with the knowledgeable person and then parrots or paraphrases to me what they said. Makes asking follow-up questions hard.

"I also end just about every interview with this question: Is there something important I forgot to ask about or did I ask a question in a way that you felt painted into a corner. If so, tell me now, please. I am looking to get the best information and don't want any preconceived notions of mine to make you say what you think I wanted you to say."

Table 5.6
Use and Value of Public Information, Scientific, and Administrative Sources, by Region
(Raw numbers and percentages represent the portion of respondents who said they talk to the source always, often, or sometimes.) (Raw numbers and percentages represent respondents who said time spent with a source has very high value, high value, or some value.)

Environment Reporters...	New England	Mountain West	South	Pacific West	Mid Atlantic	Mid Central	West Central	National*
Who do you talk to?								
Public Information	52	86	149	111	50	89	79	616/648
	96.3%	94.5%	98.7%	95.7%	94.3%	90.8%	92.9%	95.1%
Scientists	52	84	140	113	44	77	77	587/650
	94.5%	92.3%	92.7%	97.4%	83.0%	77.8%	90.6%	90.3%
Administrators	55	86	129	103	45	92	78	588/650
	100.0%	94.5%	85.4%	88.8%	84.9%	92.9%	91.8%	90.5%
Whose time do you value?								
Public Information	49	85	139	102	43	85	76	579/642
	90.7%	94.4%	92.1%	89.5%	84.3%	86.7%	90.5%	90.2%
Administrators	55	86	133	107	50	89	80	600/645
	100.0%	94.5%	88.1%	93.0%	96.2%	90.8%	96.4%	93.0%
Scientists	55	91	150	112	51	94	84	637/643
	100.0%	100.0%	100.0%	98.2%	100.0%	96.9%	98.8%	99.1%

Ok, now I'd like to know who you talk to when you call these public and private organizations for information on environmental stories.

Q: For example, how about public information officers.
Q: How about scientists? In your environmental reporting, would you say you talk to scientists...
Q: How about administrators of the government agency or private group. In your environmental reporting, would you say you talk to administrators...

Finally, we want to know whether you value the time you spend with each of these sources.

Q: How about the public information officers. Would you say the time you spend with them on a story has...
Q: How about scientists. Would you say the time you spend with them on a story has...
Q: How about administrators. Would you say the time you spend with them on a story has...

* In the national categories, the first number is the total of respondents in that category who said always, often, or sometimes. The second number in the *Who do you talk to* section is the number of reporters who answered always, often, sometimes, rarely, or never (but does not include those responding no opinion, don't know, no answer, or refused to answer). The percentage is the percentage of respondents in each category who said always, often, or sometimes. Each type of source is rank ordered nationally by mean, rather than the percent answering always, often, or sometimes. The second number in the *Whose time do you value* section is the number of reporters who answered no value, little value, some value, high value, or very high value (but does not include those responding no opinion, don't know, no answer, or refused to answer). The percentage is the percentage of respondents in each category who said some value, high value, or very high value. Each type of source is rank ordered nationally by mean, rather than the percent answering some value, high value, or very high value.

Environment Reporters and Business Issues

This project tested the sometimes heard claim that environment reporters stress nature, wilderness, and the outdoors over other potential story frames at the expense of business interests. This analysis looked specifically at how these reporters said they handled business and economic stories that might be expected to be at odds with a nature-oriented beat. How often did they use a business angle to frame a story? In choosing sources, were environmental advocacy groups preferred over business groups? Were business groups and advertisers seen as barriers to reporting on the environment? Did these reporters feel they needed to be as fair to corporations as they are to environmental activist groups? Did they feel their peers are too pro-environment in their reporting? Was there any evidence that environment reporting is too pro-business?

Given the controversy regarding environmental reporting and the business world, this study used a variety of lenses to look at the intersection of business and the environment. One key consideration is the fairness of reporters in doing stories. (The issue of whether environment reporters are balanced in their coverage of business is explored earlier this chapter and, at length, in Chapter 6, "Wrestling with Objectivity and Fairness.")

Business Angles and Business Sources

Earlier this project looked at whether environment reporters commonly said they used a business angle or framework, compared to eight other angles. While all nine angles were often or sometimes used by the average reporter, the mean scores indicate that a business framework was the third most popular angle of the nine offered (see Table 5.1).

Here, the study goes beyond that initial analysis in an effort to better understand what types of reporters were more likely to use a business angle. A linear regression was conducted to examine 29 potential independent variables that might help explain how frequently a reporter used a business frame. The variables included socioeconomic factors such as salary, race, gender, and marital status; workplace characteristics such as the number of years in journalism and the percentage of time spent covering the environment; and other issues such as how good a job the reporter felt his or her own news organization did in covering the environment. None of the 29 independent variables was significantly related to use of the business framework or angle, suggesting that the use of the business framework for stories was widespread and uniform across the hundreds of reporters interviewed.

This study also discussed whether environment reporters commonly used business sources in their stories. Respondents were asked about 29 different sources (eight federal government offices, seven state-level offices and individuals, four local offices, six environmental groups or individuals, three business-related groups or individuals, and academic researchers). Two business sources, "local manufacturers, developers, and other business leaders" and the Chamber of Commerce were commonly used by reporters, while the Chemical Manufacturers Association was near the bottom of the list. Given the business vs. environmental activist debate, it is worth noting again that "local environmental groups" and "individual, local citizens who are active on the environment" ranked second and third on the list of the 29 types of sources examined (see Table 5.3).

Finally, in Chapter 4 the researchers looked at 17 potential barriers to reporting; the reporters were asked to rate each in terms of it being always a barrier, often, sometimes, rarely, or never. Business-oriented issues such as "advertisers" (ranked sixteenth on the list) and "other business or corporate interests" (ranked eleventh on the list) were far less likely to be cited by reporters than such workplace concerns as the size of the news hole and time constraints (see Table 4.8).

Potential Problems Affecting Environment Reporting

Even after reporters decide on a framework and sources for a story, there are a variety of problems they may face in executing the final version (see Table 5.7 and 5.8). A majority of reporters (57.7 percent) said they agreed with the statement, "Environmental journalists generally concentrate far too much on problems and pollution rather than writing stories to help the public understand research or complex issues." Reporters from various regions had similar views; support for the statement ranged from 50.6 percent in the Mountain West to 60.9 percent in the Mid Central region.

A slim majority of reporters disagreed with the statement, "An environmental problem is generally a better news story than an environmental success." Only 45.4 percent of environment reporters agreed or strongly agreed. Here there was greater variance in the regions, which ranged from a low of 31.8 percent of reporters agreeing in the Mountain West to a high of 50.7 percent in the South.

There was even less support for the statement, "Environmental journalism generally centers too much on personalities and not enough on

Table 5.7
Potential Problems Affecting Environment Reporting
Reporting on Environmental Successes, Problems, Personalities, and Risks
(Raw numbers and percentages represent the actual number of respondents in each category.)

Environment Reporters...	Strongly Agree	Agree	Disagree	Strongly Disagree	Total	Mean*
Environmental journalists focus too much on problems	28 4.8%**	312 53.0%**	231 39.2%	18 3.1%	589[a] 100.1%***	2.41
Environment problem a better story than environment success	33 5.6%	236 39.8%	290 48.9%	34 5.7%	593[b] 100.0%	2.55
Environmental journalists focus too much on personality	9 1.6%**	102 17.7%**	424 73.5%	42 7.3%	577[c] 100.1%***	2.86
Environmental journalists have overblown environmental risks	9 1.6%	114 19.7%	393 68.0%	62 10.7%	578[d] 100.0%	2.89

Q: Environmental journalists generally concentrate far too much on <u>problems and pollution</u> rather than writing stories to <u>help the public understand research or complex issues</u>. Do you...

Q: An <u>environmental problem</u> is generally a better news story than an <u>environmental success</u>. Do you...

Q: Environmental journalism generally centers <u>too much on personalities</u> and <u>not enough on actual findings</u>. Do you...

Q: Environmental journalists generally have <u>overblown environmental risks</u>, unduly alarming the public. Do you...

*Sources that they talk to are ranked by mean score, lowest to highest. Index ranged from: strongly agree = 1.0 to strongly disagree = 4.0.

**The discrepancy between 57.7% national on Table 5.8 and 4.8 + 53.0 on Table 5.7 is due to rounding. When the real numbers 4.7538 and 52.9711 are added together in Table 5.8 the result is correctly 57.7%. Likewise, the discrepancy between 19.2% national on Table 5.8 and 1.6 + 17.7 is due to rounding. The real numbers add up to 19.2%

***Percentage does not total 100 because of rounding.

[a] Total does not include reporters who responded no opinion (26), don't know (33), no answer (2), or refused to answer (2).

[b] Total does not include reporters who responded no opinion (41), don't know (17), or refused to answer (1).

[c] Total does not include reporters who responded no opinion (39), don't know (33), no answer (2), or refused to answer (1).

[d] Total does not include reporters who responded no opinion (36), don't know (35), no answer (1), or refused to answer (2).

Table 5.8
Potential Problems Affecting Environment Reporting, by Region
Reporting on Environmental Successes, Problems, Personalities,
and Risks, by Region

(Raw numbers and percentages represent the portion of respondents who
said they strongly agree or agree with the statement.)

Environment Reporters...	New England	Mountain West	South	Pacific West	Mid Atlantic	Mid Central	West Central	National*
Environmental journalists focus too much on problems	30 57.7%	41 50.6%	82 59.0%	61 57.6%	27 57.4%	53 60.9%	46 59.7%	340/589 57.7%**
Environment problem a better story than environment success	25 49.0%	27 31.8%	71 50.7%	53 50.5%	22 50.0%	35 38.9%	36 46.2%	269/593 45.4%
Environmental journalists focus too much on personality	8 17.0%	12 14.6%	27 19.3%	19 19.0%	10 21.7%	21 24.7%	14 18.2%	111/577 19.2%**
Environmental journalists have overblown environmental risks	12 25.0%	14 16.9%	29 21.5%	24 22.6%	16 33.4%	17 20.7%	11 14.5%	123/578 21.3%

Q: Environmental journalists generally concentrate far too much on problems and pollution rather than writing stories to help the public understand research or complex issues. Do you…

Q: An environmental problem is generally a better news story than an environmental success. Do you…

Q: Environmental journalism generally centers too much on personalities and not enough on actual findings. Do you…

Q: Environmental journalists generally have overblown environmental risks, unduly alarming the public. Do you…

*In the national categories, the first number is the total of respondents in that category who answered strongly agree or agree. The second number is the number of reporters who answered strongly agree, agree, neither, disagree, or strongly disagree (but does not include those responding no opinion, don't know, no answer, or refused to answer). The percentage is the percentage of respondents in each category who said they strongly agree or agree with the statement. Each perspective on coverage or audience interest is rank ordered nationally by mean, rather than by the percent answering strongly agree or agree.

**The discrepancy between 57.7% national on Table 5.8 and 4.8 + 53.0 on Table 5.7 is due to rounding. When the real numbers 4.7538 and 52.9711 are added together in Table 5.8 the result is correctly 57.7%. Likewise, the discrepancy between 19.2% national on Table 5.8 and 1.6 + 17.7 is due to rounding. The real numbers add up to 19.2%.

actual findings." Only 19.2 percent of reporters agreed or strongly agreed with the statement. A regional breakdown showed few differences, with all regions in a ten-point range, from a low of 14.6 percent of reporters from the Mountain West agreeing, to a high of 24.7 percent in the Mid Central.

These three questions suggest environment reporters have a sense that they need to do more in helping their audiences understand the complexity behind stories about the environment. Most reject the idea that they focus too much on personalities and not enough on actual findings. Reporters were split on whether environmental problem stories are generally better news stories than those about environmental successes.

One of the basic elements of newsworthiness is conflict. This study examined whether environment reporters felt journalists "generally have overblown environmental risks, unduly alarming the public." To do so would be to stress conflict. Of the 578 reporters with an opinion, 78.7 percent of environment reporters either disagreed (68.0 percent) or disagreed strongly (10.7 percent) with the statement. A very low percentage, 1.6 percent, strongly agreed with the assertion, while another 19.7 percent said they agreed. Seventy-four of the 652 reporters—an unusually high 11.3 percent—responded no opinion (36), don't know (35), no answer (1), or refused to answer (2). The question may have made some respondents uneasy. While some critics such as Gregg Easterbrook and Bjørn Lomborg have decried exaggerated reporting about environmental problems, most of the journalists who actually do that reporting reject the claim.[4]

A breakdown of the results by region shows reporters in the West Central and Mountain West regions were most likely to reject the claim that environment stories are overblown and that they unduly alarm the public. Some 33.4 percent of reporters in the Mid Atlantic region agreed or strongly agreed with the statement, higher than the national average of 21.3 percent.

These potential problems may relate to the traditional standards of reporting generally prevalent in American newsrooms. Journalists are trained to think in terms of timeliness (today's news, rather than long-term issues), proximity (local, not worldwide), human interest, prominence (famous people, rather than the majority), and consequence (importance, including degree of risk), while scientists and others may view the first four of these news values as shallow at best.[5] The reporters who agreed that "environmental journalists generally concentrate far too much on problems and pollution rather than writing stories to help the public understand research or complex issues" and "an environmental problem is generally a better news story than an environmental success" may be reflecting their concern with the news media's tendency to focus on acute problems rather than long-term issues and to emphasize the negative ("If it bleeds, it leads."), rather than the positive. This study characterizes journalists who question such fundamental issues as what news is (and what news should be) as "Work Place Critics" (see Chapter 6).

Reporting Environmental Risk

Almost all of the environment reporters interviewed for this book—96.8 percent—said they always, often, or sometimes used a government angle to present or frame a story. In addition, 90 percent or more of them said they used human interest, business/economic, pollution, or nature/wilderness angles in environmental reporting. More than 80 percent said they used a health, science/technology, or political angle.

But a risk assessment angle? It ranked ninth—out of nine angles or frameworks—among the reporters interviewed. Only 70.2 percent of the environment reporters said they used it always, often, or sometimes.

Dave Flessner thinks he knows why.

"I think the media have a love and hate affair with risk," said Flessner, who covers environment stories on a regular basis as a business-oriented, special projects editor at the *Chattanooga* (TN) *Times Free Press*. "Too often in the media we are searching for the unusual, the extraordinary, the sensational. We tend to highlight stories that involve things that are extraordinarily dangerous. We don't always put that in the best assessment of risk.

"Some people get a heightened fear of a low probability of risk. If you read about kidnappings, they are extraordinarily horrific, but the instances of that are extraordinarily rare. It's probably much more common that children go out with cars and get killed. From an environmental perspective, there is a tension because you like a sensational, dramatic story, when...people are most affected in terms of life or health. But sometimes that may be more sensational and have a lower risk probability than things that affect a lot of people," said Flessner in an interview that was conducted after the national survey of environment reporters.[6]

Despite the potential for misuse, Flessner said he has no problems using a risk assessment approach to compare, say, exposure to radioactive material at a nuclear power plant to similar releases at other plants. Or comparing the radiation at a plant to the radiation a person might receive from a dental X-ray or excessive exposure to the sun.

In this study, the researchers sought to better understand how often a risk assessment angle is used by environment reporters and what variables—socio-economic, in the workplace, source-driven—might explain why some reporters are more apt to use this story framework. The authors took a close look at the question of whether environmental journalists have overblown risk stories, unduly alarming the public. Finally, they posed a series of questions to 652 environment reporters on how they look at environment problem stories, success stories, and whether they need more science in their stories.

Environment reporters have been criticized for sometimes mishandling risk and unduly frightening their readers or viewers. About one out of five of the reporters in this study agreed with the statement that environmental journalists generally have overblown environmental risks, unduly alarming the public. News stories about scientific topics often contain fewer caveats than the scientific source material on which they are based, and can convey a misleading level of certainty as to the potential outcomes of studies.[7] Other factors that may lead to exaggerated claims include problems in simplifying technical information, media competition in the race to be first, a desire to make the front page or to lead a newscast, plus space and time limitations.[8]

Michael R. Greenberg, David B. Sachsman, Peter M. Sandman, and Kandice L. Salomone noted that "journalistic news values focus reporters on events rather than issues, and on the spectacular rather than the chronic" and concluded that "the public's conception of risk is almost certainly distorted by television's focus on catastrophes and its dependence on films."[9] JoAnn Myer Valenti and Lee Wilkins offered a protocol for ethical reporting of risk to improve public understanding of science and environment issues in the news.[10] Valenti later examined ethical decision making among members of the Society of Environmental Journalists when covering risk and found that extrinsic values such as what's legal and peer evaluation were the major factors. When journalists fail to cover risk information completely and accurately, Valenti said, "the consequence is misunderstanding and poor judgments" by readers and viewers.[11]

The nature of the medium also may influence how environmental stories are covered by reporters. Greenberg, Sachsman, Sandman, and Salomone studied network evening news coverage of environmental risk and found that "risk as calculated by scientists had little to do with the amount of coverage provided by the three networks' evening news broadcasts. Instead, the networks appear to be using the traditional journalistic determinants of news plus the broadcast criterion of visual impact to determine the degree of coverage of risk issues."[12] In a separate study, the same researchers concluded that the networks "are also guided in their coverage by geographical factors (such as cost and convenience) much more than by risk."[13]

The careful, conservative nature of scientific work may be a problem for journalists as well. Sometimes scientists may be reluctant to give a clear statement of the degree of risk involved in any particular situation.

Risk as a Story Angle

Earlier in this chapter the researchers looked at the various story angles or frameworks used by environment reporters and rank ordered them based on how often reporters said they used each. A risk assessment angle was used always, often, or sometimes by 70.2 percent of the journalists surveyed, putting it in ninth place out of the nine angles examined. To help explain why some environmental journalists were more likely than others to use risk assessment, this project looked at 52 potential independent variables that the researchers grouped into seven categories—workplace characteristics, demographics, a reporter's view of the environment reporting field, barriers in doing stories, job satisfaction, how a reporter judges a job in his or her field, and sources they can use in reporting. The study cross-tabulated the variables against the use of the risk angle. For the sake of data reduction, the project computed the results as a correlation and indicated the level of statistical significance. The study used Cramer's V to compute the correlation. Cramer's V takes a Chi Square measurement (testing the hypothesis that two variables are unrelated) and places it on a more accessible format of a continuum ranging from 0 to +1.[14] It is not a measure of association, but the accompanying test of significance (p value) indicates whether the results occurred by chance.

Few of the 52 variables correlated strongly with use of the risk angle. Only three variables were both significant ($p < .05$) and had a correlation of .20 or higher.

One was job title ($g = .347$, $p < .001$). Reporters with the word "environment" in their titles were more likely to use a risk analysis framework. These reporters, on average, also had higher levels of formal education and had more years of experience as an environment reporter, which may help explain the relationship. The second variable that correlated with risk assessment was percentage of time spent covering the environment (g = .291; p < .01). Reporters who spent more time on environmental stories were more likely to use the risk framework. Finally, reporters who used a health angle or health framework in their environmental reporting were more likely to also use a risk assessment angle; they may use both angles in a single story. In sum, while risk was used on a regular basis by almost three quarters of the reporters, there were few independent variables that helped explain its use.

Environment reporters are forced to constantly evaluate scientific studies, decide on their worthiness, and then decide whether to present conflicting results from other studies.[15] Flessner is no exception. He said risk assessment stories are especially complicated, in part, because even if environment reporters talk to the best scientific experts, they must often deal with dueling scientific studies. Working with their editors, the environment reporters also have to decide how much emphasis to place on a study, he said.

"You might have some sensational study that says one day coffee leads to health problems," Flessner said. "The next day caffeine is good for you and wine is good for you. Then wine is bad for you. Sometimes the underlying data is a sub-sample of some university study of 70 or 80 or 100 people. The science wasn't bad, but it wasn't that dramatic of a study, and sometimes those small sexy studies get as much attention as the more significant studies.[16]

"In our risk assessment, sometimes bad science, lesser science, gets as much attention as better science. I think we as journalists don't sort through what is always the best science. I guess that's a continual challenge that we need to go to the best sources and get the most quantitative study. But because of the nature of what we write, we write about the extraordinary and not the natural. We don't write about planes safely landing, we write about plane crashes."

Notes

1.   Earlier version of elements of this chapter were originally written by the authors and published in:

David B. Sachsman, James Simon, and JoAnn Myer Valenti, "Risk and the Environment Reporters: A Four-Region Analysis," *Public Understanding of Science* 13 (2004): 399-416.

David B. Sachsman, James Simon, and JoAnn Myer Valenti, "Regional Issues, National Norms: A Four-Region Analysis of U.S. Environment Reporters," *Science Communication* 28 (2006): 93-121.

The final, definitive versions of the papers published in *Public Understanding of Science* and *Science Communication* have been published by SAGE Publications Ltd./SAGE Publications, Inc., All rights reserved.

2.   Mike Dunne, personal interview with James Simon, May 7, 2007 that was unrelated to the survey. Mike died July 8, 2007. He is sorely missed.

3.   Ibid.

4.   Gregg Easterbrook, *A Moment on the Earth* (New York: Penguin, 1995).
       Bjørn Lomborg, *The Skeptical Environmentalist: Measuring the Real State of the World* (Cambridge: University Press, 2001), 5; 39.

5.   David B. Sachsman, "Linking the Scientist and the Journalist," in *HazPro '85: Proceedings of the HazPro '85 Conference*, ed. Richard A. Young. Purdvan Publishing Co., 1985.

6.   Dave Flessner, personal interview with James Simon, April 16, 2007. Unrelated to the survey.

7.   S. Holly Stocking, "How Journalists Deal With Uncertainty," in *Communicating Uncertainty: Media Coverage of New and Controversial Science,* ed. Sharon M. Friedman, Sharon Dunwoody and Carol L. Rogers (Mahwah NJ: Lawrence Erlbaum, 1999), 23-42.

8.   Julie Wakefield-Albers, "Making Headlines in the Lab," *Environmental Health Perspectives* 103.6 (1995): 560-62. http://www.ehponline.org/docs/1995/103-6/spheres.html (accessed April 30, 2007). [No longer available at this address]

9.   Michael R. Greenberg, David B. Sachsman, Peter M. Sandman, and Kandice L. Salomone, "Network Evening News Coverage of Environmental Risk," *Risk Analysis* 9 (1989): 125.

10.   JoAnn Myer Valenti and Lee Wilkins, "An Ethical Risk Communication Protocol for Science and Mass Communication," *Public Understanding of Science* 18 (1995), 177-94.

11.   JoAnn Myer Valenti, "Ethical Decision Making in Environmental Communication," *Journal of Mass Media Ethics* 13.4 (1998): 229.

12.   Michael R. Greenberg, David B. Sachsman, Peter M. Sandman, and Kandice L. Salomone, "Risk, Drama and Geography in Coverage of Environmental Risk by Network TV," *Journalism Quarterly* 66 (1989): 275.

13.   Greenberg, et al., "Network Evening News Coverage of Environmental Risk," 125.

14.   Marija J. Norusis, *SPSS 7.5 Guide to Data Analysis* (Upper Saddle River, New Jersey: Prentice Hall, 1997).

15.   See Maxwell T. Boykoff and Jules M. Boykoff, "Balance as Bias: Global Warming and the US Prestige Press," *Global Environmental Change* 14 (2004): 125-36.

16.   Dave Flessner, personal interview with James Simon, April 16, 2007.

6

Wrestling with Objectivity and Fairness[1]

Tom Meersman says he thinks he knows one reason why some environment reporters are tagged with the reputation of being "too green," pro-environment, and anti-business.

"I have heard that claim and it's probably true to some degree because the definition of reporting, or of journalism these days, is not a 'bright line' in many cases," said Meersman, the environment and natural resources reporter for the Minneapolis Star-Tribune, in an interview conducted separately from this study's anonymous national survey of reporters. "There are people who are writers and who write advocacy pieces for advocacy publications and they say that they are journalists or reporters. I am not going to dispute that claim, but I would imagine that doesn't help some people's perception that if people are writing about environmental topics, they must be environmentalists to be interested in those topics."[2]

Meersman, who has been covering the environment since the 1980s, estimates he spends 95 percent of his time on environment and natural resource stories. When he writes a critical story about a local employer being held responsible for drinking water contamination, he gets complaints from "people who think we are not appreciative enough of the company's good things they have done.... I also see or receive occasional e-mails saying that reporters are not green at all, that they buy into what the corporate world says and that they are too easily influenced or spun by what politicians and government officials and company officials say."[3]

Welcome to the modern day world of environmental reporting, where it often seems that everything a journalist writes or broadcasts is examined by the political right and left for evidence—real or imagined—of bias.

The question of the objectivity and fairness of environment reporters spilled into public view in reactions to the November 2004 annual meeting of the industry's professional group, the Society of Environmental Journalists. Journalists are socialized to avoid public displays of support or opposition when covering a speech, a press conference, or other public event. Here, journalists and others in the audience gave a standing ovation to a political speech by environmental attorney Robert F. Kennedy, Jr., then a muted response to EPA administrator Mike Leavitt the next morning. In his online *Environment Writer* column, Bud Ward wrote:

> The fact is that environmental journalists have a problem perhaps unique to their calling: They are battling the perception that many of them have both inside and beyond their newsrooms of being "greens with press passes," as a former Scripps Howard reporter used to say.... The fact is that the SEJ annual meeting is the single most visible manifestation of the field. The shocking/frustrating/ disappointing/disgusting public displays of affection (PDAs) are far more visible than the very worthwhile internal soul-searching those standing Os [ovations] are triggering among the group's serious and committed members.[4]

Seth Borenstein, national correspondent for Knight-Ridder Newspapers in Washington, D.C., agreed. He opened a first-person account in *SEJournal* by writing, "I wanted to sink deep into the padded seats in the auditorium at the Carnegie Museum and disappear out of embarrassment.... Not for me, but for my profession, and more importantly for SEJ.... Our duty is to remain OBJECTIVE, non-partisan reporters. If you want to be an advocate, more power to you, but don't taint the rest of us. Don't consider yourself an environmental journalist."[5]

In 2006, SEJ President Perry Beeman reported that "a board member or two" had suggested that the Society of Environmental Journalists change its name. Why? "Because the phrase 'environmental journalists' seemed to suggest 'environmentalist journalists' to some, especially those who suspect the group has some sort of environmental agenda akin to the Sierra Club," said Beeman, a writer for the *Des Moines Register*.[6]

Beeman recalled that a reader had written to the newspaper's blog and made critical comments on a water quality story:

> The central part of this guy's message is the disturbing part. "What is an environmental journalist anyway?" I cringe at that, because I'm sure he's thinking "Birkenstock-wearing, tofu-eating Sierra Club member, green and left as can be."... I have never owned Birkenstocks. I have never tasted tofu. I have never belonged to the Sierra Club. I am white, not green. I am registered "no party."...We are diverse people with diverse interests and lifestyles. We aren't an environmental group. We need to keep reminding people. Perhaps now more than ever.[7]

SEJ has printed T-shirts that remind people: We are not environmentalist journalists. We are reporters who cover the environment.

Other journalists feel it is unfair to single out environment reporters and demand that they have no personal opinions or feelings about the subject they cover. "[M]ust a business writer declare that he or she is not a capitalist in order to have credibility?" asks Peter Thompson, an independent radio producer. "Should a political reporter purport to have no opinion on the virtues of democracy as opposed to dictatorship? Must a crime reporter strive not to care about right and wrong? For someone aspiring to work one of these beats to even suggest that they're indifferent or hostile to the basic concerns of the endeavor would guarantee that they don't get the job. And yet on our beat, we are constantly under pressure, even from within our ranks, to disavow any concern or values associated with what we cover. What's going on here?"[8]

Bob Lutgen, then managing editor for operations at the *Chattanooga Times Free Press,* said that environmental writers might start out unbiased, but that the environmental groups' public relations are just so good that stories may not appear to be objective. On the other hand, business owners are very timid about talking to environment reporters, according to Lutgen, the former managing editor of the *Arkansas Democrat Gazette*: "In Little Rock, we had an environmental writer doing a story on chicken plants, but could not get a comment from Tyson. We didn't see how we could run environmental stories without comments from business."[9]

In the long run the *Arkansas Democrat Gazette* dropped the environment beat. "We dropped the beat, but we didn't drop the coverage," said Lutgen. "The issue is very important and [generates] high readership, but it is easier to spread it around so that individual reporters don't get so close to the stories' sources that they become biased."[10]

Business advocates have complained that reporters have taken a pro-environment viewpoint on many issues that could affect business, including global warming and the proposed Kyoto treaty,[11] pesticide usage on produce,[12] air pollution standards,[13] the health of the national economy,[14] and the need for government regulation.[15] Business-related critics have faulted environment reporters for offering a "pervasive pessimism about the future that has become the hallmark of today's environmental orthodoxy"[16] and for preferring liberal activist sources for environmental information rather than conservative sources.[17] Steven F. Hayward, a fellow of the American Enterprise Institute, argues environment reporters are seen as endowing moral authority on environmental advocacy organizations while at the same time viewing industry, with its focus on profit motives, more skeptically. "This tends to lead to asymmetry in news coverage, with the claims of environmental advocates accepted at face value, while industry claims are often overlain with, for instance, the amount of campaign contributions an industry has given to political office holders (as if environmental groups don't put money into politics)."[18] Yet others feel that reporters can grow impatient with the "purist approach and quasi-religious zeal" of environmental activists.[19] Claims of anti-business bias are not restricted to environmental reporting. Business leaders have complained for decades that reporters, in general, overemphasize negative news in their business coverage.[20]

The issue of global warming, highlighted by Al Gore's Oscar-winning documentary, "An Inconvenient Truth," spurred interest in environmental reporting[21] and fueled the debate on whether the journalistic goal of balanced coverage is proper when the consensus on an issue is so lopsided.[22] Cornelia Dean, a former *New York Times* science editor, said the normal goal of objectivity can backfire if a reporter presents any uncertainty or debate over an issue as equal to the scientific consensus. "Fringe opinions" can wind up being seen as equal to the mainstream perspective in science if a reporter uses an on-the-one-hand, on-the-other-hand approach, she said.[23]

Meersman said he sometimes uses a business framework for environmental stories. He said that he has a good relationship with some companies, or business associations such as the Chamber of Commerce, but that other firms establish barriers to reporters. Some do not return phone calls, or provide only short written statements with no opportunity for reporters to ask questions. Reporters want to know details, Meersman said, including whether there are reasonable explanations for problems, or lessons learned from an environmental incident that may be valuable to other companies.

Whether they cooperate or not, Meersman said that he considers companies to be important players. "All I can say in my case is that I think that businesses are the agents of change. Once they get clear signals from consumers or government agencies about what they want—and it might be an improvement one way or another towards air or water quality or to other issues—businesses are among the first sometimes to change and to change very quickly and to take full advantage of it in terms of their public relations. So I guess I plead not guilty in my own case to being anti-business. I think business can make stuff happen."[24]

"It's just a question sometimes of them trying to figure out what's going to be required of them," Meersman said. "As we learn more about how all of our activities, whether as individuals driving cars or using a lot of disposables, there's enough for everybody to do in terms of changing

behaviors and caring a little more deeply about the effects we are having on the environment."[25] (The issue of whether environment reporters
are balanced in their coverage of business also was explored at length
in Chapter 5, "Covering The Environment.")

How Do Environment Reporters View Their Peers?

Claims about the objectivity and fairness of environmental coverage often are based, in part, on subjective analyses of environmental
stories. Another approach is to examine the attitudes of the reporters
themselves. There have been only a handful of formal research efforts
to examine those who report on the environment, and most have used
small or convenience samples.[26] This national census looked at how
environment reporters wrestle with questions of objectivity, advocacy,
and the civic journalism concept of working with community leaders to
help solve problems. Do reporters view their peers as being fair to business and environmental sources—or are they "too green" or "too brown"
in their coverage? Should their peers in environmental reporting be as
objective as other reporters? Or should they sometimes be advocates for
the environment and work toward solutions to environmental problems?
The personal views of these environmental journalists allow us to better
understand how they view the world and how their views may affect their
role as the link between scientists and the public.

Fairness vs. Pro-Environment or Pro-Business Slant

The researchers asked environment reporters two parallel sets of questions. The first set asked whether they agreed that environment reporters
in general "need to be fair to corporations" and whether they "need to
be fair to environmental activist groups." Reporters were asked whether
they strongly agreed, agreed, disagreed or strongly disagreed with the
statements. The results were almost identical, as reflected by mean
scores of 1.47 and 1.49 (1 = strongly agree, 2 = agree). An overwhelming majority of respondents agreed that environment reporters needed
to be fair both to business and to environmental activists (see Table 6.1).
A regional breakdown showed the sentiments were uniform across the
seven regions studied. In some regions (New England, Mountain West,
and Mid Atlantic), every single reporter agreed or strongly agreed with
both statements (see Table 6.2).

There was far less agreement on the second set of questions. Reporters were asked whether they agreed that environment reporters are "too
green, meaning slanted in favor of environmentalism" or "too brown,

Table 6.1

Fairness and Perceived Slant Toward Issues

(Raw numbers and percentages represent the actual number of respondents in each category.)

Environment Reporters...	Strongly Agree	Agree	Disagree	Strongly Disagree	Total	Mean*
Need to be fair to corporations	350 54.1%	293 45.3%	4 0.6%	0 0%	647[a] 100.0%	1.47
Need to be fair to environmental activists groups	338 52.1%	307 47.3%	4 0.6%	0 0%	649[b] 100.0%	1.49
Are "too green," slanted in favor of environmentalism	12 2.3%	190 35.8%	313 58.9%	16 3.0%	531[c] 100.0%	2.63
Are "too brown," slanted in favor of business and industry	0 0%	24 4.2%	496 87.0%	50 8.8%	570[d] 100.0%	3.05

Q: Environmental journalists need to be fair to sources such as corporations. Do you...
Q: Environmental journalists need to be fair to sources such as environmental activist groups. Do you...
Q: Environmental journalists tend to be too "green"—meaning slanted in favor of environmentalism. Do you...
Q: Environmental journalists tend to be too "brown"—meaning slanted in favor of business and industry. Do you...

* Statements are ranked by mean score, lowest to highest. Index ranged from: Strongly Agree=1.0 to Strongly Disagree=4.0.

[a] Total does not include reporters who responded no opinion (3), don't know (1) or no answer (1).
[b] Total does not include reporters who responded no opinion (2) or don't know (1).
[c] Total does not include reporters who responded no opinion (62), don't know (55), no answer (1), or refused to answer (3).
[d] Total does not include reporters who responded no opinion (38), don't know (38), no answer (2), or refused to answer (4).

meaning slanted in favor of business and industry." A substantial minority of reporters—38.0 percent, or 202 of 531 journalists responding—agreed or strongly agreed with the statement that environmental reporters were too green. Only 4.2 percent—24 of 570 reporters—agreed with the statement that reporters are "too brown."

This second pair of questions had one of the lowest response rates of the entire survey. A total of 121 reporters responded no opinion, don't know, no answer, or refused to answer to the question about their colleagues being "too green"; 82 responded no opinion, don't know, no answer, or refused to answer about their peers being pro-business.

Table 6.2
Fairness and Perceived Slant Toward Issues, by Region
(Raw numbers and percentages represent the portion of respondents who said they strongly agree
or agree with the statement.)

Environment Reporters...	New England (2000)	Mountain West (2001)	South (2002)	Pacific West (2002, 2004-2005)	Mid Atlantic (2003-2004)	Mid Central (2004-2005)	West Central (2004-2005)	National*
Need to be fair to corporations	54 100.0%	91 100.0%	148 99.3%	115 99.1%	53 100.0%	99 99.0%	83 98.8%	643/647 99.4%
Need to be fair to environmental activists groups	54 100.0%	91 100.0%	149 99.3%	115 99.1%	53 100.0%	99 99.0%	84 98.8%	645/649 99.4%
Are "too green," slanted in favor of environmentalism	20 46.5%	27 38.0%	56 42.1%	37 38.9%	10 23.3%	30 39.0%	22 31.9%	202/531 38.0%
Are "too brown," slanted in favor of business and industry	1 2.0%	2 2.5%	7 5.2%	6 5.9%	0 0%	5 6.0%	3 3.8%	24/570 4.2%

Q: Environmental journalists need to be fair to sources such as corporations. Do you...
Q: Environmental journalists need to be fair to sources such as environmental activist groups. Do you...
Q: Environmental journalists tend to be too "green"—meaning slanted in favor of environmentalism. Do you...
Q: Environmental journalists tend to be too "brown"—meaning slanted in favor of business and industry. Do you...

* In the National categories, the first number is the total of respondents in that category who answered strongly agree or agree. The second number is the number of reporters who answered strongly agree, agree, disagree, or strongly disagree (but does not include those responding no opinion, don't know, no answer, or refused to answer). The percentage is the percentage of respondents in each category who said strongly agree or agree. Each evaluation is rank ordered nationally by mean, rather than by the percent answering strongly agree or agree.

The responses to the two pairs of questions, taken together, appear to be pointing to a division between some of the reporters. The answers to the first set of questions suggest that environment reporters acknowledge that they need to be fair to both environmental activist groups and to corporations. The responses to the second set of questions suggest that while most of these reporters perceive no pro-business bias, a substantial minority do see evidence that some of their peers may very well be slanted in favor of environmentalists. Two hundred and two environment reporters said that their colleagues tend to be "too green," a clear indictment of journalists who acknowledge the need to be fair.

Objectivity vs. Fairness

Another way that the study sought to measure such issues as objectivity was to simply ask the reporters whether they agreed with the statement, "Environmental journalists need to be just as objective as journalists in general." Here, an overwhelming 99.4 percent of reporters (645 out of 649 responding) agreed with the need for objectivity (see Table 6.3). There was virtually no variation across regions; the positive responses ranged from 98.1 percent to 100 percent in individual regions (Table 6.4).

The researchers then focused on reporters who agreed with three statements: Journalists need to be 1) just as objective as journalists in general, 2) fair to sources such as corporations, and 3) fair to sources such as environmental activist groups. There were few dissenting voices; 637 of 644 reporters strongly agreed or agreed with all three statements. Since there was such universal agreement, the demographic makeup of such reporters differed little from the reporter pool as a whole. Objectivity and fairness seemed to be well ingrained in the decision-making process of most environment reporters, even when recognizing that some reporters may give a socially desirable response to such questions.

Should Journalists Stay Out of Stories?

The environment reporters were far more divided on companion issues that asked about their going beyond the traditional reporter's role of staying out of the stories that they cover. One question asked journalists whether they agreed, "Environmental journalists should work with community leaders to help solve environmental problems." The question was designed to tap support for a "civic journalism" approach in which news organizations go beyond a passive role of just reporting the news. Here, few reporters (4.5 percent) strongly agreed with such an approach, but another 28.4 percent said they agreed with taking such action. The majority (67.1 percent) disagreed or strongly disagreed with such an approach (see Table 6.3). Regional differences did emerge. In the West Central region, almost half of the reporters (45.8 percent) agreed or strongly agreed with taking such a step, while in the Pacific West, only 16.7 percent advocated such an approach (see Table 6.4).

Finally, the reporters were asked directly whether they agreed with the statement, "Environmental journalists sometimes should be advocates for the environment." Again, only 4.5 percent strongly agreed with such a position, while a further 32.2 percent agreed that reporters sometimes should be advocates. Another 42.4 percent disagreed with the advocacy

Table 6.3
Objectivity vs. Advocacy in Reporting Environmental Stories
(Raw numbers and percentages represent the actual number of respondents in each category.)

Environment Reporters...	Strongly Agree	Agree	Disagree	Strongly Disagree	Total	Mean*
Need to be as objective as other journalists	502 77.3%	143 22.0%	4 0.6%	0 0%	649[a] 99.9%**	1.23
Should work with community leaders to solve environmental problems	25 4.5%	158 28.4%	304 54.7%	69 12.4%	556[b] 100.0%	2.75
Sometimes should be advocates for environment	26 4.5%	186 32.2%	245 42.4%	121 20.9%	578[c] 100.0%	2.80

Q: Environmental journalists need to be just as objective as journalists in general. Do you...

Q: Environmental journalists sometimes should be advocates for the environment. Do you...

Q: Environmental journalists should work with community leaders to help solve environmental problems. Do you...

* Statements are ranked by mean score, lowest to highest. Index ranged from: Strongly Agree=1.0 to Strongly Disagree=4.0.
** Percentage does not total 100 because of rounding.
[a] Total does not include reporters who responded no opinion (1) or refused to answer (2).
[b] Total does not include reporters who responded no opinion (63), don't know (27), no answer (1), or refused... (5).
[c] Total does not include reporters who responded no opinion (46), don't know (26), no answer (1), or refused... (1).

position, and 20.9 percent strongly disagreed (see Table 6.3). Again, regional differences emerged. In the Mid Atlantic, a majority of reporters (51.1 percent) either agreed or strongly agreed with the idea of environmental journalists sometimes being advocates for the environment. In contrast, opposition was again strongest in the Pacific West, where 80 percent of reporters rejected the idea (see Table 6.4).

Objective...and an Advocate, too?

Are objectivity and advocacy polar opposites, two qualities that never overlap for most environment reporters? Or are they separate dimensions? Can reporters consider themselves to be both advocates and objective on

Table 6.4
Objectivity vs. Advocacy in Reporting Environmental Stories, by Region
(Raw numbers and percentages represent the portion of respondents who said they strongly agree or agree with the statement.)

Environment Reporters...	New England (2000)	Mountain West (2001)	South (2002)	Pacific West (2002, 2004-2005)	Mid Atlantic (2003-2004)	Mid Central (2004-2005)	West Central (2004-2005)	National*
Need to be as objective as other journalists	54 98.2%	88 98.9%	151 100.0%	116 100.0%	52 98.1%	99 99.0%	85 100.0%	645/649 99.4%
Should work with community leaders to solve environmental problems	14 30.4%	23 28.0%	52 39.4%	17 16.7%	12 31.6%	32 38.1%	33 45.8%	183/556 32.9%
Sometimes should be advocates for environment	20 40.8%	30 38.0%	59 42.8%	21 20.0%	23 51.1%	38 40.9%	21 30.4%	212/578 36.7%

Q: Environmental journalists need to be just as objective as journalists in general. Do you...

Q: Environmental journalists sometimes should be advocates for the environment. Do you...

Q: Environmental journalists should work with community leaders to help solve environmental problems. Do you...

* In the National categories, the first number is the total of respondents in that category who answered strongly agree or agree. The second number is the number of reporters who answered strongly agree, agree, disagree, or strongly disagree (but does not include those responding no opinion, don't know, no answer, or refused to answer). The percentage is the percentage of respondents in each category who said strongly agree or agree. Each evaluation is rank ordered nationally by mean, rather than by the percent answering strongly agree or agree.

some issues and in some circumstances? The study looked at whether some reporters felt they should be as objective as other reporters, but also were open to being an advocate sometimes or working to solve problems (often called a civic journalism approach) (Table 6.5). The effort was complicated by the decision of an unusually high number of reporters (150 reporters out of 652, or 23.0 percent) not to answer all three questions; perhaps they felt uncomfortable with discussions of objectivity.

As was discussed earlier, the overwhelming majority of reporters agreed that environmental journalists should be as objective as journalists in general. Of the 502 reporters responding to all three questions, 499 agreed with this statement. But from there, opinions splintered in several directions (Table 6.5):

- 95 journalists (18.9 percent) agreed that environmental reporters should be objective, agreed that sometimes they should be advocates for the environment, and agreed they should work with community leaders to help solve environmental problems. These are activist reporters, unwilling to always just passively transcribe the remarks of others in the name of objectivity.

- 90 journalists (17.9 percent) agreed that environmental reporters should be objective, agreed that sometimes they should be advocates for the environment, but disagreed that they should work with community leaders to help solve environmental problems. These reporters stress objectivity, are comfortable with sometimes assuming an advocacy role, but draw the line at getting involved with the story they are covering by working with community leaders on an issue.
- 71 journalists (14.1 percent) agreed that environmental reporters should be objective, agreed they should work with community leaders to help solve environmental problems, but draw the line at sometimes being advocates for the environment. These reporters are able to balance the goals of being objective and still working with community leaders to help solve environmental problems.
- The largest number of reporters, 243 (48.4 percent) took what might be viewed as an objectivity purist position: yes on being objective, no on advocacy, no on working with community leaders.
- Only three reporters disagreed with the notion of environmental reporters being as objective as other reporters. Two agreed they should sometimes be advocates for the environment, but not work with community leaders. The other was consistently negative: no on objectivity, no on advocacy, and no on civic journalism.

Objectivity and Fairness, Workplace Critics, and Advocates/Civic Journalists

Using multiple indicators to judge the responses by environmental reporters to such central issues as objectivity, fairness, and advocacy provides an opportunity to better understand the range of attitudes on the part of these journalists. Factor analysis was used with 12 such questions, in an effort to identify underlying variables, or factors that might explain the pattern of responses. The questions are listed at the bottom of Table 6.6.

The initial analysis used all 12 questions to sort reporters into categories. One question, "An environmental problem is generally a better news story than an environmental success," generated a factor loading of less than .500, meaning that it did not have a strong relationship with other questions, and it was eliminated. Another question, "Environmental journalists tend to be too 'brown,' meaning slanted in favor of business and industry," failed to load with any other variable and was discarded.

Table 6.5
Contrasting Views on Objectivity, Advocacy and Civic Journalism
(How did each of the 502 reporters who responded to all three questions answer them?)

Statement 1: Objectivity	Statement 2: Advocacy	Statement 3: Civic Journalism	n =	%
Environmental journalists need to be as objective as journalists in general.	Environmental journalists sometimes should be advocates for environment.	Environmental journalists should work with community leaders to help solve environmental problems.		
Agree	Disagree	Disagree	243	48.4%
Agree	Agree	Agree	95	18.9%
Agree	Agree	Disagree	90	17.9%
Agree	Disagree	Agree	71	14.1%
Disagree	Agree	Disagree	2	0.4%
Disagree	Disagree	Disagree	1	0.2%
Disagree	Agree	Agree	0	0%
Disagree	Disagree	Agree	0	0%
TOTAL			502	99.9%*

Q: Environmental journalists need to be just as objective as journalists in general. Do you...
Q: Environmental journalists sometimes should be advocates for the environment. Do you...
Q: Environmental journalists should work with community leaders to help solve environmental problems. Do you...

* Percentage does not total 100% because of rounding.

Reporters were judged to "Agree" if they agreed or strongly agreed with a statement, "Disagree" if they disagreed or strongly disagreed. 150 of the 652 reporters failed to answer at least one of the questions and were eliminated from consideration.

The analysis focused on the remaining 10 variables, each of which had a loading of more than .585 on one factor. Three underlying factors, or patterns of responses, each had an eigenvalue of more than 1.0 and were included in the analysis. Taken together, the three factors explained 56.0 percent of the variance among the 10 variables.

In Table 6.6, three questions clustered together in the first factor, each with a loading of .562 or higher, and the study looked at reporters who responded positively (above the mean score). These reporters, whom the researchers call "Objective/Fair Reporters," responded positively to: a) "Environmental journalists need to be just as objective as journalists in general"; b) "Environmental journalists need to be fair to sources such as corporations"; and c) "Environmental journalists need to be fair to sources such as environmental activist groups."

The study found 136 such reporters, out of the 299 journalists included in this analysis (Table 6.6). The results suggest that attitudes toward objectivity and fairness share a common dimension.

The second factor, which the researchers call "Workplace Critics," represented a cluster of five traditional complaints about the way environment reporters perform their duties (Table 6.6). These reporters responded positively (above the mean score) to five statements that clustered together: a) "Environmental journalists generally concentrate far too much on problems and pollution rather than writing stories to help the public understand research or complex issues"; b) "Environmental journalism generally centers too much on personalities and not enough on actual findings"; c) "Environmental journalists generally have overblown environmental risks, unduly alarming the public"; d) "Most environmental journalists are not well enough educated to cover news about environmental issues"; and e) "Environmental journalists tend to be too "green"—meaning slanted in favor of environmentalism."

This project found 153 such environment reporters. They were united in their common complaints about how stories are written, the focus of stories, and the education level of their peer reporters.

The third cluster, which we call "Advocates/Civic Journalists," included reporters who seemed to reject the notion that environmental reporters need to place objectivity in front of all other concerns (Table 6.6). They responded positively (above the mean score) to two statements that clustered together: a) "Environmental journalists sometimes should be advocates for the environment"; and b) "Environmental journalists should work with community leaders to help solve environmental problems."

There were 144 such reporters. While many civic journalists, who believe in working to help address or solve environmental problems, probably do not consider themselves outright advocates, the factor analysis suggests there is a common pattern in the responses of environmental reporters to the two positions.

Ethical Decision Making in Environmental Journalism

When Craig Pittman, a Florida native and decade-plus reporter for the *St. Petersburg Times*, pitched an investigation into why the state was losing wetlands, he spent two years trying to get his editor to support him to go after the story. Florida's wetlands kept disappearing. The U.S. Army Corps of Engineers kept handing over permits allowing developers

Table 6.6
Underlying Factors in Responses of Environmental Reporters

	1. Objective/Fair Reporters	2. Workplace Critics	3. Advocates/ Civic Journalists
Q6A objective?	**.562**	.079	-.195
Q6B advocates?	-.120	-.080	**.821**
Q6C fair to business?	**.944**	-.034	-.009
Q6D fair to activists?	**.944**	-.046	-.023
Q6F work with community?	-.085	.103	**.807**
Q6G focus too much on problems?	.049	**.676**	.070
Q6H focus too much on personality?	.090	**.629**	.055
Q6I problems overblown?	-.031	**.585**	-.101
Q6J educated enough?	-.037	**.625**	.205
Q6K too green?	-.058	**.666**	-.207

SPSS factor analysis based on Principal Component Analysis extraction method and Varimax Rotation with Kaiser Normalization. Rotation converged in 4 iterations. The process eliminates respondents who failed to answer any of the 10 questions. High missing values for some individual questions (e.g., 132 reporters failed to respond to the question about whether environmental reporters are educated enough) resulted in a final n=299 for this analysis. A comparison of reporters who answered all 10 questions and those who did not showed little difference in attitudes and socio economic status except for the question of how strong they felt about religion. A separate data analysis in which we substituted mean values for missing values, generating an n=652, generally showed minor differences in the results.

There was some overlap among the categories. While 299 reporters responded to all 10 questions and were included in the factor analysis, 134 of them answered in a way that qualified for two or more categories (usually both Objective/Fair Reporters and Workplace Critics, or Workplace Critics and Advocates/Civic Journalists). They were included in the foregoing analysis.

Q:
6A. Environmental journalists need to be just as objective as journalists in general. Do you...
    1) strongly agree with the statement 2) agree 4) disagree, or 5) strongly disagree
6B. Environmental journalists sometimes should be advocates for the environment...

6C. Environmental journalists need to be fair to sources such as corporations...

6D. Environmental journalists need to be fair to sources such as environmental activist groups...

6E. An environmental problem is generally a better news story than an environmental success...

6F. Environmental journalists should work with community leaders to help solve environmental problems...

6G. Environmental journalists generally concentrate far too much on problems and pollution rather than writing stories to help the public understand research or complex issues...

6H. Environmental journalism generally centers too much on personalities and not enough on actual findings...

6I. Environmental journalists generally have overblown environmental risks, unduly alarming the public...

6J. Most environmental journalists are not well enough educated to cover news about environmental issues...

6K. Environmental journalists tend to be too "green"—meaning slanted in favor of environmentalism...

6L. Environmental journalists tend to be too "brown"—meaning slanted in favor of business and industry...

The initial analysis used all 12 questions to sort reporters into categories. One question, 6E , "An environmental problem is generally a better news story than an environmental success," generated a factor loading of less than .500, meaning that it did not have a strong relationship with other questions, and it was eliminated. Another question, 6L, "Environmental journalists tend to be too 'brown,' meaning slanted in favor of business and industry," failed to load with any other variable and was discarded.

to drain and destroy. The fed's promise of "no net loss" under presidents Clinton and both Bushes seemed to be failing. One disgruntled Corps staffer even told him, on the record, "the whole thing's a fraud." Pittman knew he had a story.[27]

It took a new editor, a green light to file a Freedom of Information Act request, $5000 worth of new computer hardware and software, a computer-assisted reporting whiz (willing to take two college courses to help them figure out how to use GIS locations to map the needed data), and persistent interviewing to finally expose to the public what was really happening to Florida's valuable wetlands, and probably to wetlands all over the Southeast and beyond. "Vanishing Wetlands" first ran in 2005 with the final stories published in 2006. After the series ran, permits started to be denied, especially on the local level as municipal zoning boards saw the failed process. Letters-to-the-Editor praised the reporters for doing "what nobody else has the guts to do [draw the line on development]." Younger colleagues sent messages saying, "This is why I went into journalism."[28]

Pittman and Matthew Waite won awards for excellence in reporting from the state and nationally from the Society of Environmental Journalists. Pittman won a number of awards from his peers. His latest book, *Paving Paradise*, was published by the University Press of Florida in 2009 and became a top seller among books on Florida. "It [takes] an unprecedented level of commitment to do what the government is supposed to be doing," Pittman said of the wetlands story. It had taken Pittman and Waite nearly a year just to analyze the data the Corps had failed to track. "Do we just accept what the government says or do we spend money and time to do the real story?" he asks. "A promise [to the public to protect wetlands] was broken." Although he says he tries to remain neutral and let readers make up their own minds, it's hard to ignore the results of hard digging. He's uncomfortable saying flat out that the public's interest reigns over profits and property rights. But in an e-mail following the interview for this book, he noted, "[I]t would be accurate to point out that a considerable body of case law says public interest is supposed to take precedence over profits and property rights—but one of the Corps employees told us that instead of doing a 'public interest test' on permits, they did what he called a 'special interest test.' Did it benefit a special interest? Then the permit was approved." Hanging on to neutrality—the ethical stance of journalism culture—is tough. Who else, armed with facts and charged with informing the public, will stand up for the water, for the swamps? "After ten years, I'm finally hitting my stride [on the environment beat]," Pittman says.[29]

Water issues are becoming key, above-the-fold stories across the country. Water has always been controversial in Florida. While waiting for the go-ahead on the wetlands investigation, Pittman and Julie Hauserman, another award-winning environment journalist then also at the *Times*, got a tip on a serious breach in the process of managing the state's water. And one of the "bad guys" in the story just happened to be the president and CEO of their newspaper. Well, not exactly bad guys, just a powerful group of state leaders called the Council of 100 ready to siphon water from elsewhere in the fragile peninsula to supply the ever expanding population of South Florida. And to do it secretly. Moving water around, secrets or not, is surefire controversy. And the paper's boss sure looked to be in a conflict of interest position. With their editor's blessing, and full cooperation from the paper's CEO (who agreed to be interviewed) a special report on Florida's water ran in 2003. The public was outraged. The "secret" plan vanished, for the time being. Florida's water got at least a brief reprieve. Interviewing his CEO, who favored the secret water deal but spoke candidly with Pittman as the story evolved, was "thorny," he admits, but part of the necessary process. Whatever it takes to get the story.[30]

Going the distance to cover an environment issue, putting the public's interest first, and reporting that wins respect and recognition from their colleagues are hallmarks of ethical decision making in journalism. This chapter reported findings on what motivates ethical decision making among environmental journalists.

A recent book aimed primarily at science communication specialists— targeting especially, current genetic science—asserts that research scientists should embrace open and rational discourse to find common ground with other communities on the ethical, legal, and social implications of science and technology.[31] No one would risk such a suggestion to journalism professionals, whose implied code of ethics is tough to nail down. Attempts at ethical analysis of journalists and their products—based on philosophy—can be found throughout mass communication literature (see for example Philip Patterson & Lee Wilkins, William L. Rivers & Cleve Mathews),[32] yet arguments over who even qualifies as "journalist" abound, particularly in regard to the growing online/blog world and a host of cable commentators. There is little discussion, for example, of moral standing or moral outrage as might apply to the media or to media consumers. When the point person on endangered species at the Interior Department, a political appointee, was found by the inspector general's office to be "heavily involved" in editing scientific documents and leaking confidential information to industry groups, the ethical breach seemed clear and was widely reported.[33] What constitutes ethical behavior should always be so clear-cut. *The Washington Post*'s David Broder agrees with U.S. Senator Lamar Alexander's lament, "More than ever, the media, outside interest groups, and [political] party structures reward conflict and the taking of irreconcilable positions."[34] Where indeed is attention to reconciling principled positions? Some, addicted to the balancing act of objectivity, might even ask, is that media's role? Clearly defining media ethics in this era of convergence and corporate ownership affords new challenges, just as measuring public opinion has become more uneven. As leading media ethicist Lee Wilkins argues, the public is of more than one mind on most issues, and so the authors of this book argue, it may often seem, are individual journalists.

Consider for example how journalists might report making human eggs from stem cells, not typically the purview of an environment reporter, but as this study indicates, those who cover the environment often also write on health, medicine, and other topics. In the United States, women are allowed to sell eggs for clinical use, but there remains much debate about the ethics of altruistic donation or research use. Cow or rabbit eggs are more likely to be used in U.S. research, resulting in "cybrid" stem cell lines. Cytoplasmic hybrids are quite controversial in other countries, and in the United Kingdom, women undergoing in vitro fertilization are allowed to donate eggs for clinical or research use. Whose ethical stance is reported or presented as "correct," or reported at all? If the goal is what has been termed "solution reporting," responsible reporting should mean reporting not only choices in the traditional inverted pyramid, but an effort to synthesize or make sense of conflicting claims.[35] Covering the environment should be as much about problem solving as problem exposure. Reporting that the world's top scientists have confirmed climate change impacts, then adding that some experts or politicians continue to disregard global warming as a serious threat, confounds and confuses rather than informs or empowers the public. Environmental journalism invites a re-thinking of some traditional news values.

Rachel Carson's *Silent Spring*, first released in a series of magazine articles, did for the environment, perhaps the environmental movement, what Ida Tarbell's series of articles in *McClure's Magazine*, then published as a book, did to Standard Oil, John D. Rockefeller, and all future corporate behemoths. Truth told in a comprehensive narrative can trigger change. Journalists, as do most nonfiction or fiction writers, understand the power of words. Journalism at its origins is about reporting empowering information, news that informs decision making. Environmental journalists have been railed against, just as have the mainstream media overall, for bias, lack of objectivity, prejudice (in any number of directions), and ideological advocacy. There is no need to argue that objectivity is possible; to be human implies subjectivity. Fairness comes from the choices made by reporters and their editors about what stories to cover, who to use as sources, what makes it to the lead, or the overall emphasis of the piece. As Evan Thomas recently rehashed in "The Myth of Objectivity," news people are typically unaware of their own biases. What really drives perceived press bias is a "yen for scandal," a drive to expose conflict and human drama. That's what gets audience attention, and some will argue, that's what sells the product, rewards the advertisers. Thomas also notes that when mainstream media failed to rouse the public over global warming, Al Gore made use of the Internet and independent filmmakers, winning a Nobel Prize and an Oscar for "An Inconvenient Truth."[36]

Science and environment journalists, probably more so than other beat specialists, recognize the risk of bias in their reporting. Ethical choices are made daily. National Public Radio's Joe Palca openly shared with an American Association for the Advancement of Science audience at the AAAS 2007 annual meeting some of the potential pitfalls journalists face when covering the complexity of science topics, particularly controversial subjects such as cloning, stem cell research, or genetic manipulation.[37] Language can be co-opting. Somatic cell nuclear transfer—science jargon—doesn't even mention cloning, the controversial term more familiar to the general public. Even more confounding for journalists covering environmental or science topics is the balance trap. While reporters are traditionally trained to cover all sides of a story, unlike in politics, issues in science are often more settled, the facts are in the data. Deciding when the data are indeed all in overwhelming agreement, and whether the sources are credible, that's the work of a journalist tackling the what and why of a story. She or he relies on internal and external ethical guides to make choices.

Honesty, trustworthiness, consideration, and loyalty are traditionally highly valued character virtues, moral virtues. Internalized norms of social behavior, how we behave in public, and private moral predispositions interact to influence ethical outcomes. In research using behavioral game theory, most individuals fall somewhere between selfishness and public-spiritedness.[38] A single selfish individual in a group can have an alarming impact on fairness. An ethic of altruism and sacrifice is easily toppled. The culture of journalism imbues ideals of public service, honesty, accuracy, and collegial recognition. Stanford professor Stephen Schneider, a senior climatologist, urges scientists to support their arguments by "clearly identifying which opinions are personal values and which are based on professional judgments."[39] Journalists serve as the message conveyors; their opinions have no standing in a news story; opinion/commentary writers occupy another floor in the building. And yet, choices are made in every step of the reporting/writing/editing process. This study attempted to uncover how environment reporters see themselves as they make these routine ethical decisions.

Although journalists bring a degree of individuality to their reporting, professional values in the field, centered on truth, timeliness, relevancy, fairness and so on, provide a strong foundation for making judgments throughout the process. Research points also to external heuristic guides such as the law, peer evaluation, and internal motivations such as religious or moral beliefs as reasons for journalists' behavior.[40] Using Michael

Singletary et al's ethical motivation scale as a tool to study decision making among environmental journalists, studies indicated a reliance on extrinsic guides: what is legal, what is considered by the profession to be ethical standards of practice, and what other journalists would approve of.[41] In the census study reported in this book, an adapted version of the ethical motivation scale was included among the survey questions. Interviewed environmental journalists were asked to react to a series of statements in terms of whether each statement sounded "very much like you," "like you," or "not at all like you." Findings supported a high overall reliance on extrinsic guides and, among some of these journalists, attention to intrinsic guides.

Relying on extrinsic guides, 94.9 percent of those responding said the following statement was either very much like them or like them: "My ethical decisions are based on what I perceive to be the ethical standards prevailing in American journalism today." Nearly 99 percent (98.9 percent) responded equally positively to the statement: "Being ethical in pursuit of environmental news will win the trust of the audience." Nearly 92 percent (91.8 percent) also agreed that: "When environmental news judgments involve matters of professional ethics, I want my fellow staffers to approve of my decisions." However, agreement was weaker (63.3 percent) with another external value statement: "My ethical decision making is based more on what I know is legal rather than on what my instinct sometimes tells me is right."

Measures of concerns for intrinsic motivations such as personal advancement and religious beliefs were somewhat mixed. Some 63.8 percent of those responding rejected the statement: "Ethical considerations are of secondary importance to the public's need to know." And 88.2 percent disagreed with the statement: "Codes of ethics are not very important to me in my environmental news decision making." However, half of the journalists (51.7 percent of those responding) said it was like them that, "If there's an environmental story that needs to be reported, I would do whatever was needed to get the facts, even if I had to use some debatable tactics." And 94.5 percent saw themselves in the statement: "The harder it is to get information from officials, the harder I try to get it, by whatever means necessary." The impact of religious or moral beliefs on ethical decision making seemed consistent with demographic information on religious affiliation for this group of specialty beat reporters. Two-thirds (66.7 percent) of those interviewed did not see themselves in the statement: "Religion is the true basis for professional ethics." One-third (33.3 percent) of these journalists said the statement was indeed like them.

The ethical motivation scale was developed to examine the relationship between Internal Work Motivation and Extrinsic Guides. Early research on journalism students and professional editors indicated that using extrinsic guides motivated good job performance. Those who used personal advancement concerns were not motivated to perform well on the job, and those who relied on religion/moral beliefs as the basis for motivation faced ethical dilemmas. It should be noted that the original scales involved from 11 to 13 "motives" with 5-7 items per motive. Later research specifically aimed at measuring ethical values among environmental journalists and their scientist sources used a validated, much smaller scale. Those items with the strongest measures were again whittled down for the lengthy interview used in this census study. The modification in this application weakens the ability to test for statistical significance. The findings should be viewed as descriptive.[42]

"You offend God...by ruining the environment," announced Vatican Bishop Gianfranco Girotti.[43] Eco-abuse appears on the Roman Catholic Church's new list of deadly sins. Also joining the list of mortal sins are obscene consumerism and genetic manipulation. The internal ethical dilemmas for multitudes face fearful ratcheting up. Journalists have no access to the confessional, but religious beliefs promise to confound further the decisions made by some scientists and those in the media.

During the interview with Pittman (in the *St. Petersburg Times* newsrooms), he was working on general assignment on a Saturday, another sign of industry cutbacks and these specialty beat reporters' widely diverse assignments. Before he was called off to cover a tip that a mother had stabbed her teenage son during a supervised visit at a local clinic, he reflected, "Any job where they pay you to go ride around in a boat or walk in the woods is a great job. There's drama on the crime beat...but everything's part of the environment beat, it encompasses everything... it's intellectually challenging." And as his wife teases him, "just hold up a sign that says 'will work for compliments.'"[44]

Discussion

While much has been written about a perceived bias or tilt in environmental reporting, little has been written about how these reporters themselves feel about the issue. This project probed their attitudes using a variety of measurements.

The concept of objectivity seemed important to these reporters; 645 of 649 said environmental journalists should be as objective as journalists in general. There was far less support for the idea that reporters should sometimes be advocates for the environment (36.7 percent agreed) or that they should work with community leaders to help solve environmental problems (32.9 percent agreed).

Almost all of the environment reporters (650 out of 652) agreed with the statement that environmental reporters need to be fair to corporations and to environmental activist groups. While most (62.0 percent) rejected the statement that environment reporters are "too green" or too slanted in favor of environmentalism, the remaining 38.0 percent agreed or strongly agreed with the statement. Nearly everyone (95.8 percent) rejected a statement suggesting environment reporters were "too brown" and slanted in favor of business.

The environment reporters surveyed do not, in their reported work habits, evidence the anti-business bias claimed by critics. These reporters commonly use a business/economics framework for their stories (see Table 5.1 in Chapter 5). Local business-oriented sources (local manufacturers, Chamber of Commerce) are routinely used (see Table 5.3). Advertisers or other business interests were not seen as barriers to their reporting (see Table 4.8 in Chapter 4). Results found overwhelming support among environment reporters for the need to be fair to both business and environmental activist sources.

Nevertheless, a substantial minority of the reporters (38.0 percent) agreed with the statement that their peers are too green. Thus, many environment reporters appear to be wrestling with the question of objectivity and fairness.

This study demonstrates that environmental journalists recognize the importance of the business community. Their stories include a business angle and routine use of business sources. Still, a substantial minority of these environment reporters think their colleagues "tend to be too green." Whether or not significant numbers of environment reporters are truly biased, the perception of reporter bias clearly exists inside the newsroom as well as among industry leaders.[45]

The concepts of objectivity and advocacy were not mutually exclusive in the minds of some of these reporters. Almost half—48.4 percent—preferred a purist approach: they felt environment reporters should be objective, should not be advocates for the environment, and should not work with community leaders to help solve environmental problems. But another 17.9 percent said environment reporters should be pro-objectivity, pro-advocacy, and anti-civic journalism. Another 14.1 percent said environment reporters should be pro-objectivity, pro-civic journalism, but anti-advocacy. A final 18.9 percent can be seen as activist reporters who attempt a balancing act: protect objectivity, sometimes be advocates for the environment, and work with community leaders to solve environmental problems.

The factor analysis suggests these environment reporters have a nuanced, multi-layered view of their profession. The group this project calls Objective/Fair Reporters responded in a common, uniform way to questions about objectivity and fairness. The second group of reporters, whom the researchers called Workplace Critics, agreed with several traditional complaints about the way environment reporters perform their duties. They were united in their common complaints about how stories are written, the focus of stories, and the education level of their peer reporters.

Finally, the Advocates/Civic Journalists seemed willing to go beyond the traditional concept of objectivity and to frame their roles differently. They responded positively (above the mean score) to two statements that clustered together: a) "Environmental journalists sometimes should be advocates for the environment"; and b) "Environmental journalists should work with community leaders to help solve environmental problems."

So while almost all of the environment reporters interviewed agreed that objectivity was needed, half (51.0 percent) were willing to go beyond that one goal. For example, is objectivity the primary goal on an issue such as climate change when a resulting story may be out of balance with the scientific consensus? Many of the reporters here seemed willing to include elements of advocacy or civic journalism, presumably when it would aid their readers or viewers. This broader view, going beyond objective, on-the-one-hand approaches to stories, may be consistent with Maxwell Boykoff and Jules Boykoff's warning of "balance as bias"– that press coverage of global warming has led to popular discourse on global warming diverging from scientific discourse.[46]

Whatever their feelings about advocacy or civic journalism, environment reporters believe they are using extrinsic guidelines—the ethics of the journalism profession—when making decisions about environmental reporting. Relying on these extrinsic guides, more than nine out of every ten environment reporters said the following statements were either very much like them or like them:

- "My ethical decisions are based on what I perceive to be the ethical standards prevailing in American journalism today."
- "Being ethical in pursuit of environmental news will win the trust of the audience."
- "When environmental news judgments involve matters of professional ethics, I want my fellow staffers to approve of my decisions."

Back in the newsroom at the *Minneapolis Star Tribune*, Tom Meersman said he struggles with issues of objectivity, fairness, and balance almost every day. "There are folks who definitely feel…that the media is so mainstream that it relies on conventional sources and it is not open enough to challenging the status quo and the people who are making the decisions and who are involved in many news items," he said.[47]

Reporters who want to avoid a tag of being biased need to work hard to add depth to their stories, said Meersman.

"One thing I always keep in mind as a rule of thumb is: always make that extra call. You can do a story even under time constraints with a minimum of reporting. Or you can push out every day as far as you can to get that extra call and get that different perspective. And sometimes it can make a difference in terms of what the story is or adding quality to the story…. Make that extra call. Sometimes it also is a springboard. People will say I don't know that much about that, but you really ought to look at this."[48]

Notes

1.   Elements of this chapter were published first in David B. Sachsman, James Simon, and JoAnn Myer Valenti's "Wrestling with Objectivity and Fairness: U.S. Environment Reporters and the Business Community," *Applied Environmental Education and Communication* 4 (2005): 363-73.
2.   Tom Meersman, personal interview with James Simon, 10 April 2007.
3.   Ibid.
4.   Bud Ward, "Just thinking," *Environment Writer* (November, 2004). http://www.environmentwriter.org/resources/think/1104_think.htm (accessed December 20, 2004).
        Sachsman, Simon, and Valenti, "Wrestling with Objectivity and Fairness," 364.
5.   Seth Borenstein, "Rousing Ovation for Kennedy Taints Even Those Who Sat," *SEJournal* 16.2 (Winter 2004): 6.
6.   Perry Beeman, "No Matter the Name, the Only Agenda is Pure Journalism," *SEJournal* 16.2 (Summer 2006): 2
7.   Ibid., 2, 14.
8.   Paul Thompson, "A Business Writer Can be a Capitalist, so…," excerpt in "Are We Fooling Ourselves," *SEJournal* 12.4 (Spring 2003): 23.
9.   Bob Lutgen, personal interview with David Sachsman, December 12, 2004.
10.   Ibid.
11.   Media Research Center, Free Market Project, "Clamoring for Kyoto: The Network's One-Sided Coverage of Global Warming," May 7, 2001. http://secure.mediaresearch.org/specialreports/fmp/2001/globalwarming.html (accessed December 20, 2004). [No longer available at this address]
12.   Free Market Project, Media Research Center, "Media Aid Environmental Hit Job on ABC Reporter," *MediaNomics* 8.1 (August 29, 2000).
13.   L. Brent Bozell, III. "Flat Earth Environmental Reporting," Syndicated Column,

Creators Syndicate, July 10, 1997. http://www.mediaresearch.org/BozellColumns/newscolumn/1997/coll9970710.asp (accessed December 20, 2004). [No longer available at this address]

14.   "How Media Bias Colors the News," *Investor's Business Daily*. Lexis Nexis (October 25, 2004). http://web.lexisnexis.com/universe/document?_m=499e136769c770d6&_md5=36ee9fcba09d7bab4533aac925684416 (accessed December 16, 2004). [No longer available at this address]

15.   S. Robert Lichter, Stanley Rothman, and Linda S. Lichter, *The Media Elite* (Bethesda, MD: Adler & Adler, 1986).

16.   Stephen F. Hayward, "Mixed Atmospheres: Good and Bad Environmental Reporting Swirl Together," *The American Enterprise* (July/August, 2003): 36

17.   S. Robert Lichter, Linda S. Lichter and Stanley Rothman, *Watching America* (New York: Prentice Hall, 1991).

18.   Hayward, 36.

19.   Everett E. Dennis, "In Context: Environmentalism in the System of News," in *Media and the Environment*, eds. Craig L. LaMay and Everett E. Dennis (Washington, D.C.: Island Press, 1991): 62.

20.   Lisa Barchie, *Business and the Media*, (Columbia, MO: Freedom of Information Center FOI-463, 1982).

Robert K. Goidel and Ronald E. Langley, "Media Coverage of the Economy and Aggregate Economic Evaluations: Uncovering Evidence of Indirect Media Effects," *Political Research Quarterly* 48.2 (1995).

Chad Raphael, Lori Tokunaga, and Christina Wai, "Who is the Real Target?: Media Response to Controversial Investigative Reporting on Corporations," *Journalism Studies* 5.2 (2004).

21.   Bud Ward, "Al Gore's Movie and Book: Spur to More Climate Change?" *Environment Writer* (June, 2006).

22.   Maxwell T. Boykoff and Jules M. Boykoff, "Balance as Bias: Global Warming and the US Prestige Press," *Global Environmental Change* 14 (2004): 125-36.

Bill Dawson, "In Climate Change Coverage, Researchers Say Balance Equals Bias," *Environment Writer* (September 2004): http://www.environmentwriter.org/resouces/think/0904_think.htm (accessed April 10, 2007).

Chris Mooney, "Blinded by Science: How 'Balanced' Coverage Lets the Scientific Fringe Hijack Reality," *Columbia Journalism Review* (November/December 2004): http://web.lexis-nexis.com/universe/document?_m=05ef6cd0700de4465e ab442646f48d21&_docnum=1&wchp=dGLbVlb-zSkVA&_md5=c081af030306 0d31233af953165d6247 (accessed April 15, 2007).

Paul D. Thacker, "Has Balance Warped the Truth," *SEJournal* 16.1 (Spring 2006): 14

Bud Ward, "Just Thinking," *Environmental Writing* (June 2006), http://www.environmentwriter.org/resources/think/0606_think.htm (accessed April 10, 2007).

Bud Ward, "Climate Scientists, Reporters Swap Insights at Wilson Center Public Meeting," *Environment Writer* (August, 2006), http://www/environmentwriter.org/resources/articles/0706_wilsonctr.htm (accessed April 10, 2007). [No longer available at this address]

23.   Bud Ward, "Media at Nieman Session Weigh Climate Change, Water Resource Issues," *Environment Writer* (August, 2004), http://www.environmentwriter.org/resources/articles/0704_nieman.htm (accessed April 10, 2007).

24.   Meersman, personal interview.

25.   Ibid.

26.	See examples in JoAnn Myer Valenti, "Ethical Decisions Making in Environmental Communication," *Journal of Mass Media Ethics* 13.4 (1998): 219-31.

	JoAnn Myer Valenti and Lee Wilkins, "An Ethical Risk Communication Protocol for Science and Mass Communication," *Public Understanding of Science* 4 (1995): 177-94.

	Michael Greenberg, David Sachsman, Peter Sandman, and Kandice Salamone, "Risk, Drama, and Geography in Coverage of Environmental Risk by Network TV," *Journalism Quarterly* 66.2 (1989): 267-76.

	Holly Stocking and Jennifer Pease Leonard, "Greening of the Press," *Columbia Journalism Review* 29.4 (1990): 37.

	Kandice Salamone, Michael Greenberg, Peter Sandman, and David Sachsman, "A Question of Quality: How Journalists and News Sources Evaluate Coverage of Environmental Risk," *Journal of Communication* 40.4 (1990).

	Eleanor Singer, "A Question of Accuracy: How Journalists and Scientists Report Research on Hazards," *Journal of Communication* 40.4 (1990): 102-116.

27.	Craig Pittman, personal interview with JoAnn Myer Valenti, March 22, 2008. Unrelated to the survey.

28.	Ibid.

29.	Pittman, personal interview; e-mail to Valenti after March 22, 2008.

30.	Pittman, personal interview.

31.	George Gaskell and Martin W. Bauer, eds., *Genomics and Society: Legal, Ethical and Social Dimensions* (London: Earthscan, 2006).

32.	Philip Patterson and Lee Wilkins, *Media Ethics* 2nd ed. (Madison, WI: Brown and Benchmark, 1991).

	William L. Rivers and Cleve Mathews, *Ethics for the Media* (Englewood Cliffs, NJ: Prentice Hall, 1988).

33.	Erik Stokstad, "Endangered Species Act: Appointee 'Reshaped' Science, Says Report," *Science* 316 (2007): 37.

34.	David Broder, "Thankless Bipartisanship," *Washington Post*, May 3, 2007, A18.

35.	JoAnn Myer Valenti, "Environmental Communication: A Female-Friendly Process," in *Women Transforming Communications: Global Intersections,* eds. Donna Allen, Ramona Rush and Susan Kaufman (Thousand Oaks: Sage Publications, 1996).

36.	Evan Thomas, "The Myth of Objectivity," *Newsweek,* March 10, 2008, 36-38.

37.	Joe Palca, paper presentation, presented to American Association for the Advancement of Science annual meeting, February, 2007, San Francisco, CA.

38.	Benedikt Herrmann, Christian Thöni, and Simon Gächter, "Antisocial Punishment Across Societies", *Science* 319 (2008): 1362-67.

39.	Benjamin Somers and Becky Ham, "Scientists 'Uniquely Positioned' to Assist Climate Policy-Makers," *Science* 319 (2008): 1200.

40.	Michael W. Singletary, Susan Caudill, Edward Caudill and H. Allen White, "Motives for Ethical Decision-Making," *Journalism Quarterly* 67 (1990): 964-72.

	H. Allen White and Michael Singletary, "Internal Work Motivation: Predictor of Using Ethical Heuristics and Motivations," *Journalism Quarterly* 70 (1993): 381-92.

41.	JoAnn Myer Valenti, "Ethical Decision Making in Environmental Communication," *Journal of Mass Media Ethics* 13.4 (1998): 219-31.

	JoAnn Myer Valenti and Jack Welch, "Embracing Similarities, Not Differences, to Improve Science Communication: Using an Ethical Motivation Scale to Examine Potential Professional Communication Barriers," paper presentation, presented at the Annual Conference of the International Communication Association, San Francisco, CA., 1999.

42. Ibid.
43. Vatican Bishop Gianfranco Girotti, wire services March 8, *Newsweek*, March 24, 2008, 27.
44. Pittman, personal interview.
45. Sachsman, Simon, and Valenti, "Wrestling with Objectivity and Fairness," 371-72.
46. Maxwell T. Boykoff and Jules M. Boykoff, "Balance as Bias: Global Warming and the US Prestige Press," *Global Environment Change* 14.2 (2004): 125.

    Bud Ward, "Media at Nieman Session Weigh Climate Change, Water Resource Issues," *Environment Writer* (2004a, August). http://www.environmentwriter. org/resources/articles/0704_nieman.htm (accessed April 10, 2007).
47. Meersman, personal interview.
48. Ibid.

Part III

The Craft: Telling the Environment Story

7

On the Beat:
Environment Reporters at Work

The hundreds of environment reporters who contributed to this study have many different approaches to their craft. Some rely on their strong backgrounds in science. Others try to cope with their lack of science background through meticulous background research. Some immerse themselves in arcane government reports, trying to bring trends to light that would otherwise go unnoticed. Others rely on strong interviewing skills and story-telling ability.

Whatever their approach, these reporters appear to have discovered the special qualities of the environment beat. Peter Nelson, one-time editor-in-chief of Greenwire, an environmental news service, lists many of these qualities. He writes that environmental reporting "is _broad_, embracing nothing less than life itself. It is _interdependent_ with other fields, such as politics, culture, and the economy. It is _complex_, and therefore resistant to simple explanations and equations. It is _technical_, which means it requires some expertise. Environmental news reporting is _imprecise_ because environmental _science_ is imprecise—imprecise in its sources, data, scientific methodology and solutions. And it is _emotional_ in the effect it has on people." (Emphasis in the original.)[1]

This chapter looks at many of the elements cited by environment reporters as they perform the juggling act of addressing all these concerns.

Getting a Handle on the Environment

Communication scholars met in Hamburg, Germany in 2000 to focus on media's apparent reluctance to cover emerging environmental issues. One of this book's authors was among the gathered researchers from around the world focused on how to present sustainability to the public through the media. A consensus emerged, led by the U.S. scholars, that for the media, the concept and the term itself (sustainability) lacked "an acceptable, coherent definition, resulting in skepticism and an emphasis on political conflict rather than a fuller understanding of the substantive issues." They noted that there was a time when editors confused radon with radar. Or, more recently, when few could clearly state the difference between climate change, global warming, and the Greenhouse Effect. Science often generates new lingo, sometimes lengthy words even without the Latin terminology. Space-conscious editors and journalism's dictate for clarity can easily hit a brick wall when it comes to unfamiliar terms and the uncertainty inherent in science. In time, however, news reports of issues such as radon, hantavirus, climate change, and even sustainability entered the culture. It just takes time and a lot of persistent communication.[2]

The Internet and other information sources have made it easier for environment reporters to research stories and try to stay current in the field. Philip Shabecoff covered the environment for the *New York Times* from 1977 to 1991 and has since written several books about the environment. Looking back on his long career, he wrote:

> If covered properly, the environment encompasses an astonishing range of subjects. I had to give myself crash courses in environmental science and environmental law and get to know the workings of the government departments and agencies that administered the laws. I had to become acquainted with the nongovernmental environmental groups and how they functioned and with the lobbying groups that spoke for business and industry in the often bitter and prolonged battles over environmental policy. Only after I plunged into the job did I begin to understand how much policy was intertwined with politics and economics and with ideology and broad social issues such as race and poverty. I knew virtually nothing about the history of environmentalism, and there was little in the literature to teach me....[3]

Although the rise of the World Wide Web in the mid-1990s made research easier, it introduced another set of problems. James Bruggers, who covers environmental stories for the *Louisville Courier-Journal*, says there is now too much information available from the Internet and other sources for any individual reporter to handle. Getting a handle on the flood of information is only the start; an effective reporter then has to determine how to weigh the information. Bruggers said he now is more concerned with the human element—how environmental problems affect people—than when he started. "And I find the environmental beat more expansive, more complicated, more contentious and more difficult to manage than it has ever been. I don't think I'm alone," he writes.[4]

Andrew Revkin, who covered the environment for the *New York Times* for 15 years, said there are additional reasons why the beat has become more difficult. Major environmental issues once were "iconic" because of their worldwide notoriety, he said. The Love Canal chemical contamination site in New York State dominated headlines, as did the federal Superfund cleanup laws that were approved in its wake. The industrial disaster in Bhopal, India, that killed thousands of people led to right-to-know laws that allow neighbors and community officials to know

---

Convergence

Today's coming together of previously separate media forms is forcing more environment reporters to collect their information, then decide whether to present it as text, in a multimedia package, as a blog or as a podcast. Paul Rogers, a natural resources and environment writer at the *San Jose (CA) Mercury News*, would have preferred to continue his nationally recognized writing full-time for the daily newspaper. But newspaper staffs are shrinking and science stories are getting softer. So he decided to try working in the converged media world of both newspapers and TV. He works four days a week at the *Mercury News* and one day with KQED, the local public television station, where he is managing editor of Quest, a 30-minute prime time weekly science and environment show.

Eric Simons in *Columbia Journalism Review* suggests the Quest program "offers a glimpse of the future" on several levels:

> First of all, Quest is multiplatform, and in a really good way. It creates original content for TV, radio, and the Web, then promotes one medium on the others. The idea is that each platform appeals a bit more to a certain demographic, but that if the content is good, you can convince your audience to play around a bit with different mediums. The Web acts as the catch-all, with an archive of all the audio, video, and extras. The TV and radio segments attract a fairly traditional PBS audience, but the Web has more potential to bring in readers and viewers who may not turn to public broadcasting. And Quest has capitalized on that by offering its videos in an easy-to-embed format and sending them out via an almost viral marketing campaign to science and technology Web sites. (The embedded format allows people to watch or listen without clicking away from the site they're on.) Rogers says that 500,000 people downloaded programs in the first six months of season one.[5]

"I wanted to keep being a newspaper reporter," Rogers told Bud Ward in *SEJournal*. "But with all the different types of media converging together," Rogers sees his KQED/*Mercury News* positions as "an extension of where all the media are going anyway." He encourages other print reporters to look at potential tie-ins with local broadcasters.[6]

about chemicals used by local industry. The Chernobyl nuclear power incident in the then-Soviet Union generated new worries that built on concerns stemming from the Three Mile Island nuclear plant accident in Pennsylvania. When the *Exxon Valdez* ran aground in Alaska and spilled its oily cargo, that single incident galvanized international concern about transporting oil in sensitive areas.[7]

Today, environmentalists worried about oil spills also are concerned about less dramatic non-point sources of pollution such as runoff from lawns or farm fields, said Revkin. These environmental threats might not catch the public attention as much as an oil-soaked bird in Alaska, but they still have a significant negative impact on the environment. Revkin writes: "Now, however, the nature of environmental news is often profoundly different, making what was always a challenging subject far harder to convey appropriately to readers. By appropriately, I do not just mean accurately. Any stack of carefully checked facts can be accurate but still convey a warped sense of how important or scary or urgent a situation might be. Therein lies an added layer of responsibility—and difficulty—for the reporter."[8]

The Basics of the Beat

Many reporters say they started out their environment reporting career with stories that largely looked at traditional, nature-oriented themes and news pegs. They quickly learned that there are many other ways to frame an environmental story and that they needed to approach a story from multiple angles and overlapping perspectives. Margaret Kriz, the energy and environmental correspondent for the *National Journal*, writes that reporters "need to become experts on—or at least willing students of—science, government policy, economics, business practices, health impacts, and civil rights issues. Writers must analyze the tradeoffs between a community's economic and environmental needs, examine regional planning issues that impact suburban sprawl, and delve into racial and cultural problems that result when polluting factories locate in low-income neighborhoods."[9]

Government has long been the dominant source for environment reporters. Government reports, timetables, and actions provide reporters with a steady stream of spot stories. In Chapter 5, this book looked at a list of 29 sources of information for environment reporters and found many state agencies and local government offices in the top half of the list, with the local state Department of Environmental Quality ranking number one.

The many, often competing layers of government provide opportunities for reporters to pit state health officials announcing new regulations against local health officials who may be less than thrilled to have to implement them. Local officials who issue a report on an environmental problem can face challenges from state and federal government officials who would see a problem more broadly. The various layers of government also give reporters a chance to counter punch if a rival news organization receives a scoop. At one time in Boston, Massachusetts, the *Boston Globe* was the preferred outlet for longer take-outs on environmental issues, and therefore federal and state environmental officials often would leak stories and news pegs to *Globe* reporters. In response, the competing *Boston Herald* gave prominent treatment to stories offered by municipal officials who dealt with environmental or health issues. Counter-punching also can take the form of using outside advocacy groups to knock down stories leaked to a rival.[10]

Traditional news ingredients like conflict and human interest remain important to environment reporters, such as in the battle between environmental and business interests. Christy George created the business and environmental desk for the Los Angeles-based national business show "Marketplace," distributed by National Public Radio. She writes: "Simply put, there exists a fundamental clash between the goals of business and the way nature works. This beat gave me room to explore it all." Science stories in general can be a hard sell to editors, "who are attuned to the fast and the new.... But all stories worth telling are ultimately about people, including stories on this beat, and for television, complex and challenging business stories about the environment can be visually rich."[11]

Environment reporters say they need to develop some expertise on complex issues and avoid the temptation to try to fudge it in the hope that readers and viewers, who know even less, will not catch on. "It is easy to nod your head while sources babble on, pretending to understand their remarks," writes Peter Nelson, the one-time editor-in-chief of Greenwire. "Many journalists are afraid to admit their ignorance or ask a silly question. For journalists, there are no silly questions. There are unnecessary ones, however. Obviously, one doesn't ask a world-renowned scientist how to spell his name."[12] He said finding some neutral third parties to guide reporters in their work and serve as sounding boards can be valuable as can searching for college "faculty expert" guides online.

The environmental beat also is filled with scientific jargon that can quickly convince readers and viewers to move on to another story. "Think of environmental jargon as a foreign language, which it is for many readers...," Nelson said. "But even experts find jargon difficult to read or listen to. And experts themselves are sometimes unclear as to the exact meaning of a technical term. Everyone prefers clear and well-structured stories to stories muddied by bureaucratic language."[13]

Some reporters use jargon in stories because they themselves don't know what the terms mean. Nelson asks the source to provide a translation, to simplify the material for a broader audience. An alternative technique is for the reporter to try to translate the jargon, then read back the simplified description. Nelson quotes a reporter saying to an expert source, "'So, if I understand you correctly, biodiversity is the variety of life at all levels, including the number of species and differences within species.' If a reporter has misinterpreted something, the source will have a chance to explain it again."[14]

Former Associated Press environment reporter James Simon, a coauthor of this book, said he often would write with a reader or viewer in mind—maybe a middle aged woman in a neighboring town without much scientific background—and make stories understandable to such a person. He would anticipate what questions this reader might have and answer them. If much more background was needed to make a story understandable, he would consider a sidebar and go into greater detail without bogging down the flow of the main story, or mainbar. Simon focused on the question: Will this reader find the story relevant or interesting? If Simon thought the reader might respond with an acidic, "so what," he would try to do a better job of making the story relevant.[15]

Simon said environment reporters also have to avoid taking the easy way, i.e., merely reporting facts rather than seeking empirical truth. It is a fact that scientists can publicly claim that they know how to reverse the effects of global warming, for example. Reporters could write a story based on the fact that scientists made that claim, but reporters should take the next step and see if there is evidence to support such a claim, Simon said. This problem also can be seen in "he said, she said" reporting, where an environment reporter provides equal space to two competing scientific claims and places the burden on readers to discern the truth. Reporters who have the time should research the competing claims, perhaps finding a qualified third party who gives readers or viewers a sense of the scientific consensus on the given issue, he said.[16]

Shrinking newsrooms can lead reporters to adopt an assembly line approach to story writing that fails to pay attention to the kind of depth and nuance often needed for environmental pieces. Jennifer Kaylin, a former news producer at WTNH TV, Channel 8 in New Haven, Connecticut, warned that because so many environmental journalists have to do one or two stories every day, "they produce kind-of pseudo-environmental stories." There is an inclination to think too big, she says, focusing on insurmountable problems like population control and global warming. Reporters may want to focus on smaller pieces of such large problems, small enough so that they can include the many other considerations— politics, health, business—that may be at play.[17]

Kaylin said that when reporters have the time to complete in-depth research, they may be tempted to feel they should include all of their data instead of just boiling it down into one paragraph or even one sentence. While data is important, people want drama. They don't want to read an endless list of facts and numbers. "You need to think about the human element," she said.[18]

The Workplace

Newspapers and television stations are changing workplaces, where cutbacks have been severe and the newshole keeps shrinking. Reporters who take over the environment beat in this period of change may not be given the time to learn its basics, develop sources and interviewing style, and handle complex risk analysis stories. In Chapter 4, environmental journalists reported high job satisfaction, but expressed concern about barriers to reporting like time constraints, financial, travel, or other resource constraints, and the size of the newshole. They relished the high level of autonomy most enjoyed and the chance to help people. But some worried that environment stories were less important to their editors or audience members than they were to the reporters themselves.

Journalists need to find ways to overcome such barriers to their environment reporting. In this study, reporters were asked about 17 potential barriers, including editors, time constraints, competition in the local media market, and pressure from advertisers. This study found that everyday, practical journalistic process concerns were far more likely to be rated as always or often a barrier than, say, dealing with their editor, or competitive pressure. Time constraints received a far higher score than any of the 16 other reasons offered. The next highest rated was financial, travel, or other resource constraints, while problems with editors or supervisors ranked ninth of the 17. Other factors such as colleagues, advertisers, competition in the local media market, and university sources of information were seen as posing the lowest barriers to reporting on environmental stories.

Finding and Interviewing Sources

Environment reporters collect information through background research, by crunching numbers themselves, and by visiting sites and using their senses—especially sight, sound, smell, and touch. But interviews are their major source of information.[19] Robert McClure, an environment reporter at the *Seattle Post-Intelligencer*, writes that "Interviewing is neither the first thing nor the last thing reporters do. But it's arguably the most important."[20]

Reporters are used to the willingness of public relations and communication professionals to talk to them. They may become baffled when other sources—such as scientists—are less willing. Robin Mejia, a reporter who has written for *Science* and *Mother Jones*, said, "Unlike politicians, contractors and environmental group leaders, their prestige is tied to their research publications, not quotes in the popular press. Some actually fear the press."[21]

Mejia said she explains to scientists how she works, addressing such issues as whether the scientists will get to review their quotes or the whole story ahead of time. She said reporters should take time to build a relationship instead of calling in a rush and saying they need material because a deadline nears. While journalists may prefer sexy headlines, they should realize that scientists state their conclusions in qualified terms that might help reporters avoid overstating the value of a study.

Mejia meets in scientists' offices, if possible, rather than over the phone, hoping that sources will communicate visually with her. "Repeat back what you think you heard," Mejia advises. "Most scientists' biggest concern is that you'll get something wrong, you'll attribute it to them, and it will make them look stupid in print."[22]

Instead of being surprised that scientists and journalists don't always agree, it may be more useful to understand the nature of their different perspectives. Nelson writes:

> Part of the problem is that scientists and journalists are guided by somewhat different principles. Scientists are supposed to look for the truth, while reporters look not only for the truth but also for *news*.... Environmental journalists spend much of their time reacting to news—a chemical spill, a new law, etc. But most of the important scientific work is not dramatic or even very controversial. However, it is still *important*. By only reporting accidents and isolated 'findings,' journalists can give the impression that environmental news is just a series of random accidents and grim predictions. What are needed are more overviews—reports that educate readers about the state of scientific knowledge of an environmental problem.[23]

The most recent research on the science-media relationship may put to rest the widespread and persistent assumption that the journalist-scientist interaction is troubled. In an international survey conducted by scholars from five countries (the United States, Germany, Japan, France and England), researchers found a positive relationship between scientists and journalists. Interestingly, the scientists surveyed rated their own experiences with media in a more positive light than media coverage of science in general. Peters et al. hypothesize that, "A few problematic encounters may shape the general image of the science-media relationship more than the many less visible but unproblematic encounters."[24]

Sara Thurin Rollin, coauthor of *Guide to Environmental Laws: From Premanufacture to Disposal*, suggests dealing with scientists on three different levels. She has one set of scientists whom she uses as teachers. For example, when working on a story on the health reassessment of dioxin, she needed sources who could expertly explain to her chemical-cell interaction and the significance of background levels of exposure. The information was not directly included in the article, yet provided several benefits. Rollin writes: "First, I have gained an understanding of the issue (often the interview evolves into an oral exam). Second, I may win the trust of a scientist because I participated in this learning-exercise, and this often leads to a comment on the record." The second use of scientists is for conventional, on-the-record explanation of a study or issue. Finally, she has developed what she calls "secret scientists," experts she can call on deadline to double check a phrase or an editor's changes. She also uses them on a deep background basis to give her early warnings about emerging issues and to give her not-for-attribution tips about problems in the research of other scientists.[25]

Rollin's procedure lends itself to the use of a snowball technique in which one asks the original source: whom else should I talk to about this? Who else has some expertise? Finally, building a personal relationship with knowledgeable sources helps one ward off the temptation to quote the first person who calls back instead of cultivating the most knowledgeable source.[26]

Some reporters say they feel overmatched when dealing with the knowledge of scientists. Veteran environment reporter Andrew C. Revkin of the *New York Times* says science writing is difficult for many reasons, including pressures to publish exclusives, constraints on how much space and time one has to do a story, and competition for top placement of a story. Reporters can be too quick to frame stories in a simplistic "he said, she said" approach in which the reader is left with the responsibility—but no guidance or scientific background—to decide which side is closer to the truth. Revkin said journalists and scientists need to communicate better. The two professions have elements in common—they are both competitive, both want to get to a story or a finding first, and both are engaged in a pursuit toward the truth. He said scientists should not feel the need to suppress the passion they may feel for their work; refusing to show such emotion "can help foster counter productive stereotypes of scientists as being remote and aloof from the public and society."[27]

Environment Reporters versus Environmental Communicators:
The View From the Other Side

One day a reporter wants information on, say, air quality permits, and the state official is reluctant to provide it, perhaps fearing the release of proprietary information. Another day, the same state official wants a story to publicize a new initiative, and the reporter is too busy, too uninterested, or too afraid of being seen as too friendly toward the source. Other times, both the reporter and state official are eager to get news out, such as, say, approval of an open space bond issue.

The uneven give and take between environment reporter and environmental communicator varies by the issue. They get angry at each other, may at times disdain one another, but often find they need one another. "I think obviously there are occasions when you need the reporter, you need that interface, you need that relationship to get your point across," said Phillip Burgess of the Tennessee Valley Public Power Association. "Conversely, there are those times when they need you. And those needs are not always at the same time."[28]

Building a relationship with a reporter can give an environmental communicator confidence to provide background information and more than just a talking points memo on the news event. Burgess said he has established a trusted relationship with a couple of energy reporters. "I am comfortable going to background sessions with them, knowing full well our discussions are off the record. And to this point I have not been disappointed." Burgess said how a reporter phrases questions is a tip-off to whether they are interested in a serious story or just want quotes to fill out a story angle they have already chosen.[29]

"Being former media myself, I go into those situations with a positive attitude that hopefully I am dealing with a reporter who is not biased in some manner. But I am smart enough to quickly discern by wording of questions...if that is true or not. They show me their hand relatively quickly and I know whether I can be a bit more open or be more guarded in our comments."[30]

Does he "work the refs"—complain to reporters about unfavorable stories in hopes of getting better coverage next time? "I think so, without a doubt, I think so. Let's face it. They are the outlet to a much larger audience. You are always working the corners and the angles."[31]

Burgess said some reporters assume environmental issues should be approached on a national scale, despite differences at the local level. "I tend to look at different prisms. I don't think a one-size approach is necessarily the right way to go. It's been my experience that typically, many of the environment reporters I have worked with over the years tend to take a big picture approach to their topics, and it's problematic in that they don't always realize there are diversities, especially in the electric utility industry, and regional differences.[32]

"That's one thing I deal with on a continual basis in the southeast United States. We do not have a lot of renewable energy capabilities. The environmental reporter tends to think that's a cop out, but you can't compare Tennessee to Colorado in terms of wind generation. The terrain is different; the existing wind patterns are different. There are a lot of elements to that subject that make it sound like a utility is making excuses. But we are looking at it by a state by state basis and they are looking at it on a national perspective."[33]

While James Gomes was president of the advocacy group Environmental League of Massachusetts, his experiences paralleled many of those of Burgess, who represents industry. Gomes said he was far more likely to trust a veteran reporter who covered the environment as a beat. He says many environmental communicators take advantage of the lack of experience of part-time environment reporters and "the incredibly short memory of the press. You could roll a study out today that you rolled out five years ago, and as long as you said 'a new study says today,' nobody would know. It is a pernicious form of recycling here. Just take the same old stuff, repackage it, and it will play as news again because most reporters and editors don't have any historical context for what you are trying to do."[34]

Gomes said these reporters are generally interested in the environment and can be pro-green, but any such tendency is often intertwined with their training to be skeptical. "They have to have their skeptic's hat on as reporters in general, but the barrier for them usually is pretty low. They will tend to believe stories from environmental public officials or environmental advocates because they comport with their view of how the world is. Having said that, it sometimes is difficult to have a normal relationship with a reporter because of the skepticism…. I have had the experience of having a really good story, good facts, and having a reporter who doesn't want to believe what you are saying, doesn't want to take your angle on it, even if your angle is pretty good…. A lot of good reporters have their defenses up. They don't want to be spun by you; they don't want to feel they are shilling for you. Even if you bring them a perfectly good, interesting, and novel angle on something that's backed up by facts, they tend to want to present it differently so they don't feel they are regurgitating your stuff. One thing it suggests for advocates [and all environmental communicators] is don't give reporters your line right from the top, but help them discover it themselves."[35]

Gomes said that for some news stories, he would suggest to reporters the names of other worthwhile sources and groups, whom he expected to back up his position. "They were all ready to get their quotes in the story, which made the reporters happy, which made the story better, and which made those groups happy with us because we steered them to the press."[36]

Gomes said he was reluctant to lean on personal friendships with reporters. "I really felt I would be crossing the line, that it would get their defenses way up if they thought I was trying to prevail via friendship rather than coming to them with stuff that was good on its own merits."[37]

Is there a "favor bank," a way of helping a reporter and being owed a favor? "There may be, but in my experience the bank that was more important is the reliability/trustworthiness bank. Reporters would want to hear what we had to say because usually we had good stuff and we didn't come to them overhyping a particular study or fact, and I think that counts for a lot with reporters."[38]

Gomes said that getting a favorable story is only a part of a broader communication effort. "You can generate a story that gets you more ink or a better placement, but the question we always ask is: how will that help us pass a bill or get the bill out of committee or whatever," Gomes said. "Getting a story to run does have value for us organizationally—you can bundle together some of your press clips as evidence that you are influential, that you get your name in the paper. This can be helpful to your fundraising. But it's not the same as truly bringing about change."[39]

Gomes said a more effective story is to link a single event with a strategy to get legislation approved. "One of the things we always try to do is if we are trying to get more money for parks, let's find a scruffy park in the district of the chair of the Ways and Means Committee. Let's use that rundown park as an example in our story on parks. So when it appears, the staff member on Ways and Means will say, 'Look here, our local park is in bad shape. We should be in favor of that $3 million more for parks.'" Gomes called that framing of a story, as both a political and local story, "a two cushion shot."[40]

This study found that environment reporters tended to talk more to public information officers than to scientists or administrators (see Chapter 5). The higher usage of PIOs reflects the journalistic reality that they often serve as gatekeepers; the reporters cannot reach the scientists or top administrators until they first talk to the PIOs. When the same reporters were asked to rate how much value they placed on time spent with public information officers, scientists, and administrators, scientists topped the list with a mean score of 1.64 (range of 1 to 5), followed by administrators (2.37), and PIOs (2.74). The similarity in scores for the value of talking to administrators and PIOs again runs against the stereotype of reporters complaining that they cannot get around a PIO in order to talk to the top person at an agency or at other organizations. Overall, more than 90 percent of reporters indicated they either used or valued all three sources (using them, perhaps, for different needs).

The relationship between environment reporters and environmental communicators is clearly symbiotic. Burgess says, "I think obviously there are occasions when you need the reporter, you need that interface, you need that relationship to get your point across. Conversely, there are those times when they need you. And those needs are not always at the same time."[41]

Reporter's Stance: Objectivity Purist? Advocate? A Blend?

This project's survey of reporters shows that journalists are divided as to whether they should be advocates for the environment, and/or whether they should work to help solve problems, in addition to the traditional approach of holding up a mirror and reflecting what they see. One social norm that reinforces the traditional, objective approach is the desire by reporters to be seen as neutral and not "in the pocket" of any special interest, whether it be a particular politician, government agency, advocacy group, or other environmental actor. Reporters may be criticized if they are consistently pro-environmental or pro-business in their coverage.[42]

Case Studies of Environment Reporting

How do environment reporters cover the environment? Here are detailed case studies of how two journalists, a magazine editor and a television reporter/producer, put together very different stories about climate change.[43]

Brita Belli pushed back from her desk with a sigh. She had been working for a week, trying to get a handle on the resurgence in environmental activism on U.S. college campuses. It was scheduled as the cover story in *E/The Environmental Magazine*, to be accompanied by five sidebars. It would eat up the entire newshole for feature stories in the magazine, and she was a bit overwhelmed as she tried to sort out all the information.[44]

"The most difficult thing is the large scope of the topic," said Belli, editor of the magazine and occasional lead writer. "There are changes happening in the classrooms in terms of the actual things that kids are learning. Then there are buildings that are getting LEED (Leadership in Energy and Environmental Design) certified. Then there are cafeterias serving organic food, and campus climate activism. There are just so many facets to it..."[45]

Three thousand miles away and a year earlier, Christy George, a reporter and producer for Oregon Public Broadcasting, had had a different problem. Five years had gone by since she first had the idea of focusing on the skepticism of some television meteorologists and state climatologists about the impact of humans in causing global warming—the issue former Vice President Al Gore later depicted in *An Inconvenient Truth*. The good news was that she finally had an airdate for an hour-long environmental news documentary: October 2007. And that was the bad news, too, because she had to back-time the reporting, editing, and production process so everything was completed before that date. "If I'm going to air a one-hour show on October 25, 2007, I know that in March, April, May, something like that, I'll need twelve weeks of editing. And before those twelve weeks start, I'm going to need to back-time a month's worth of logging my tape and writing my script, and before that I need to back-time all my shooting and researching. So when I started in December 2006 and back-timed everything from October 2007, I didn't have enough time. I mean, this was not a journalistic crisis. This was a time crisis."[46]

The two environment journalists—one print, one television—took very different approaches to their stories and faced different problems, some unique to the medium of communication they were using. But in doing so, they used many of the techniques outlined in the preceding chapter. Each produced a prominent story geared to the needs of their specific medium. Here is a brief profile of each reporter, then an inside look at how the two environment reporters constructed their stories. The reporters take us through the process of conceptualizing a story, bringing it to life, then reconsidering it a year later. They take us through such steps as building on a story idea, casting a wide net for information, considering the audience and sources, the all-important lead, pacing the story, and dealing with jargon, the experts and your editor. A full version of Belli's story is available at http://www.emagazine.com/view/?4103. George's hour-long show can be viewed online at Forecast Cloudy (http://news.opb.org/forecastcloudy/#).

Brita Belli is the editor of *E/The Environmental Magazine*, the largest independent magazine dedicated to green issues. Prior to joining *E*, Belli was the arts editor at the *Fairfield County Weekly* where she won numerous awards for her writing from the Association of Alternative Newsweeklies, New England Press Association, and Connecticut Society of Professional Journalists. Her stories have been featured in the books *Notes from the Underground: the Most Outrageous Stories from the Alternative Press* and *Best AltWeekly Writing and Design 2006*. She writes a green column for *Connecticut Home & Garden* and her articles have appeared in such sites as *Plenty Magazine*, MSN.com, and Treehugger.com. She has appeared on numerous TV programs as an eco-expert, and she maintains a blog on sports and the environment at www.PlayItGreen.com.[47]

Christy George produces special projects for radio and television at Oregon Public Broadcasting. She won an Edward R. Murrow award in 2008 and a Gracie Allen award in 2007 for her weekly radio show, Oregon Territory, which ran from 2003 to 2007. In 2009, she was elected president of the Society of Environmental Journalists. She started at OPB in 1997, creating a bureau covering the intersection of business and the environment for the Los-Angeles based national business show, *Marketplace*. George's special, "Liquid Gold," on how water is being bought, sold, and marketed like any other commodity, was part of *Marketplace*'s 1998 winning submission for a Columbia-DuPont Silver Baton award. Before that, George edited foreign and national news for the *Boston Herald* and covered politics for WGBH-TV, where she won her first Emmy, for an investigative documentary about Massachusetts political corruption. She started out as a journalist in 1976, covering noise and air pollution and neighborhood encroachment by Logan Airport for the *East Boston Community News*—which she calls a dream beat. She was a 1990-91 John S. Knight Journalism Fellow at Stanford University.[48]

1. Building on a Story Idea

Belli, 30, was looking for potential stories for her magazine when she read about "PowerShift" in 2007. It was billed as "the first national youth summit to solve the climate crisis," the biggest gathering of college students ever to oppose climate change. The event was at the University of Maryland, about a six-hour drive from the magazine's offices in Norwalk, Connecticut.[49]

"I really wasn't aware of this larger movement about climate change and just how widespread it was on college campuses," she said in an interview. "So I knew I wanted to attend that and meet some of the main players in this movement. Once you start looking into green initiatives on college campuses it's really a question of where do you stop because there's so much happening on so many levels."[50]

The broad issue of the greening of college campuses was a good topic for her magazine because a substantial portion of its audience is made up of college-age readers. Then in its 16th year, *E/The Environmental Magazine* billed itself as "a bimonthly clearinghouse of information, news and resources for people concerned about the environment." She and the other editors decided on a spring issue because readers might be looking for information to help guide them on a college choice.[51]

"I think that decision was already made, when I was going to the festival, that this would be part of a larger piece on green initiatives on college campuses. It was something that we decided in-house that we wanted to do."[52]

As a newcomer to environmental issues, Belli has had to rely on extensive background reading—from the latest green websites like Treehugger.com and the *New York Times'* green blog, DotEarth (www.dotearth.blogs.nytimes.com), to poring through the extensive library of environmental titles that arrive weekly at *E*'s office. She also joined the Society of Environmental Journalists and subscribed to their listserv. "SEJers," as the widespread group of reporters, producers, editors, and freelancers are known, engage in constant e-mail conversation on green topics, from the highly technical to the humorous, with a focus each Friday on filing Freedom of Information actions.[53]

In Oregon, George's story began when she, like many veteran journalists, attended a mid-career training session to try to stay current in her field. In 2001, she received an MIT Science-Journalism Fellowship that featured a week-long intensive boot-camp on climate change.[54]

"The last speaker they had was a guy who had been a TV meteorologist and who was a Ph.D. journalism professor at the University of Texas in Austin.... Kris Wilson had studied the attitudes...of TV meteorologists about climate change. And what he discovered was that, even though they understood the science of climate change, they failed to believe in it. He came to the conclusion that something was contaminating their understanding of climate change. He didn't know what it was, but he definitely concluded there was a problem there.[55]

"And I thought that was so interesting: why don't weather people on TV believe in climate change? That was really intriguing to me. So I filed it away in the back of my head, and thought: 'good story.'"[56]

George said Oregon Public Broadcasting was looking for stories that lent themselves to multiplatforming: taking a topic and presenting it in different ways in different media, whether TV, radio, or the web. In talking with her editor, "we wanted to look for something enterprising to do, and so we talked about the broadcast meteorologists and the state climatologist issue, which was the other half of the show. We have our own state climatologist who is quite famous as a climate skeptic, not skeptical of climate change—nobody's skeptical anymore that Earth is getting warmer—but skeptical of the human cause: that we can blame humans for climate change."[57]

There were several local angles. The governor of Oregon had gone after George Taylor, the state climatologist, a few months before. Christy George recalled the study of TV weathercasters from the MIT conference, and found there were some meteorologists in Portland, Oregon, who might be climate skeptics. "So, that was the genesis of it. And we thought, 'well, they're two different kinds of weather people, let's follow both. And let's do it for TV.'"[58]

She realized she would struggle with the issue of how to illustrate an abstract concept like climate change in a medium that usually rewards an "If it bleeds, it leads" mentality. Former network correspondent Jim Upshaw, who now teaches journalism at the University of Oregon, told her: "If you can't hold a story in your hand, if you can't turn it over in front of the camera, if you can't get people to speak emotionally about it—not just about the argument about whether there is global warming but about how it is here in our town—then you don't really have what they call 'good television' in the business."[59]

Another problem would be her lack of formal scientific background.

"My training is almost completely on the job. I never went to college, but I had a journalism sabbatical at Stanford in 1990-91. At the time I was still a political reporter, but I was drawn to audit a handful of science classes—everything from basic geology to a seminar on how scientists were preparing for life on the space station. Once I started covering the environment for *Marketplace*, I needed to get up to speed, fast. I joined the Society of Environmental Journalists and went to the next conference SEJ held, where I discovered a terrific group of working journalists, who were collegial about sharing both their how-to tips and background about the beat. I've never missed a conference since, and I'm now on SEJ's board of directors.[60]

"I tend to come at environmental stories at an angle—business and environment, or politics and environment—so my stories aren't about a specific peer-reviewed study, but rather about how environment and science are playing in society."[61]

2. Casting a Wide Net for Information

Belli said that at the PowerShift meeting in Maryland she was looking for both factual material to drive the story and observational details and color to give the reader a sense that they were there. She started writing furiously when Brianna Cayo Cotter, communications director for the Energy Action Coalition, announced, "Climate change is our generation's civil rights movement.... We're at a crucial moment in history. Climate change is an issue that's already impacting us, from the destruction of the Appalachian Mountains to the wildfires in California. We get that the resource wars and super storms are connected. And we get that the steps taken today will end up being the future for tomorrow."[62]

But she also jotted down that Cotter drank from a tall cup of coffee while speaking, that she talked fast, that she raked her fingers through her hair, that it was thick and wavy hair, that she was staring intently, that she seemed to be on a caffeine jag.[63]

The facts were plentiful: the group said so many college students across the nation logged on to register that its server crashed. On Halloween night alone, they hit 5,500 registrants. Students attended hundreds of workshops ranging from lobbying and communicating a winning message too running an energy-efficiency campaign in your house of worship.[64]

The observational details were also plentiful: the commercial side to the event included foldout tables where organic T-shirts, cloth bags, environmental magazines and activist pamphlets were displayed. Students grabbed the kind of complimentary tote bags that their parents would receive at standard business conferences.[65]

"That's the beauty of going to something firsthand and meeting people and seeing things and being able to pick up on those details," Belli says. "I know when I'm reading, that's something that would draw me into a story. You want to give people the color and the character, which especially helps when you are dealing with a lot of technical issues."[66]

The in-person interviewing and colorful observational details are supplemented by research, usually from the Internet. The research can range from search engines such as Google to restricted information sources such as Nexis, from college web pages to blogs.[67]

"I love Nexis. It's a great tool.... In terms of listing colleges and their green programs, I went onto college websites and college blogs. A detail I included about Wesleyan College, students taking a dance class in response to climate change, I had read about on the blog Gawker.com, where they were basically making fun of it. But it stood out to me as, 'Wow that's just so unusual. They're dancing about climate change.' So if I could squeeze it in, I wanted to. I just thought it was interesting."[68]

Belli says her magazine still "believe[s] in some of the old fashioned techniques of actually meeting and calling people. But, I did some interviews by e-mail, too and it's nice to have it as an option. The college kids you're communicating with now are used to e-mailing, and it's a quick way to contact a group of people at once.[69]

"In terms of the basic technique, it's funny because, I'm often taking notes with a pen and paper and making phone calls much the same way, I think, as you would be doing 10 years ago. We're seeing that with the interns that come to E, in getting them to realize you've got to pick up a phone –you can't rely on information from the web."[70]

A "snowball" technique also worked well: ask each source who else to call, then ask those additional sources whom else to call, replicating a snowball that rolls down a wintery hill and gets bigger and bigger. "Once I started making connections among students, they would then pass me on to other students. Or say, 'Oh, I know of somebody who's doing this, I know of someone who's doing that.' And I was particularly interested in talking to as many students as possible, student leaders. So often I think there are stories about college students where very few students are actually interviewed. So I wanted to be sure that I did speak to them, and the networking worked well."[71]

The preparation was much different for the Oregon story. Normally, George says, she starts by talking to sources, asking each to name several additional people she should interview. But to speed up the process, George had to start videotaping before she finished her research. Again—the dilemma that reporters face is the issue of back-timing when there isn't enough time.[72]

Her first shoot was at the annual conference of the American Meteorological Society in January 2007, where scientists were meeting simultaneously with broadcast meteorologists for the first time in 12 years. A Portland TV weathercaster, Mark Nelsen, was chairing the broadcasters' meeting, which cemented the local angle.[73]

Given the expense of shooting television, decisions about who and what to shoot are critical. "On a local station's budget, there's little room for error," George says. "So I look early on for the main characters. In documentary, you're looking for drama, for a story arc—you know, Hollywood stuff. So I committed to Mark Nelsen, from KPTV, as my likely main character, but I left myself open a little because there were a couple of other meteorologists from Portland going to that conference. But Mark turned out to be everything you could want: articulate, friendly, and honest."[74]

Nelsen gave George strong quotes on the impact of climate change on Oregon and how he bristles when he hears someone minimizing the problem. "I don't like it when I hear radio talk show hosts who say 'It's just a crock. There's no such thing,'" she quotes Nelsen as saying. "Well, our climate is warming, and it's possible we aren't changing it that much, but it's quite possible we are, so we should at least say what would happen if we are changing it and would those actions actually help?" But he later admitted, "I rarely have talked about it within my weathercasts."[75]

There was no hesitation for George when it came to choosing her other main character, state climatologist George Taylor. He freely admits he received $2,500 from the fossil fuel industry for eight stories he wrote on climate change over eight years. But Christy George concludes, "He's not a skeptic because Exxon paid him to be, but because of a combination of factors—including a distrust of weather models, scientific data that shows part of the country cooling, and maybe even partly because of his own religious beliefs." In the program, Taylor stresses that there is a level of uncertainty in all scientific endeavors, which, in this case, prevents anyone from reaching a conclusion with certainty.[76]

George wrestled with the fact that she was working with two separate stories that were interwoven. "The truth is, Mark Nelsen, though he chaired the AMS conference, was not the best choice if I had wanted to show two climate skeptics. He certainly is not a skeptic, but on the other hand, you could argue that he was well-chosen because he inadvertently ended up illustrating something that's going on with a lot of broadcasters: self-censorship. He has his own realization at the end of the show that maybe he self-censors a little bit because he knows deep down that if he talked about it more than he does, his bosses might do the censoring—which I think is true of a lot of people on TV, actually. A lot of TV meteorologists feel that they better not go out on a limb politically, even if they feel that climate change is real; that for them to talk about it could come back to haunt them. I think that's a very real thing they think about and worry about."[77]

Many of the TV meteorologists were experts themselves, yet they were trained as journalists not to give their own personal opinion. George said many felt, "It's just that—my opinion—and I shouldn't be talking about my opinion. But there are some good and strong reasons why they should talk about climate change during the weathercast. The AMS is the premiere credentialing group for broadcast meteorology, and lately the AMS has been saying to broadcasters, 'You guys are where science resides in your newsrooms and you should become your station's science reporter.... You can explain why weird weather is happening. You're the science guy.' The AMS wanted to formalize that 'station scientist' concept, but it hasn't happened. Things are not that different then they were a year ago."[78]

3. The Audience and Sources

Belli knows that the typical *E* reader is apt to be someone who has already converted to the green message, and expects environmental stories that are thorough, in-depth, and more serious in tone. With its long history of covering environmental topics of every variety, *E* has established a reputation as a real resource for those in the movement, and Doug Moss, *E*'s founder and publisher, often reminds staff that *E* was the "environmental paper of record" and the stories in it had to carry weight and importance. At the same time, as environmental stories went mainstream and a host of new green publications took root—from print magazines like *Plenty* to online sites like Grist.com and Treehugger.com—*E* was looking to evolve and reach a broader audience. As editor, Belli needs to walk a fine line—cover topics that would appeal to a more mainstream and younger audience without alienating *E*'s core readers.[79]

Gathering expert sources is critical to an *E* story. During the course of researching a topic, Belli will keep a running list of expert names and contact information. For a feature-length story, it would likely have some 20 people. These will include the representatives of environmental organizations, researchers, activists, and company (or, in this case, college) spokespeople. She consciously seeks a variety of voices—in ages, backgrounds, and gender—and typically will use only a handful of quotes from each person. But all that extra material still has its purpose—it informs the story and educates the author, it provides the framework and many of the ideas that shape the final piece.[80]

At OPB, George says her audience is older than the general public, more affluent and better educated. "So I assume my typical viewer has already read the local daily paper, *The Oregonian*, and probably *The New York Times*, along with listening to NPR, and maybe watching some television news as well. We're a statewide TV and radio system, so we reach all Oregonians. Politically, our viewers are all over the map.[81]

"Oregon is a red state with a blue strip running through the Willamette Valley, where the big cities are. But rural Oregonians aren't hicks. These days, Oregon loggers and ranchers have masters' degrees. They watch public television and listen to public radio. So I don't talk down to our viewers. Who do I write for? Often for whoever is in the show—which means when there are adversaries, I have to tell the story so that everybody recognizes it as the truth.[82]

"In TV, everything has to be on videotape, or it effectively didn't happen. Producing television can be expensive: a videographer, a sound engineer and me, all traveling somewhere for a week, multiplied by a handful of shoots. But tape is cheap, so once you're there, you might as well keep rolling until you get the perfect soundbite. The ratio in documentary can go as high as sixty to one—one hour of tape for every minute you use. For Forecast Cloudy, we shot about 90 tapes, each about 40 minutes long. So information I gather may end up in my narration but not on your screen. Or in one of the companion radio interviews we did, or on the Forecast Cloudy website we created.[83]

"I try to pre-interview as much as possible, to be sure an interview is worth doing. But there's serendipity, too. The Society of Environmental Journalists board met in Atlanta while I was working on the program, so I hired a crew and was able to shoot a panel discussion on weather-casting and climate change, and interviewed Weather Channel anchor Heidi Cullen, senior Weather Channel meteorologist Stu Ostro, and the man who started me on this project six years earlier, Kris Wilson."[84]

4. The Lead

Magazine editor Belli debated how to pull the reader into the story. She decided to open with a quote:[85]

"Climate change is our generation's civil rights movement," says Brianna Cayo Cotter, communications director for the Energy Action Coalition, swilling from a tall cup of coffee. Cotter talked fast and raked her fingers through her thick, wavy hair, staring intently, as though she'd been on a steady diet of nothing but caffeine for the last few days. This was PowerShift 2007, held at the University of Maryland, the largest gathering of college students ever assembled to fight climate change, a weekend of non-stop workshops and speakers and rallies brought together by Energy Action staff.[86]

"That idea struck me right from the get-go. As soon as she said it, I thought, 'Wow, that's a major statement to make.' And I brought that out as an idea, drawing that parallel between the sixties and today. And I asked people later on, other people that I interviewed, what they thought about that. And some thought, we're not there yet, people aren't angry enough yet. But it was a very interesting point about how seriously college students today take the issue of climate change."[87]

She used a political angle or "frame" (climate change = civil rights), then combined it with the human interest angle that comes out of the narrative lead, thrusting the reader into Brianna Cayo Cotter's passion for climate change. She also could have framed it as a government story (college students prep on how to lobby for climate change); a nature angle (opening with students getting involved in an anti-coal campaign to block mining that removes mountaintops); a science and technology angle (schools compete for most green school building projects), or several of the other frames discussed in Chapter 5 of this book.[88]

Television reporter George recognized that covering climate change generated strong feelings in her diverse audience. But when it came to the so-called "debate" about whether humans are causing climate change, she sidestepped the common journalistic problem of automatically giving equal time to two sides of an issue. Instead, she adopted the point of view of the scientific consensus: global warming is real. In a story about skeptical weather forecasters, that immediately created conflict, the lifeblood of storytelling. The hour-long piece opens with cross-faded audio of Portland weather-casters from off-screen newscasts, and then George begins a voice-over:[89]

The debate over why Earth is warming is essentially over. But some skeptics—contrarians—are still arguing about whether people are changing the planet. And some of the most prominent climate skeptics are TV meteorologists and state climatologists....

Portland weatherman Bruce Sussman: "You know we have trouble with the 7-day forecast. Now you're telling me I have to base everything and panic on a 70-year forecast? How accurate can that really be?"

Skeptics don't challenge basic science. They agree that without greenhouse gases, like carbon dioxide, or CO_2, all the Sun's energy would go back into space.

They agree the greenhouse effect is what makes the planet habitable. And that Earth is getting warmer. And they agree humans have burned a staggering amount of oil, gas and coal, which all release carbon dioxide. Study after study has concluded that fossil fuel burning is the only way to explain the warming Earth—but skeptics say it's something else. Anything else. Natural variability, the sun, water vapor, land use changes, underground nuclear reactions or cosmic rays.

The people you rely on most to tell you what's happening with the weather may be on the trailing edge of climate science.... As long as skeptics debate the cause of climate change, they delay the debate about what to do.

Oregon Governor Ted Kulongoski says on camera: "I'm trying to do things on bio-fuels, bio-mass, a whole series of things. What the other side was saying is you don't have to do those—it's just a naturally occurring event. And I think that's not true."

Why are weather experts skeptical about the human role in climate change? What role should meteorologists play in the climate debate?... And if weather-watchers aren't talking about climate change, how will you know when it's affecting your life?[90]

5. Pacing the Story

Belli gathered so much information that it soon became apparent that the piece would be the cover story. What should they do with substantial issues that didn't fit into the mainbar? College cafeterias are trying to buy local produce. Colleges are trying to save water. Colleges are trying to create their own sustainable solutions in conserving energy and using alternative sources. All these became sidebars to a large package that used up the entire 7,400-word feature section of the magazine, and Belli was able to use the expertise of the magazine's interns by giving several of them a sidebar in which they could generate a fresh perspective.[91]

"In terms of an article like this taking up the entire feature well, it really has to do with, how much there is to say about this topic, how important is it, and how definitive do we want to be. And I think this is one of those ones where we really wanted it to cover all the bases with this topic. And there's just so much to say."[92]

The author knew *E* was known for lists such as "the greenest schools" and end-of-story contact lists for additional information. "I think it's really about being a resource so people can really tap in and get involved."[93]

She spent several weeks gathering the information, then spent about a week writing out two or three full drafts and revisions. "I definitely do a lot of the gathering first and then I usually sketch an outline, especially for a big feature. And I do have to say that I start at the beginning and follow it through. I do agonize over a lead. I don't really know who doesn't."[94]

Environment reporters at *E* face the same kind of convergence pressure as their counterparts in other media. While Belli views herself primarily as a magazine writer, she is constantly looking for ways to illustrate her stories. She has no problem taking out a digital camera on assignment and snapping away. "If I go somewhere, I would take pictures. I think it helps because we're so small staffed. I'm responsible for finding pictures for most of the magazine, with the exception of features that I haven't written. At a small publication, you have to wear a lot of different hats, and, as the writer, you've got the contacts already, so you're already dealing with the PR people from the schools or whoever might have access to high resolution images."[95]

In Oregon, George was challenged with the goal of combining two specific stories: one on TV weather forecasters, the other on state climatologists.

"It was two stories inter-woven. That's very hard to do and I continue to wonder if I shouldn't just have done two half-hours—one on TV meteorologists, one on state climatologists. I don't know if it would have been effective. There were great similarities between the groups and they were both very important weather people. So it made sense to put them in the same box, but man…"[96]

George noted that this chapter was constructed in much the same way: two stories of environment reporters doing stories, interwoven.

"Be careful. It's very hard.

"I mean, I used the chronological story-telling method and again there were similarities like the state climatologists not believing climate models because they know the failings of weather models and the TV meteorologists don't believe in weather models either, because they don't work beyond five days for a day-to-day weather forecasting. But climate models are totally different. They don't say 'It will be this temperature on this day in 2047.' They say 'We'll see this kind of temperature increase globally in 2047.' And the other thing is that weather happens on the surface of the Earth, while the greenhouse effect happens in the upper atmosphere. Climate change science is really not about surface temperature—at least not now. It's about emissions of carbon dioxide that intensify the greenhouse effect. Eventually that manifests as surface temperatures, but it's really mostly about upper-atmosphere stuff right now. Both groups—TV meteorologists and state climatologists—aren't climate scientists. And they're similar in that way.[97]

"And the other great similarity was that both groups came under fire from their own colleagues and peers for remaining skeptical in the face of so much evidence. That was a major development of 2007. So there were great reasons for putting the two stories together, but it made the storytelling difficult, I think, to go back and forth."[98]

She looked for a consistent thread to tie together the hour-long piece. She found one in the basic principle that "science is built on data." First she reports that scientists in the Pacific Northwest (PNW) "are already seeing troubling signs—signals from the environment that the climate is changing." This gives her a chance to show compelling video of the melting snowpack in Oregon and to report the latest data showing that the PNW snowpack is down by 25-30 percent, albeit with some natural variability.[99]

"Science is built on data," she says again, allowing her to report that when the snowpack drops "farmers and fish are the big losers."[100]

George reasons that because the weather segment on local television is part of the newscast, it should be considered journalism. She wants to address the issue of false balance—presenting both sides of an issue and implying they are of equal weight. Professor Kris Wilson tells her on camera, "Balance in this issue is not 50-50, because that's not accurate and fair reporting. The balance should reflect the scientific weight, and that is how science has evolved over time."[101]

She concludes the piece by looking ahead to the prospect of an even more bleak future on climate change. "This summer, the Northwest Passage was completely free of sea ice. If climate change keeps playing out as the scientific consensus forecasts, it will be the biggest news story of the 21st century. And then, commercial television executives will see climate change quite differently. They'll see it as ratings gold."[102]

6. Dealing with Jargon, the Experts, and Editors

Dealing with statistics and climate science issues requires a learning curve. As someone new to environmental journalism, Belli began by taking on story topics that weren't overly technical in nature. As she developed more confidence with denser subject matter—renewable energy advances, toxic chemicals in plastic products—she relied on the best science data she could find, and in talking to consumer and science-based groups about their research and what it meant. Because her audience is largely well-versed in environmental issues, Belli knew that they were looking for the real particulars—a misstated temperature range or a wrong recycling code would be immediately challenged, and a "gee whiz" attitude toward the subject matter wouldn't work.[103]

Though Belli didn't possess a strong science background, as the former editor at an alternative newsweekly, she had covered a range of topics, from political scandals to genetically modified crops, and had learned how to dig for facts, how to ask questions, and how to track down sources. When she found herself overwhelmed by particularly science-heavy subject matter, or inside jargon, she would ask those she knew about their own interpretations.[104]

Her primary mentor was *E*'s longtime former editor, Jim Motavalli, who was editor at the time Belli, then managing editor, was writing the college activism article. In his more than 10-year editorship at *E*, Motavalli had become adept at environmental topics from hybrid cars to hydrogen power. For the piece on campus sustainability, the subject matter didn't require special inside knowledge, but when questions arose, she could turn to the university professors who she quoted in the story for the best information on the campus climate movement.[105]

Meanwhile, George said that throughout her show, she tried to steer clear of jargon, but embraced core scientific concepts "as part of my storytelling—the search for data, scientific uncertainty as a normal part of the search for results that can be replicated, the constant review and re-testing of theories—to the point that things as basic as evolution and even gravity are still technically theories.[106]

"A phrase you'll barely hear in the show is 'anthropogenic global warming.' Everyone I talked to used that expression all the time, and I cut it out every time, except once—when George Taylor is asked what it means during a climate change debate at Oregon's Museum of Science and Industry. He explained it means 'human-caused' global warming and then jokes, 'Hello, anthros.'[107]

"The other big issue was what to call it—global warming or climate change? Years ago, everyone called it global warming, but in 2003, Republican pollster Frank Luntz wrote a famous paper on how conservatives should deal with environmental issues. Luntz is the master of GOP wordsmithing—he coined the phrase 'Contract for America' for Newt Gingrich's 1994 takeover of Congress—and he suggested that conservatives adopt 'climate change' because 'global warming' sounded more catastrophic, while 'climate change' sounded less emotional and easier to fix. Despite the politics, our news director decided that 'climate change' is more accurate, since a warmer world is only part of what climate change will bring. It will also be a wetter world and above all, scientists say, the weather will be much more variable and volatile—so, warm and wet most places, but sometimes cold, or dry, too."[108]

George said, "The language of television is images—the pictures you see on the screen. So we set out to shoot images of weather in flux—raindrops splatting into puddles and clouds scudding across the sky. We show you weather that's volatile, always in motion, to symbolize a changing climate. And then, to underscore the theme of weather forecasters, we sped up the weather pictures, just like TV meteorologists do with the sky show they include with the weathercast at 11.[109]

"One of my biggest barriers was getting all the permissions I needed. One I expected to be hard was finding video from a White House event back in 1997, but the Clinton Library turns out to be a terrific resource. I also wanted to use video from actual Portland weathercasts recorded off the air, which meant getting permission from four news directors to record and use anything I wanted. I credit all four for trusting OPB enough to grant us permission. But hardest of all, I wanted to use local car dealership ads off the air to illustrate the high stakes for local TV newsrooms when it comes to covering climate change. The number one advertisers during the local TV news are people who would prefer that no legislation ever be passed imposing a tax on carbon dioxide, or capping CO_2 emissions. At first our lawyer was adamant that we couldn't run any ads without permission. That's standard for documentary production, but when a show is very newsy—which mine was—the 'news use' doctrine comes into play. Essentially, if your story revolves around something that is protected by copyright, as mine did, journalists have a strong argument for using a small portion of the copy-protected material. In the end, one auto dealer said yes, and our lawyer gave the okay to run short excerpts of the others, as long as we didn't show the dealership names.[110]

"Another critical issue for me was not burning either of my main characters, Mark Nelsen or George Taylor. Both had been extremely generous with their time, and both had trusted me to understand the nuances of their situations. It takes more time to get into nuances, but in an hour-long show, there's no excuse not to try."[111]

7. Reconsidering the Stories

Looking back, Belli said she was pleased she did not use the easy story frame of how colleges are in competition to be considered the most green.[112]

"It's easy to portray this as the schools battling for the top green honors. I did have to change some of the way I'd phrase things when I felt myself falling into that. In talking to the students at these schools, it seemed like they were actually working together and learning from one another and sharing. That may not be as exciting to read about, but it's the truth."[113]

Belli said it was helpful to be out of school for less than 10 years and still able to communicate easily with college students. "I certainly felt comfortable approaching college students, and I think it helps that I really do value where they're coming from and I can draw that comparison to when I was in school.... I was impressed that these students were so passionate about things like climate change and ending coal and really aware of these issues beyond their campuses. It was quite different than when I was in school...."[114]

E/The Environmental Magazine is read by people interested in the environment, and Belli said it is possible to lose your perspective in writing for readers already committed to a cause. "We're so immersed in it that it's hard to have that outside view. We do appeal to a core group that is passionate about these issues." She said the magazine also struggles with how to reach a more mainstream audience while still serving its core readership.[115]

Looking back on the Oregon piece, George was surprised by the unlikely role that Al Gore played in encouraging skepticism among some forecasters and climatologists.[116]

"Al Gore has a great impact in this whole debate for these guys. He is a loathed figure. It is amazing. They hate him so much—both groups of skeptics. They just cannot stand him. This was one of Kris Wilson's realizations. When he did his study of skeptical TV meteorologists, they kept bringing up Al Gore and the White House.[117]

"So he did a little bit of research and discovered that Bill Clinton and Al Gore had called a meeting shortly before the Kyoto global warming treaty conference in 1997. They invited a hundred TV meteorologists to the White House to talk about the climate crisis. And what happened was that the hundred people who were invited felt like they were being spun and a thousand other weathercasters who didn't get invited felt like they were being snubbed. That one incident might have been the mysterious something beyond science that predisposed a lot of weathercasters to be skeptics. And to hate Al Gore."[118]

George said she and her executive producer discussed how to approach objectivity without misleading the viewer.[119]

"We want to be objective without false balance. False balance is when you say, 'So-and-so says this, So-and-so says that, you figure it out—we're not going to mediate.' We want to do a little better than that. We want to mediate. What's the point otherwise? We [my boss and I] made a courageous decision to say, 'Our point of view on this is that climate change is real. Human cause. Period. End of conversation.

We're with the IPCC [the United Nations' Intergovernmental Panel on Climate Change], we're with the scientists who are widely respected on this. And not only that, we have a lot of nationally prominent scientists in Oregon who are looking at specific issues in the state. We've got a Dead Zone in the Pacific Ocean off the Oregon coast, we've got forest issues—drought and fire and insects, we've got snowpack and water and fish issues, and people here are studying those things and starting to take it very seriously—our governor, our legislature in particular are taking climate change very, very seriously.[120]

"And so as journalists, we just said we're not going to be namby-pamby about this at all," George said. "We're saying it's real and these guys are wrong for not taking it seriously. And that allowed us to move beyond that tired old debate about whether climate change is real, and into the conflict about what weather forecasters' role should be in informing the public about the on-the-ground consequences of climate change."[121]

Notes

1.   Peter Nelson, *Ten Practical Tips for Environmental Reporting* (Washington, D.C.: International Center for Journalists, 1995), vii–viii.
2.   JoAnn Myer Valenti, "A Review of the President's Council on Sustainable Development (U.S.): Building Networks, Throwing Pebbles at a Goliath Media" in *Environmental Education, Communication and Sustainability*, ed. Walter Leal Filho (Peter Lang GmbH: Frankfurt am Main, 2000), 121.
3.   Philip Shabecoff, "The Environment Beat's Rocky Terrain: Editors Often Don't See these Stories as 'Traditional News,' and Reporters Tread on Sensitive Ground Inside the Newsroom," *Nieman Reports* (Winter, 2002): 34-35.
4.   James Bruggers, "The Beat is a Tougher One Today: Reporting on the Environment Requires More and Better Training of those Who Do It," *Nieman Reports* (Winter, 2002): 37-39.
5.   Eric Simons, "Vision Quest: KQED's New Science Program Offers a Glimpse of the Future," *Columbia Journalism Review* (2007). http://www.cjr.org/behind_the_news/vision_quest.php?page=all&print=true (accessed June 5, 2008).
6.   Bud Ward, "E-Journalists May Fit Well into Complex, Converged Media Future," *SEJournal* (Spring, 2007) 4, 7.
7.   Andrew Revkin, "The Environment," in *A Field Guide for Science Writers*, 2nd ed., ed. Deborah Blum, Mary Knudson, and Robin M. Henig (New York: Oxford University Press, 2006), 222-28.
8.   Ibid., 223.
9.   Margaret Kriz, "The Environment Beat in the Nation's Capital: Reporters Sort Through Promises of Politicians and Claims of Advocates" *Nieman Reports* (Winter, 2002): 73.
10.   James Simon, Assistant Secretary of the Environment, Executive Office of Environmental Affairs, Commonwealth of Massachusetts, 1987-1989; reporter and editor, The Associated Press, 1974-1978, 1979-1987.
11.   Christy George, "A Beat About Business and the Environment: A Broadcast Journalist Starts to See Stories Through a More Complicated Lens" *Nieman Reports* (Winter, 2002): 73-74.

12. Nelson, *Ten Practical Tips, x.*

13. Ibid., 13-14.

14. Ibid., 15.

15. James Simon, reporter and editor, The Associated Press, 1974-1978, 1979-1987; Assistant Secretary of the Environment, Executive Office of Environmental Affairs, Commonwealth of Massachusetts, 1987-1989.

16. James Simon, reporter and editor, The Associated Press, 1974-1978, 1979-1987; Assistant Secretary of the Environment, Executive Office of Environmental Affairs, Commonwealth of Massachusetts, 1987-1989.

17. Jennifer Kaylin, Remarks delivered at conference on "'Sound' reporting: Journalism Techniques and Scientific Tools for Reporting on Long Island Sound and the Environment," (April 9, 1999), Fairfield University, Fairfield, CT.

18. Ibid.

19. James Simon, reporter and editor, The Associated Press, 1974-1978, 1979-1987; Assistant Secretary of the Environment, Executive Office of Environmental Affairs, Commonwealth of Massachusetts, 1987-1989.

20. Robert McClure, "Tips on Interviewing from Some of the Best," *SEJournal*, 10, 24, http://www.sej.org/resource/tools.htm#toolbox (accessed May 20, 2008). [No longer available at this address]

21. Robin Mejia, "Interviewing Scientists: A Primer on Finding and Building a Stable of Science Sources," *SEJournal* 13.3 (Winter, 2003): 1, 22.

22. Ibid., 1, 22.

23. Nelson, *Ten Practical Tips,* 29-30.

24. Hans Peter Peters, Dominique Brossard, Suzanne Cheveigne, Sharon Dunwoody, Monika Kallfass, Steve Miller, and Shoji Tsuchida, "Science-Media Interface: It's Time to Reconsider," *Science Communication* 30.2 (2008): 270.

25. Sara Thurin Rollin, "Getting Scientists to Talk," *SEJournal* (Summer, 1998): 12.

26. James Simon, reporter and editor, The Associated Press, 1974-1978, 1979-1987; Assistant Secretary of the Environment, Executive Office of Environmental Affairs, Commonwealth of Massachusetts, 1987-1989.

27. Andrew C. Revkin, "Times' Revkin Points to Challenges, Opportunities in Boosting Media Coverage of Science Issues," *Metcalf Institute Science Writer,* April 2004. http://www.environmentwriter.org/resources/articles/0404_revkin.htm (accessed April 15, 2008).

28. Phillip Burgess, personal interview conducted by James Simon, September 3, 2008.

29. Ibid.

30. Ibid.

31. Ibid.

32. Ibid.

33. Ibid.

34. James Gomes, personal interview conducted by James Simon, August 14, 2008.

35. Ibid.

36. Ibid.

37. Ibid.

38. Ibid.

39. Ibid.

40. Ibid.

41. Phillip Burgess, personal interview.

42. James Simon, reporter and editor, The Associated Press, 1974-1978, 1979-1987; Assistant Secretary of the Environment, Executive Office of Environmental Affairs, Commonwealth of Massachusetts, 1987-1989.

43.   Elements of this section have been taken from personal interviews: Brita Belli, personal interview conducted by James Simon, July 17, 2008; Christy George, personal interview conducted by James Simon, April 21, 2008. These interviews are unrelated to the survey research conducted for the study reported in this book.
44.   Brita Belli, personal interview.
45.   Ibid.
46.   Christy George, personal interview.
47.   Brita Belli, personal interview.
48.   Christy George, personal interview.
49.   Brita Belli, personal interview.
50.   Ibid.
51.   Ibid.
52.   Ibid.
53.   Ibid.
54.   Christy George, personal interview.
55.   Ibid.
56.   Ibid.
57.   Ibid.
58.   Ibid.
59.   Ibid.
60.   Ibid.
61.   Ibid.
62.   Brita Belli, personal interview.
63.   Ibid.
64.   Ibid.
65.   Ibid.
66.   Ibid.
67.   Ibid.
68.   Ibid.
69.   Ibid.
70.   Ibid.
71.   Ibid.
72.   Christy George, personal interview.
73.   Ibid.
74.   Ibid.
75.   Ibid.
76.   Ibid.
77.   Ibid.
78.   Ibid.
79.   Brita Belli, personal interview.
80.   Ibid.
81.   Ibid.
82.   Ibid.
83.   Christy George, personal interview.
84.   Ibid.
85.   Brita Belli, personal interview.
86.   Brita Belli, "Cleaner, Greener U," *E/The Environmental Magazine*, March 27, 2008. Accessed April 1, 2009 from http://www.emagazine.com/view/?4103.
87.   Brita Belli, personal interview.
88.   Belli, "Cleaner."
89.   Christy George, personal interview.
       Forecast Cloudy, writ. and narr. Christy George, OPB, October 25, 2007. Accessed April 1, 2009 from http://news.opb.org/forecastcloudy/#.

90. *Forecast Cloudy*.
91. Brita Belli, personal interview.
92. Ibid.
93. Ibid.
94. Ibid.
95. Ibid.
96. Christy George, personal interview.
97. Ibid.
98. Ibid.
99. Christy George, personal interview.
    Forecast Cloudy.
100. Christy George, personal interview.
101. Christy George, personal interview.
    Forecast Cloudy.
102. Christy George, personal interview.
103. Brita Belli, personal interview.
104. Ibid.
105. Ibid.
106. Christy George, personal interview.
107. Ibid.
108. Ibid.
109. Ibid.
110. Ibid.
111. Ibid.
112. Brita Belli, personal interview.
113. Ibid.
114. Ibid.
115. Ibid.
116. Christy George, personal interview.
117. Ibid.
118. Ibid.
119. Ibid.
120. Ibid.
121. Ibid.

8

Environment Reporters
in a Time of Change

The future of environment reporting has more to do with the future of news than it does with the future of newspapers. Environmental journalism will survive as long as people want public affairs information on the environment and the world around them, but the form of delivery may be very different.

In the first decade of the 21st century, most of the best environment reporters worked for daily newspapers. Throughout this period, the newspaper business as a whole was in a state of economic decline, a decline brought on by the digital age and worsened by the drying up of credit and the American-induced worldwide recession that began in 2008. Downsizing of staff, upswings in blogging, and a rise in convergence of media outlets have had an impact on specialty beats. Local television stations also have been in economic decline, but since they rarely supported environment reporters before the decline, there may be little change in local TV environmental reporting in the next few years.

A Golden Age of Environmental Journalism?

Were the first five years of the 21st century a golden age of environmental reporting, given the cutbacks already occurring? They certainly were good years, as demonstrated by the satisfaction felt by environment reporters throughout the period and the multi-person environmental reporting staffs at some mid-sized and larger newspapers. But few of these reporters were covering the environment full time, and the very part-time nature of the environmental beat already reflected the systemic change in the newspaper business. And some environment reporters were moving on to other aspects of the information business, including the Internet (either doing public relations, public information, or news), a trend that would increase as layoffs increased.

The Environment Reporters

In this period, daily newspapers were much more likely than television stations to employ an environmental journalist, and newspapers with higher circulations were most likely to employ environmental writers and to have more than one. There were some regional differences. Daily newspapers in the Pacific West, New England, and the Mountain West were more likely to employ environmental journalists, while the region with the largest number of small newspapers, the West Central, had the lowest percentage of newspapers with environmental writers. Journalists who covered environmental issues had a number of different job titles and these reporters spent an average of 43.0 percent of their time on environmental news. Again, there were regional differences. In the two most western regions, the percentage of time was 50.0 percent and above. The environmental journalists were reporters first; nearly half were simply called reporters, general assignment reporters, or staff writers.

In terms of personal characteristics, the environmental journalists were very similar to U.S. journalists in general. They were particularly alike in age, years in journalism, and gender. And their similarities outweighed their differences in religion, importance of religion, ethnicity, political affiliation, media usage, and education. The most popular major among both groups was journalism/communication, but many of the future environment reporters, unlike their colleagues, studied the sciences extensively in college.

Overall, this study found that environmental journalists shared many individual characteristics with U.S. journalists in general. Environment reporters are journalists first, perhaps due in part to their similar personal characteristics and experiences, including the basic professional training received by most journalists. The differences that exist between some environment reporters and U.S. journalists may be related to differences existing in their college studies. This supports a more basic concept, that *journalists* are journalists first, linked to their peers by their similar backgrounds and the professional training and practices they share in common. Such a theory of journalism education is worth further study because it might explain the similarities that exist among American journalists regardless of their age, ethnicity, gender, or politics. And it might also explain the conflicts that occur between journalists and their news sources, who are trained differently and often have very different educational backgrounds.

The findings that daily newspapers employ more specialized reporters than television stations and that the bigger the newspaper, the more specialists, points to a more general concept, that bigger is better for specialized reporting. This is not always true, given regional differences, but it appears to be the case often enough to be worth consideration, especially at a time when the fate of some newspapers is threatened by corporate readjustments and economic recession. The idea that bigger is better supports the belief that big newspapers (and the number of working reporters) should be sustained, despite the cost of operation.

Walter E. Hussman, Jr., the CEO of WEHCO Media, a diversified communications company with interests in newspapers, cable television, and the Internet, explains:[1]

We believe that we have a lot of really valuable people at our papers and one of the greatest assets we have is our personnel. So if we were to cut back on our personnel that would hurt. So we are resisting that as much as we possibly can, even though this is the biggest downturn in my lifetime working in newspapers for 38 years. There have been pressures to reduce staff, but we look at that as sort of a last resort and we're hopeful that we can come out of this economic downturn and not have to have any layoffs. We have had to have a wage freeze and a hiring freeze, but that is one of the milder measures that have taken in our industry.

Our philosophy is something that my dad always said. You have different constituencies that you serve as a newspaper: You have readers, advertisers, employees, creditors and shareholders. If you keep those constituencies in that order, then in the long run the shareholders will do quite well. But if you put any of those groups in a different order, things don't seem to operate as well. The shareholders of our company are going to get considerably smaller dividends than they have in the past, at least for a few years. But we think that is what we have to do, even if we take a hit in our profits, to help our employees as much as we can.[2]

Environment reporters and U.S. journalists in general usually were satisfied with their jobs. Men were more satisfied than women in both groups. The job satisfaction levels of environment reporters in all regions and in every year from 2000 to 2005 were remarkably similar, a clear indication that the year in which they were interviewed did not affect their responses. Job satisfaction related highly with job characteristics. For example, reporters with an official title including the word "environment" and those spending at least two-thirds of their time on the environment were more likely to be satisfied than their colleagues. The study also found relationships between job satisfaction and various measures of autonomy, such as the freedom to select stories and the freedom to follow up on a story. Similarly, when asked how they judge jobs in their field, environment reporters valued autonomy, the chance to help people, the editorial policies of their media, and job security. Interestingly, "the chance to get ahead in the organization" was at the bottom of their lists.

Environment reporters actually may have somewhat less autonomy in the newsroom than other U.S. journalists. When asked if they are almost always able to get a story covered, if they have almost complete freedom in selecting stories, and if they have almost complete freedom in deciding which aspects of a news story should be emphasized, fewer environment reporters said they had "almost complete" freedom than U.S. journalists. The environmental journalists were asked about seventeen potential barriers to reporting, including editors, time constraints, and pressure from advertisers. The problem of time constraints led the list and the second most common barrier was financial, travel, or other resource constraints. Editors or supervisors ranked ninth of the seventeen barriers on the list.

The environment reporters used a variety of news angles in their stories. A government angle was most frequently used, followed by a human-interest angle, business or economic, pollution, nature or wilderness, science or technology, political, health, and risk assessment angle. Even the least used framework, risk assessment, was used at least sometimes by 70.2 percent of reporters.

In terms of sources, state departments of environmental quality ranked first and local environmental groups second. Local manufacturers, developers, or business leaders were ranked seventh and the Chemical Manufacturers Association, the National Health and Safety Administration, and Greenpeace were at the bottom of the list.

After reporters decide on a framework and sources for a story, they may face a variety of problems in executing the final version. This project asked environment reporters how well they thought their colleagues did in facing such challenges. A majority of reporters said they agreed with the statement, "Environmental journalists generally concentrate far too much on problems and pollution rather than writing stories to help the public understand research or complex issues." A slim majority of reporters disagreed with the statement, "An environmental problem is generally a better news story than an environmental success." There was even less support for the statement, "Environmental journalism generally centers too much on personalities and not enough on actual findings." These three questions suggest environmental journalists have a feeling that they should do more to help their audiences understand the complexity behind environmental stories. Most reject the notion that they focus too much on personalities, and they split on whether environmental problems generally make better stories than those about environmental successes. In addition, nearly 80 percent of environment reporters disagreed that journalists "generally have overblown environmental risks, unduly alarming the public."

Do environmental journalists use the best possible standards of newsworthiness? This question involves the traditional standards of reporting generally prevalent in American newsrooms. Journalists are trained to think in terms of timeliness (today's news, rather than long-term issues), proximity (local, not worldwide), human interest, prominence (famous people, rather than the majority), and consequence (importance, including degree of risk), while scientists and others may view the first four of these news values as shallow at best.[3] The reporters who agreed that "environmental journalists generally concentrate far too much on problems and pollution rather than writing stories to help the public understand research or complex issues" and "an environmental problem is generally a better news story than an environmental success" may be reflecting their concern with the news media's tendency to focus on acute problems rather than long-term issues and to emphasize the negative ("If it bleeds, it leads."), rather than the positive. This study characterizes journalists who question such fundamental issues as what news is (and what news should be) as "Work Place Critics" (see Chapter 6).

Does reliance on traditional standards of newsworthiness cause environment reporters to sometimes sensationalize the issues they cover? While scientists are more concerned with the fact that traditional standards of newsworthiness have little to do with scientific concerns, corporate and government leaders sometimes agree with those environment reporters (21.3 percent) who say that environmental journalists "generally have overblown environmental risks, unduly alarming the public," the very definition of sensationalism.

This study looked at how environment reporters wrestle with questions of objectivity, advocacy, and the civic journalism concept of working with community leaders to help solve problems. Almost all the reporters agreed that environmental journalists need to be just as objective as journalists in general, fair to sources such as corporations, and fair to sources such as environmental activist groups. But while few felt that reporters were too pro-business, more than one-third of those responding agreed with the statement that environmental reporters tend to be too green, clearly questioning the behavior of journalists who recognize the need to be fair.

The question of objectivity, advocacy, and community involvement is far more complex than the endorsement of objectivity and fairness might imply. Slightly more than one-third of the respondents agreed that environmental journalists sometimes should be advocates for the environment and slightly less than one-third (though not all the same people) felt that environmental journalists should work with community leaders to help solve environmental problems. While a majority of the respondents appear to view objectivity and advocacy (and objectivity and civic journalism) as polar opposites, substantial minorities may be perceiving objectivity and advocacy (and objectivity and community involvement) as separate values that can exist together in certain circumstances.

This study shows that environment reporters recognize the importance of the business community. Their stories include business angles and sources. Still, many of these journalists think their colleagues tend to be too green. Whether or not significant numbers of environmental journalists are actually biased, the perception of reporter bias clearly exists inside the newsroom as well as among business leaders.

Environment reporters also were found to be heavily reliant on environmental communicators. A symbiotic relationship exists between these environment journalists and their frequent sources.

This academic study, like all such studies, might have turned out differently if it had asked different research questions. The project chose to focus on newspaper and TV reporters; the study would have received richer information if it also included the hundreds if not thousands of magazine writers, freelancers, book authors, and bloggers who write about the environment. The researchers focused on the first half of the 2000-2010 decade, comparing environment reporters to U.S. journalists in general. This comparative data might have been enhanced if there had been data about environmental journalists from an earlier time. This is the nature of descriptive, baseline data. The authors hope future researchers will be able to build on this work and chronicle changes in the field, which seem likely to occur as people continue to obtain their environmental news in different technological ways.

Time of Change

In this era of increased environmental awareness (think Al Gore) and attitudes (think Green everything), one might expect environmental journalism to hold steady if not increase, despite the tumult that has rocked the news industry. Yet some changes have already occurred. Environmental news is deeply linked to other news categories, such as energy and economic recovery. Global warming, like energy before it, is now a separate topic. Even hybrid and electric cars now stand alone. Such issues in need of coverage will require the expertise and experience of environment and science reporters.

Google and the other search engines have made this the golden age of information—and therefore the golden age of environmental information as well. If one Googles "mountaintop removal" or "global warming," much more information is provided than can possibly be absorbed. Newspapers had been losing their dominance of the information business for many years with the development of new media from radio to television and now to the Internet. But throughout the 20th century, the best (though not the fastest) place to find news was in newspapers. In the 21st century, information has shifted dramatically to the Internet, and news—including environmental news—is moving there as well.

Many of the best and brightest newspaper environment reporters who emerged in the 1980s and 1990s have either retired—some pushed into early retirement, having accepted bailout packages—or been among the many journalists laid off under economic duress. Whither they will take their talents, whether others will take their place perhaps in new media, these are the questions that cannot yet be answered.

The newspaper business can and probably will survive, although its form of delivery may be very different. Other media have been able to change (and survive) in response to new media. Radio changed almost completely in response to the rise of television. The film industry responded to television by finding its place in television, on tape, on disks, and now on the Internet. Television itself changed greatly in the 20th century, from a handful of general-interest channels in each market to perhaps 200 or more specialized channels, and it is now finding its place on the Internet.

In television and radio, news executives have broadened the definition of what constitutes an environmental story to stress consumer, health, and investigative stories. The Radio-Television News Directors Association advises members:[4]

> Ask most any news manager, and he or she will tell you that the environment is no longer a hot story. But ask the public and you will hear a very different response.
>
> One reason for this discrepancy may be that the public has very different views about what constitutes an "environmental story." In newsrooms, we still view coverage of the environment in traditional ways: the birds and bunnies pieces, the recycling stories, the "jobs versus the environment" stand-offs. But out there, the times have changed.

The stories that the public cares about today are health, consumer and investigative stories. Today's environmental stories are about our quality of life: our children's health, the traffic we endure, the places we live, work and shop, the air we breathe, the water we drink—the points at which the environment touches our daily lives.

Stories about why our children have learning disabilities, why there is so much traffic, why our downtowns are deteriorating, why cases of asthma are on the rise, why the weather is changing—these are today's environmental stories. They are about people, about families, about communities.

Public demand for these stories is high. Yet, localizing a big environmental story, finding local contacts and translating conflicting science and statistics can be a very tough assignment. Helping your community understand how the changing environment has a local impact is an important and challenging task.[5]

On the environmental communication front, the war between competing public relations interests used to be fought primarily in terms of competing public relations releases being sent to newspapers. Now these competing groups and institutions have enormous Internet web sites, use video news releases, blogs, and PR Newswire to often bypass newspapers and seek to have a direct effect on public opinion.

Issues that result from the changing media landscape are not limited to environment reporting. In the January-February, 2009 issue of *The Atlantic*, contributing editor Michael Hirschorn wrote an obituary for the *New York Times*, the undisputed leader among U.S. elite newspapers. He warned that the *Times* was "destined for significant and traumatic change" as the print edition heads for non-existence.[6] Rather than a slow emergence of convergence—predicted by most academics—Hirschorn predicted an imminent collapse, caused in part by the general economic crisis facing all media, but forced to warp speed by readers' move to the Internet. Digital-only distribution, he says, is already supported by readership data: nytimes.com ranks in the top five online news sites with some 20 million unique users; that familiar folded product lands in the hands of only a million readers a day. The death throe change, he forecasts, will mean 80 percent of *Times* reporters will be looking elsewhere for employment. "The best journalists will survive and eventually thrive," he writes, perhaps for blogs like *The Huffington Post*, other online news outlets, or freelancing.[7] The mounting freelance membership list at the Society of Environmental Journalists, and the National Association of Science Writers' overwhelming majority of freelance writers also illustrate the current changes.

Environment Reporting Outlets:
From Mass Media to Niche Media?

Four of the best known environment reporters pondered such changes in February 2009 at the Woodrow Wilson International Center for Scholars in Washington D.C. in talks on "The Future of Science and Environmental Journalism." Associated Press environment reporter Seth Borenstein was one of several speakers who noted the passing of the old guard of veteran journalists and the rise of writers for smaller, specialized outlets. He recalled being interviewed by Curtis Brainard of the *Columbia Journalism Review* for a story on science reporting:[8]

> ...And when he talked to me, I guess it was the summer of last year (2008), I was going, "No, you know, science journalism is doing probably better than many others in journalism." I pointed to John Noble Wilford and Larry Altman at *The [New York] Times* and Warren Leary at *The [New York] Times*, and Robert Boyd at *McClatchy* [a newspaper chain], David Perlman of the *San Francisco Chronicle*. What you'll find with all these gentlemen, I think they're all (well, not Warren) in their 70s or above. They showed the newspapers recognized that smart, intelligent, experienced science, medical writers were worthwhile, and they only get better.
>
> Now, actually Curtis didn't finish that story, thank God. I called him up last December saying, "Please, if you're going to write it, I have changed everything, please let me tell you what I think now." I don't believe any of that anymore. I think we're in as deep if not more trouble. John Noble Wilford, I believe, took the buyout, [and] is doing part-time stuff there. Larry Altman left. Warren Leary left. You know, right there, in just those three at *The Times*, you lose an incredible amount of knowledge.
>
> There are hot spots for new niche reporting. E&E Publications are expanding where the rest of us are shrinking, opening up bureaus. And ClimateWire, I highly recommend; John Fialka, the editor of ClimateWire, is right there. That's showing that niche publications—and on the Web, Mother Nature Network, where Peter is—are growing. The trouble is when you're looking at niches, you're not getting the broad picture you get from a John Noble Wilford or a Warren Leary.[9]

Another panelist, Peter Dykstra, former head of CNN's environmental unit, said the traditional desire to attract bigger ratings and audiences for newspaper and television is greater these days due to companion Internet sites that measure success by clicks on the web version of stories. Instead of focusing on the quality of the reporting as an indicator of a story's success, success is now measured by the number of clicks on the Internet version of the story. In this new metric, environmental issues can suffer because some news editors seeking bigger audiences view them as polarizing; 20 percent of Americans still doubt the seriousness of global warming, Dykstra said, and any story on the subject runs the risk of alienating one side or the other and reducing the potential audience. So it is safer for news organizations to present stories that can attract a wide audience. Dykstra gave several examples. The biggest NASA story of the past few years? "The astronaut who put on adult diapers and drove from Houston to Orlando in an attempt to kill her romantic rival." The top wildlife/biology story? "…The two security guards in Georgia who put a gorilla suit in the freezer and claimed to have discovered Big Foot. That was later found out to be a hoax. Now, that's journalism."[10]

Dykstra and the other panelists noted the growth of web sites on specialized topics like the environment "tends to draw those who choose to be engaged rather than drawing an audience of the general public… And in a sense, to the extent that our mission as journalists is to inform and educate, it may leave us primarily educating those who are already relatively educated, and leaving those who may not be so educated in the dark."[11]

Elizabeth Shogren of National Public Radio told the conference that this trend is exacerbated by many of these sites catering to an even more elite audience that must pay for access to these specialized web sites:[12]

> I still see a lot of reporters at global warming hearings. They're up on the Hill. If you go there, you will see all those press spots are filled, but they are representing different organizations. There are a lot fewer reporters from newspapers there, and there are more people from online services. And many of these online services are really interesting coverage, but it's a different kind of thing. A lot of times it's a subscription service that you have to pay a lot of money to have access for, and I'm thrilled that those people are still there covering the news, but it's not quite the same, I think, as old-time journalism, and I'm concerned about what [this] means for what the public gets to learn. I think that if you're an expert, or if you're an advocate, you can find out what you want to learn, much more than you were ever able to find out five or ten years ago, and so there is more information available online, and especially if you'll pay for it.… But what about the person who is not particularly interested? Will they just run across it in the newspaper that they pick up and read?[13]

The comments by veteran environment reporters Seth Borenstein, Peter Dykstra and Elizabeth Shogren illustrated what The Project for Excellence in Journalism in 2009 called "The New Washington Press Corps," also known as "the rise of the niche":[14]

> If the mainstream media have shrunk so dramatically, even before the last year, how is it that the overall numbers of journalists in Washington have not?

> The answer is that a new Washington media have evolved, but they are far from the more egalitarian or citizen-based media that advocates of the digital age might imagine. Instead, this new Washington media cohort is one substantially aimed at elites, often organized by industry, by corporate client, or by niche political interest.

> It represents the dramatic expansion of a once small niche sector of the Washington press corps—a group that as recently as a decade ago amounted to a couple of Capitol Hill newspapers that covered the nuts and bolts of Congress for staffers and lobbyists

and a disparate collection of trade magazines and print newsletters that tracked narrow issues for those working industries ranging from aviation and health care, to energy and construction. For the most part, mainstream media journalists—and much of Washington itself—looked down upon the work of these publications as both boring and peripheral to the "real" challenge of covering Washington politics. The dream of many niche sector journalists was to land work with a major mainstream outlet.

Not any more. Today, many of Washington's most experienced and talented journalists no longer explain the workings of the federal government to those in the general public, but to specialty audiences whose interests tend to be both narrow and deep.

These are publications with names like ClimateWire, Energy Trader, Traffic World, Government Executive and Food Chemical News. Their audiences vary, but most readers find the content increasingly important—even crucial—for their job, their business and their industry. Because of this, readers—usually with employer support—are willing to pay significant subscription fees—high enough that some are profitable with small readerships and little advertising.

The editor of one niche organization, Kevin Braun of Environment & Energy Publishing says his subscribers include state governments, law firms, lobbyists, corporations active in the field and non-profit environmental groups....

Most of these publications are far less known to the general public. Over the past decade, for instance, Environment & Energy Publishing has grown from a print-only weekly dealing with environment and energy legislation in Congress put out by a handful of reporters and a readership of about one thousand. Now, it's a stable of six editorial online products, including a daily webcast that carries interviews and analysis with influential figures in the energy and environment field. The group's first foreign bureau—in Brussels—is scheduled to open in early 2009, and a second in Asia is planned within the next year. The combined readership is just 40,000....

Another case is the Platts Division of the McGraw-Hill Companies, which once comprised little more than a daily oil pricing service and a two-page print newsletter of developments in the oil industry. Today, Platts has 15 different editorial products providing information to those working across the energy field, including natural gas, electricity, nuclear power and coal. Most of them consider Washington reporting crucial to their success. One biweekly newsletter called Inside NRC, with a basic subscription price of $2,495 per year, reports on developments in the important, yet arcane, subject of the nuclear power industry. As the newsletter's name implies, its primary focus is the Nuclear Regulatory Commission, a federal agency covered by no mainstream media as a full-time beat....[15]

Meanwhile, the rise of independent sources of environment reporting on the web provides readers with the kind of coverage they once received from larger newspapers. In the Yale Forum on Climate Change and the Media, Lisa Palmer summarized some of the varied approaches (as of early 2009):[16]

- Among the independent, new media newsrooms is the non-profit ProPublica [http://www.propublica.org], which focuses on public interest investigations with "moral force." Led by former *Wall Street Journal* managing editor Paul Steiger, ProPublica is funded by grants, partnerships with media outlets, and individual donations—a model not unlike that of National Public Radio. ProPublica's mission: "Carry forward some of the great work of journalism in the public interest that is such an integral part of self-government, and thus an important bulwark of our democracy." ...ProPublica.org went live last summer [2008], and it has co-published wide-ranging articles on its website. An energy series by reporter Abrahm Lustgarten was made available to a broad audience through media partnerships at WNYC radio in New York, *The Albany Union*, the now-defunct *New York Sun*, and *San Diego Union Tribune*, and also through outlets such as *Business Week* and Grist.org. His reports also appear on propublica.org. (ProPublica's stories can be republished free of charge under a Creative Commons license.)

- As mainstream news media move away from using international correspondents, the new GlobalPost [http://www.globalpost.com] may be among those trying to pick up the slack. The Boston-based news group that started publishing in January [2009] focuses solely on international reporting. Leading its climate coverage is independent journalist Stefan Faris, author of *Forecast: The Consequences of Climate Change from the Amazon to the Arctic, from Darfur to Napa Valley* (Henry Holt and Co., 2008).... Multiple streams of revenue will support the mission of GlobalPost, including web advertising, syndication and paid membership of a premium content service called "Passport." About 70 contributors get a monthly stipend, and some have been offered shares of the privately owned company.

- Also launched in January [2009] is the Mother Nature Network [http://www.mnn.com], which covers environmental stories in ways intended to be understandable to a broad readership, but one clearly self-identifying as being interested in environmental issues. Rather than focus on experts and science-heavy reporting, it provides six channels of lively environmental content aimed at mainstream America. Accessible content is the goal. Co-founded by Rolling Stones keyboardist Chuck Leavell, an intrepid environmentalist, the site features "ecollywood" features along with coverage of the new Obama administration. Mother Nature Network CEO Joel Babbit says his company, which is headquartered in Atlanta, has benefited from some unfortunate timing coincidences. "CNN laid off its environmental team; and with the acquisition by NBC, The Weather Channel followed suit," he said. As a result, many of the former CNN and Weather Channel staffers (also Atlanta-based) now comprise his 15-person newsroom. Together, they create 60 percent original content for mnn.com. The rest of the content is derived from the news aggregator Mochila.

- Lifestyle and sustainability topics have long been the realm of online publications such as Grist [http://www.grist.org], TreeHugger [http://www.treehugger.com], and PlanetGreen [http://planetgreen.discovery.com]. The three outlets produce witty content and blogs on green issues and sustainability for the masses. Grist, an independent, non-profit entity, announced last summer a new affiliation with *The Washington Post*. Grist now syndicates some of its articles to washingtonpost.com. Other syndication partners with Grist include MSN, MSNBC, and *The Huffington Post*.

- Finally, at least one traditional media outlet continues to play a leading role on global climate topics. The *New York Times* [http://www.nytimes.com] in a December 17, 2008, memo announced it is expanding its science and environment coverage, and in mid-January it officially assembled its new reporting team comprised of reporters and editors whose expertise runs the gamut of disciplines: Science, National, Metro, Foreign, and Business.[17]

Another nonprofit, online venture in environment reporting is Yale Environment 360 [http://e360.yale.edu], which went live in June 2008. The web site has no advertising and says it is committed to original features. Reporter Russ Juskalian described the concept as "money is better spent on reporters than dead trees and postage."[18] Editor Roger Cohn, former editor of the print publications *Mother Jones* and *Audubon*, said that with limited resources and three years of initial grant monies, an online source can produce better environmental reporting if it does not overextend itself by also offering a print magazine complement.[19]

This environment reporting in online form has a major advantage that it usually allows readers to respond, and often contribute useful context and analysis, to the story. It is no longer a top down process where the environment reporter is the source of all wisdom and the reader or viewer just a passive recipient. A final panelist at the Woodrow Wilson event, Jan Schaffer, director of the J-Lab, said ordinary people "want to be able to contribute and participate in some way in the news media ecosystem. And it may be somewhat passive by commenting. It may be much more active, actually creating the news. But we're seeing a fairly robust sphere of activity happening here."[20]

In this period of decline for traditional newspapers, Schaffer said citizens are starting "hyper-local news initiatives" where they provide news coverage for under covered communities "or niche subject initiatives that may cover a special topic like science or environmental journalism, or maybe investigative journalism, or maybe international journalism—a fairly robust sphere happening." One example she cited was Newwest. net, which covers 10 Rocky Mountain states and provides stories on environment, science and growth along with publishing related magazines and hosting conferences.[21]

As environment reporters try to avoid becoming an endangered species themselves, they may get help from journalism programs around the country. With funding from the Carnegie Corporation, the Knight Foundation, and the universities themselves, News21[22] established an impressive record during its first three years with coverage of the 2008 election. (The deans at the schools involved select the topic.) Five universities—the University of California, Berkeley; Columbia University; the University of Southern California; Harvard University; and Northwestern University—led the first round of training to foster "in-depth journalism in the 21st-century multimedia environment."[23] In 2009, News21 coordination moved to Arizona State University with an expanded effort among eleven major journalism schools. In time, News 21 is likely to deal with the "e" issues—economy and environment—and topics such as offshore drilling for oil, "clean" coal, new energy, re-emerging nuclear sites, and the ever-threatening climate change. These news items now fall into the beat of the environment reporter, who may be the journalist best suited to inform the public accurately, fully, and fairly.

Notes

1.   Dave Flessner, "Hussman: City's Love of 2 papers Won Hussman's Notice," *Chattanooga Times Free Press* (Jan. 6, 2009), accessed 2-25-2009 at <http://www.timesfreepress.com/news/2009/jan/06/hussman-citys-love-2-papers-won-hussmans-notice/>.
2.   Ibid.
3.   David B. Sachsman, "Linking the Scientist and the Journalist," in *HazPro '85: Proceedings of the HazPro '85 Conference*, ed. Richard A. Young. Purdvan Publishing Co., 1985.
4.   Environmental Journalism Center. Radio-Television News Directors Association. Accessed 3-4-09 from http://www.rtnda.org/pages/media_items/environmental-journalism-center262.php.
5.   Ibid.
6.   Michael Hirschorn, "End Times," *The Atlantic*, (Jan./Feb. 2009): 41-44.
7.   Ibid.
8.   Seth Borenstein, "The Future of Science and Environmental Journalism." (Edited transcript); (2009, Feb. 12); accessed 3-2-2009 at http://www.wilsoncenter.org/events/docs/Borenstein%20Edited%20Transcript.pdf.
9.   Ibid.
10.   Peter Dykstra, "The Future of Science and Environmental Journalism." (Edited transcript); (2009, Feb. 12); accessed 3-2-2009 at http://www.wilsoncenter.org/events/docs/Dykstra%20Edited%20Transcript.pdf.
11.   Ibid.
12.   Elizabeth Shogren, "The Future of Science and Environmental Journalism." (Edited transcript); (2009, Feb. 12); accessed 3-2-2009 at http://www.wilsoncenter.org/events/docs/Shogren%20Edited%20Transcript.pdf.
13.   Ibid.
14.   "The New Washington Press Corps: A special report on the rise of the niche," *Project for Excellence in Journalism*, (2009, Feb. 11); accessed 3-2-09 from http://journalism.org/print/14681.
15.   Ibid.
16.   Lisa Palmer, "What Lies Ahead as Mainstream Outlets Shrivel?" *Yale Forum on Climate Change and the Media*, (2009, February); accessed 3-2-09 from http://www.yaleclimatemediaforum.org/2009/02/potential-abounds-but-will-they-delivernew-media-and-coverage-of-environment/.

17.   Ibid.
18.   Russ Juskalian, 'Launch: Yale 360," *Columbia Journalism Review* accessed 3-3-09
      from http://e360.yale.edu/.
19.   Ibid.
20.   Jan Schaffer, "The Future of Science and Environmental Journalism." (Edited
      transcript); (2009, Feb. 12) accessed 3-2-2009 at
      http://www.wilsoncenter.org/events/docs/Schaffer%20Edited%20Transcript.pdf.
21.   Ibid.
22.   The News21 2008 Project, http://news21project.org.
23.   John Mecklin, "The New New Media," *Miller-McCune Magazine* (Oct. 2008),
      pp. 8-11.

Appendix A

The Survey

Introduction:

This is _____ from _____ University in _____. I am part of a team of journalists and researchers from three universities that is interviewing every environmental reporter in _____.

We want to get a sense of:

- o   how important environment issues are these days,
- o   who you talk to when gathering information for an environmental story, and
- o   whether you have to fight with your editors to get environmental stories on page one or to lead a newscast.

The survey takes about 25 minutes to complete, and we will be reporting only the overall results, not how you feel individually.

Is this a good time to talk to you?

RECORD TIME STARTED: _____

1a. First, what is your exact job title at (NAME OF ORGANIZATION)?

1b. Do you work full-time there? 1. Yes   2. No

1c. Do you cover the environment on a regular basis as part of your reporting duties?

(IF NO TO 1B OR 1C, THANK AND TERMINATE)

2. Looking back on the past year, about what percentage of your time has been spent on reporting environmental stories (however you want to define them). _____%

2A. (IF ZERO PERCENT): So in the last year, you have spent close to zero percent of your time on environmental stories?

(IF YES TO ZERO), thank and terminate.

> *Great. Let's start by talking about environmental reporting in general.*

1. To what extent do you think environmental stories are important and worthy of prominent play? In general, do you see them as:
1) very important   2) important   3) neither important nor unimportant
4) not important   or 5) not important at all   (7 DK 8 NA 9 RF)

2. How about your editors? To what extent do your editors feel environmental stories are important and worthy of prominent play? In general, do they see them as
1) very important   2) important   3) neither important nor unimportant
4) not important   or 5) not important at all   (7 DK 8 NA 9 RF)

3. How about the public? To what extent does the public feel environmental stories are important and worthy of prominent play? In general, do they see them as:
1) very important   2) important   3) neither important nor unimportant
4) not important   or 5) not important at all   (7 DK 8 NA 9 RF)

> *Now I would like to read two statements about your (readers, viewers). Tell me if you strongly agree, agree, disagree, or strongly disagree with these statements. If you are neutral or have no opinion, just say so.*

4. (Readers, viewers) are more interested in the day's breaking news about environmental issues than in analysis of those environmental issues. Do you:
1) strongly agree   2) agree   4) disagree   or 5) strongly disagree
(6 neutral 7 DK 8 NA 9 RF)

5. The majority of (readers, viewers) have little interest in (reading about, viewing) problems such as the environment.
1) strongly agree   2) agree   4) disagree   or 5) strongly disagree
(6 neutral 7 DK 8 NA 9 RF)

Now I'd like to read you a series of statements. Tell me if you 1) strongly agree with the statement, 2) agree, 4) disagree, or 5) strongly disagree. If you are neutral or have no opinion, just say so.

6a. Environmental journalists need to be just as objective as journalists in general. Do you...
1) strongly agree   2) agree   4) disagree   or 5) strongly disagree
(6 neutral 7 DK 8 NA 9 RF)

Here's another one...
6b. Environmental journalists sometimes should be advocates for the environment. Do you...
1) strongly agree   2) agree   4) disagree   or 5) strongly disagree
(6 neutral 7 DK 8 NA 9 RF)

6c. Environmental journalists need to be fair to sources such as corporations. Do you...
1) strongly agree   2) agree   4) disagree   or 5) strongly disagree
(6 neutral 7 DK 8 NA 9 RF)

6d. Environmental journalists need to be fair to sources such as environmental activist groups. Do you...
1) strongly agree   2) agree   4) disagree   or 5) strongly disagree
(6 neutral 7 DK 8 NA 9 RF)

6e. An environmental problem is generally a better news story than an environmental success. Do you...
1) strongly agree   2) agree   4) disagree   or 5) strongly disagree
(6 neutral 7 DK 8 NA 9 RF)

6f. Environmental journalists should work with community leaders to help solve environmental problems. Do you...
1) strongly agree   2) agree   4) disagree   or 5) strongly disagree
(6 neutral 7 DK 8 NA 9 RF)

6g. Environmental journalists generally concentrate far too much on <u>problems and pollution</u> rather than writing stories to <u>help the public understand research or complex issues</u>. Do you…
1) strongly agree   2) agree   4) disagree   or 5) strongly disagree
(6 neutral 7 DK 8 NA 9 RF)

6h. Environmental journalism generally centers <u>too much on personalities</u> and <u>not enough on actual findings</u>. Do you…
1) strongly agree   2) agree   4) disagree   or 5) strongly disagree
(6 neutral 7 DK 8 NA 9 RF)

6i. Environmental journalists generally have <u>overblown environmental risks,</u> unduly alarming the public. Do you…
1) strongly agree   2) agree   4) disagree   or 5) strongly disagree
(6 neutral 7 DK 8 NA 9 RF)

6j. Most environmental journalists are <u>not well enough educated</u> to cover news about environmental issues. Do you…
1) strongly agree   2) agree   4) disagree   or 5) strongly disagree
(6 neutral 7 DK 8 NA 9 RF)

6k. Environmental journalists tend to be too "green" – meaning slanted in favor of environmentalism. Do you…
1) strongly agree   2) agree   4) disagree   or 5) strongly disagree
(6 neutral 7 DK 8 NA 9 RF)

6l. Environmental journalists tend to be too "brown" – meaning slanted in favor of business and industry. Do you…
1) strongly agree   2) agree   4) disagree   or 5) strongly disagree
(6 neutral 7 DK 8 NA 9 RF)

OK, Let's switch gears.

I'd like to find out whether certain people, problems and institutions are <u>a barrier</u> in reporting on environmental stories. For example,

---

7a. **The size of the news hole**. Would you say the size of the news hole is...
1) always a barrier in reporting on environment stories, 2) often a barrier
3) sometimes a barrier   4) rarely a barrier   or 5) never a barrier.
(7 DK 8 NA 9 RF)

How about...

7b. Your lack of technical knowledge on environmental issues. Would you say that is...

1) always a barrier in reporting on environment stories, 2) often a barrier
3) sometimes a barrier   4) rarely a barrier   or 5) never a barrier.
(7 DK 8 NA 9 RF)

7c. The audience's lack of technical knowledge on environmental issues. Would you say that is...

1) always a barrier in reporting on environment stories, 2) often a barrier
3) sometimes a barrier   4) rarely a barrier   or 5) never a barrier.
(7 DK 8 NA 9 RF)

7d. The need to give stories "a human face." Would you say that is...

1) always a barrier in reporting on environment stories, 2) often a barrier
3) sometimes a barrier   4) rarely a barrier   or 5) never a barrier.
(7 DK 8 NA 9 RF)

7e. Ethical concerns. Would you say they are...

1) always a barrier in reporting on environment stories, 2) often a barrier
3) sometimes a barrier   4) rarely a barrier   or 5) never a barrier.
(7 DK 8 NA 9 RF)

7f. Legal concerns. Would you say they are...

1) always a barrier in reporting on environment stories, 2) often a barrier
3) sometimes a barrier   4) rarely a barrier   or 5) never a barrier.
(7 DK 8 NA 9 RF)

7g. Your publisher, station manager or owner. Would you say they are...

1) always a barrier in reporting on environment stories, 2) often a barrier
3) sometimes a barrier   4) rarely a barrier   or 5) never a barrier.
(7 DK 8 NA 9 RF)

7h. Your editors or supervisors. Would you say they are...

1) always a barrier in reporting on environment stories, 2) often a barrier
3) sometimes a barrier   4) rarely a barrier   or 5) never a barrier.
(7 DK 8 NA 9 RF)

7i. Your colleagues.   Would you say they are...

1) always a barrier in reporting on environment stories, 2) often a barrier
3) sometimes a barrier   4) rarely a barrier   or 5) never a barrier.
(7 DK 8 NA 9 RF)

7j. **The Competition (in the local news market).** Would you say they are...
1) always a barrier in reporting on environment stories, 2) often a barrier
3) sometimes a barrier   4) rarely a barrier   or 5) never a barrier.
(7 DK 8 NA 9 RF)

7k. **Advertisers.** Would you say they are...
1) always a barrier in reporting on environment stories, 2) often a barrier
3) sometimes a barrier   4) rarely a barrier   or 5) never a barrier.
(7 DK 8 NA 9 RF)

7l. **Other business or corporate interests.** Would you say they are...
1) always a barrier in reporting on environment stories, 2) often a barrier
3) sometimes a barrier   4) rarely a barrier   or 5) never a barrier.
(7 DK 8 NA 9 RF)

7m. **Environmental activists.** Would you say they are...
1) always a barrier in reporting on environment stories, 2) often a barrier
3) sometimes a barrier   4) rarely a barrier   or 5) never a barrier.
(7 DK 8 NA 9 RF)

7n. **Government sources**. Would you say they are...
1) always a barrier in reporting on environment stories, 2) often a barrier
3) sometimes a barrier   4) rarely a barrier   or 5) never a barrier.
(7 DK 8 NA 9 RF)

7o. **University sources.** Would you say they are...
1) always a barrier in reporting on environment stories, 2) often a barrier
3) sometimes a barrier   4) rarely a barrier   or 5) never a barrier.
(7 DK 8 NA 9 RF)

7p. **Time constraints**. Would you say they are...
1) always a barrier in reporting on environment stories, 2) often a barrier
3) sometimes a barrier   4) rarely a barrier   or 5) never a barrier.
(7 DK 8 NA 9 RF)

7q. **Financial, travel, or other resource constraints.**   Would you say they
are...
1) always a barrier in reporting on environment stories, 2) often a barrier
3) sometimes a barrier   4) rarely a barrier   or 5) never a barrier.
(7 DK 8 NA 9 RF)

7r. **Are there <u>any other major barriers</u> to your reporting on environmental stories?**
(For each) Would you say they are...
1) always a barrier in reporting on environment stories, 2) often a barrier
3) sometimes a barrier   4) rarely a barrier   or 5) never a barrier.
(7 DK 8 NA 9 RF)

Now I'd like to find out how important a number of things are to you in judging jobs in your field, not just your job.

8a. For instance, how much difference does <u>the pay</u> make in how you rate a job in your field – is pay
1) very important   2) important   3) neither important nor unimportant
4) not important   or 5) not important at all   (7 DK 8 NA 9 RF)

How about...
8b. <u>Fringe benefits?</u> Are they
1) very important   2) important   3) neither important nor unimportant
4) not important   or 5) not important at all   (7 DK 8 NA 9 RF)

8c. <u>The editorial policies of the organization?</u> Are they
1) very important   2) important   3) neither important nor unimportant
4) not important   or 5) not important at all   (7 DK 8 NA 9 RF)

8d. <u>Job security?</u> Is it
1) very important   2) important   3) neither important nor unimportant
4) not important   or 5) not important at all   (7 DK 8 NA 9 RF)

8e. <u>The chance to develop a specialty?</u> Is it
1) very important   2) important   3) neither important nor unimportant
4) not important   or 5) not important at all   (7 DK 8 NA 9 RF)

8f. <u>The amount of autonomy you have?</u> Is it
1) very important   2) important   3) neither important nor unimportant
4) not important   or 5) not important at all   (7 DK 8 NA 9 RF)

8g. <u>The chance to get ahead in the organization?</u> Is it
1) very important   2) important   3) neither important nor unimportant
4) not important   or 5) not important at all   (7 DK 8 NA 9 RF)

8h. <u>The chance to help people</u>? Is it
1) very important   2) important   3) neither important nor unimportant
4) not important   or 5) not important at all   (7 DK 8 NA 9 RF)

8i. <u>The chance to influence public affairs?</u> Is it
1) very important   2) important   3) neither important nor unimportant
4) not important   or 5) not important at all   (7 DK 8 NA 9 RF)

On a related question…

---

9. All things considered, how satisfied are you with your present job – would you say
1) very satisfied   2) fairly satisfied   3) somewhat dissatisfied or
4) very dissatisfied?   (7 DK 8 NA 9 RF–go to 11)

10. What are the most important reasons you say you are (satisfied/dissatisfied) with your present job?

11. How good a job does your own news organization do in enhancing the public's understanding of environmental issues? Would you say
1) outstanding   2) very good   3) good   4) only fair   or 5) poor?
(7 DK 8 NA 9 RF)

12. How much freedom do you usually have in selecting the stories you work on? Would you say:
1) Almost complete freedom   2) A great deal of freedom   3) Some freedom
4) Not much freedom   or 5) none at all   (7 DK 8 NA 9 RF)

13. How much freedom do you usually have in deciding which aspects of a story should be emphasized? Would you say
1) Almost complete freedom   2) A great deal of freedom   3) Some freedom
4) Not much freedom   or 5) none at all   (7 DK 8 NA 9 RF)

14. If you have a good idea for a subject which you think is important and should be followed up, how often are you able to get the subject covered? Would you say:
1) Almost complete freedom   2) A great deal of freedom   3) Some freedom
4) Not much freedom   or 5) none at all   (7 DK 8 NA 9 RF)

15. How much editing do your stories get from others at (FILL IN ORGANIZA-TION)? Would you say:
5) a great deal   4) a considerable amount   3) some   2) little or 1) none at all   (7 DK 8 NA 9 RF)

> *Let's switch gears. Sometimes environmental stories deal only with the environment. Sometimes they also deal with other issues.*

16a. Looking back on the stories you have done, how often would you say they also **involve a business or economic angle**. Would you say your environmental stories
1) always have a business or economic angle   2) often do   3) sometimes do
4) rarely do   or 5) never have a business or economic angle?
(7 DK 8 NA 9 RF)

How about...
16b. **a government angle.** Would you say your environmental stories
1) always have a government angle   2) often do   3) sometimes do
4) rarely do   or 5) never have a government angle?   (7 DK 8 NA 9 RF)

16c. **a political angle.** Would you say your environmental stories
1) always have a political angle   2) often do   3) sometimes do
4) rarely do   or 5) never have a political angle?   (7 DK 8 NA 9 RF)

16d. **a human interest angle.** Would you say your environmental stories
1) always have a human interest angle   2) often do   3) sometimes do
4) rarely do   or 5) never have a human interest angle?   (7 DK 8 NA 9 RF)

16e. **a pollution angle.** Would you say your environmental stories
1) always have a pollution angle   2) often do   3) sometimes do
4) rarely do   or 5) never have a pollution angle?   (7 DK 8 NA 9 RF)

16f. **a nature or wilderness angle.** Would you say your environmental stories
1) always have a nature or wilderness angle   2) often do   3) sometimes do
4) rarely do   or 5) never have a nature or wilderness angle?   (7 DK 8 NA 9 RF)

16g. **a science or technology angle.** Would you say your environmental stories
1) always have a science or technology angle   2) often do   3) sometimes do
4) rarely do   or 5) never have a science or technology angle?   (7 DK 8 NA 9 RF)

16h. **a health angle.** Would you say your environmental stories
1) always have a health angle   2) often do   3) sometimes do
4) rarely do   or 5) never have a health angle?   (7 DK 8 NA 9 RF)

16i. **a risk assessment angle.** Would you say your environmental stories
1) always have a risk assessment angle   2) often do   3) sometimes do
4) rarely do   or 5) never have a risk assessment angle?   (7 DK 8 NA 9 RF)

> *Now I want to read you another series of statements. This time, tell me*
> *whether each of the following statements sounds "very much like you,"*
> *"like you," "not like you," or "not at all like you."*

For example...
17a. My ethical decisions are based on what I perceive to be the ethical standards
prevailing in American journalism today. Does that sound...
1) very much like you   2) like you   4) not like you   or 5) not at all like you
(3 DK 3 NA 9 RF)

Here's another one...
17b. Ethical considerations are of secondary importance to the public's need
to know.
1) very much like you   2) like you   4) not like you   or 5) not at all like you
(3 DK 3 NA 9 RF))

17c. Being ethical in pursuit of environmental news will win the trust of the
audience.
1) very much like you   2) like you   4) not like you   or 5) not at all like you
(3 DK 3 NA 9 RF)

17d. If there's an environmental story that needs to be reported, I would do whatever was needed to get the facts, even if I had to use some debatable tactics.
1) very much like you   2) like you   4) not like you   or 5) not at all like you
(3 DK 3 NA 9 RF)

17e. Religion is the true basis for professional ethics.
1) very much like you   2) like you   4) not like you   or 5) not at all like you
(3 DK 3 NA 9 RF)

17f. When environmental news judgments involve matters of professional ethics, I want my fellow staffers to approve of my decisions.
1) very much like you   2) like you   4) not like you   or 5) not at all like you
(3 DK 3 NA 9 RF)

17g. Codes of ethics are not very important to me in my environmental news decision making.
1) very much like you   2) like you   4) not like you   or 5) not at all like you
(3 DK 3 NA 9 RF)

17h. My ethical decision making is based more on what I know is "legal" rather than on what my instinct sometimes tells me is "right."
1) very much like you   2) like you   4) not like you   or 5) not at all like you
(3 DK 3 NA 9 RF)

17i. The harder it is to get information from officials, the harder I try to get it, by whatever means necessary.
1) very much like you   2) like you   4) not like you   or 5) not at all like you
(3 DK 3 NA 9 RF)

Now I am going to read you a list of potential _sources_ that you might use on environmental stories. Please tell me if you always use the source in your reporting, often use it, sometimes use it, rarely use it, or never use it.

18a. For example, the federal **Environmental Protection Agency.** Would you say that you
1) always use EPA as a source   2) often use it   3) sometimes use it
4) rarely use it   or 5) never use it.   (18 DK 8 NA 9 RF)

How about these other federal agencies:
18b. **The Food and Drug Administration.** Would you say that you
1) always use FDA as a source   2) often use it   3) sometimes use it
4) rarely use it   or 5) never use it.   (18 DK 8 NA 9 RF)

18c. **The Centers for Disease Control and Prevention.** Would you say that you
1) always use CDC as a source   2) often use it   3) sometimes use it
4) rarely use it   or 5) never use it.   (18 DK 8 NA 9 RF)

18d. **The Department of Energy.** Would you say that you
1) always use DOE as a source   2) often use it   3) sometimes use it
4) rarely use it   or 5) never use it.   (18 DK 8 NA 9 RF)

18e. **The Department of Transportation.** Would you say that you
1) always use DOT as a source   2) often use it   3) sometimes use it
4) rarely use it   or 5) never use it.   (18 DK 8 NA 9 RF)

18f. **Agency for Toxic Substances and Disease Registry**. Would you say that you
1) always use ATSDA as a source   2) often use it   3) sometimes use it
4) rarely use it   or 5) never use it.   (18 DK   8 NA   9 RF)

18g. **National Health and Safety Council.** Would you say that you
1) always use NHSC as a source   2) often use it   3) sometimes use it
4) rarely use it   or 5) never use it.   (18 DK   8 NA   9 RF)

18h. **National Science Foundation.** Would you say that you
1) always use NSF as a source   2) often use it   3) sometimes use it
4) rarely use it   or 5) never use it.   (18 DK   8 NA   9 RF)

18i. **Are there any other federal agencies that you use**? _____
(For each) Would you say that you
1) always use it as a source   2) often use it   3) sometimes use it
4) rarely use it   or 5) never use it.   (18 DK   8 NA   9 RF)

18j. **Are there any other federal agencies that you use**? _____
(For each) Would you say that you
1) always use it as a source   2) often use it   3) sometimes use it
4) rarely use it   or 5) never use it.   (18 DK   8 NA   9 RF)

How about these state government agencies:
19a. **Your state Department of Health (or Public Health).** Would you say that you
1) always use it as a source   2) often use it   3) sometimes use it
4) rarely use it   or 5) never use it.   (7 DK   19 NA   9 RF)

19b. **Your Department of Environmental Quality (or Environmental Management).** Would you say that you
1) always use it as a source   2) often use it   3) sometimes use it
4) rarely use it   or 5) never use it.   (7 DK   19 NA   9 RF)

19c. **Your Dept. of Natural Resources.** Would you say that you
1) always use it as a source   2) often use it   3) sometimes use it
4) rarely use it   or 5) never use it.   (7 DK   19 NA   9 RF)
(6 don't have a DNR; circle this and ask what their equivalent agency is called, then insert it in 19h and re-ask)

19d. **Your state Dept. of Transportation.** Would you say that you
1) always use it as a source   2) often use it   3) sometimes use it
4) rarely use it   or 5) never use it.   (7 DK   19 NA   9 RF)

19e. **Your state Department of Food and Agriculture.** Would you say that
you
1) always use it as a source   2) often use it   3) sometimes use it
4) rarely use it   or 5) never use it.   (7 DK   19 NA   9 RF)

19f. **The governor's office.** Would you say that you
1) always use it as a source   2) often use it   3) sometimes use it
4) rarely use it   or 5) never use it.   (7 DK   19 NA   9 RF)

19g. **Legislative offices.** Would you say that you
1) always use it as a source   2) often use it   3) sometimes use it
4) rarely use it   or 5) never use it.   (7 DK   19 NA   9 RF)

19h. **Are there any other <u>state government</u> agencies that you use?**

_____

(For each) Would you say that you
1) always use it as a source   2) often use it   3) sometimes use it
4) rarely use it   or 5) never use it.   (7 DK   19 NA   9 RF)

19i. **Are there any other <u>state government</u> agencies that you use?**

_____

(For each) Would you say that you
1) always use it as a source   2) often use it   3) sometimes use it
4) rarely use it   or 5) never use it.   (7 DK   19 NA   9 RF)

And on the local level:
20a. **The mayor or top municipal official in local cities and towns.**
Would you say that you
1) always use such officials as a source   2) often use them   3) sometimes
use them   4) rarely use them   or 5) never use them. (7 DK   8 NA   20 RF)

20b. **Local City or town <u>council offices</u>.** Would you say that you
1) always use such officials as a source   2) often use them   3) sometimes
use them   4) rarely use them   or 5) never use them. (7 DK   8 NA   20 RF)

20c. **Local departments of health.** Would you say that you
1) always use such officials as a source   2) often use them   3) sometimes
use them   4) rarely use them   or 5) never use them. (7 DK   8 NA   20 RF)

20d. **County administrators.**   Would you say that you
1) always use such officials as a source   2) often use them   3) sometimes
use them   4) rarely use them   or 5) never use them. (7 DK   8 NA   20 RF)

20e. **Are there any other <u>local government</u> offices that you use?**

_____
(For each) Would you say that you
1) always use such officials as a source   2) often use them   3) sometimes
use them   4) rarely use them   or 5) never use them. (7 DK 8 NA 20 RF)

How about these environmental organizations:
21a. **Sierra Club.** Would you say that you
1) always use Sierra Club as a source   2) often use them   3) sometimes
use them   4) rarely use them   or 5) never use them. (7 DK 8 NA 20 RF)

21b. **Audubon Society.** Would you say that you
1) always use Audubon as a source   2) often use them   3) sometimes use
them   4) rarely use them   or 5) never use them. (7 DK 8 NA 20 RF)

21c. **Greenpeace.** Would you say that you
1) always use Greenpeace as a source   2) often use them   3) sometimes
use them   4) rarely use them   or 5) never use them. (7 DK 8 NA 20 RF)

21d. **Natural Resources Defense Council.** Would you say that you
1) always use NRDC as a source   2) often use them   3) sometimes use
them   4) rarely use them   or 5) never use them. (7 DK 8 NA 20 RF)

21e. **Local environmental groups.** Would you say that you
1) always use them as a source   2) often use them   3) sometimes use
them   4) rarely use them   or 5) never use them. (7 DK 8 NA 20 RF)

21f. Are there **any other environmental organizations you use?**

_____
(For each) Would you say that you
1) always use the organization as a source   2) often use it   3) sometimes use it
4) rarely use it   or 5) never use it.   (7 DK 8 NA 9 RF)

21g. Are there **any other environmental organizations you use?**

_____
(For each) Would you say that you
1) always use the organization as a source   2) often use it   3) sometimes use it
4) rarely use it   or 5) never use it.   (7 DK 8 NA 9 RF)

21h. Are there **any other environmental organizations you use?**

_____

(For each) Would you say that you
1) always use the organization as a source   2) often use it   3) sometimes use it
4) rarely use it   or 5) never use it.   (7 DK   8 NA   9 RF)

21i. Are there **any other environmental organizations you use?**

_____

(For each) Would you say that you
1) always use the organization as a source   2) often use it   3) sometimes use it
4) rarely use it   or 5) never use it.   (7 DK 8 NA 9 RF)

21j. Are there **any other environmental organizations you use?**

_____

(For each) Would you say that you
1) always use the organization as a source   2) often use it   3) sometimes use it
4) rarely use it   or 5) never use it.   (7 DK 8 NA 9 RF)

21k. And how **about individual, local citizens who are active on the environment?**
Would you say that you
1) always use them as a source   2) often use them   3) sometimes use them
4) rarely use them   or 5) never use them.   (7 DK 8 NA 9 RF)

How about business-related organizations, like...
22a. **The Chemical Manufacturers Association.** Would you say that you
1) always use the CMA as a source   2) often use it   3) sometimes use it
4) rarely use it   or 5) never use it.   (7 DK 8 NA 9 RF)

22b. **The Chamber of Commerce.** (local or national if they ask) Would you
say you
1) always use the Chamber as a source   2) often use it   3) sometimes use it
4) rarely use it   or 5) never use it.   (7 DK 8 NA 9 RF)

22c. **Local manufacturers, developers or other business leaders.** Would you
say that you
1) always use them as a source   2) often use them   3) sometimes use them
4) rarely use them   or 5) never use them.   (7 DK 8 NA 9 RF)

22d. **Are there any other business-related organizations that you use?**

_____

(For each) Would you say that you
1) always use the organization as a source   2) often use it   3) sometimes use it
4) rarely use it   or 5) never use it.   (7 DK 8 NA 9 RF)

23. And how about **academic officials, professors and researchers at colleges and universities**? Would you say that you
1) always use them as a source   2) often use them   3) sometimes use them
4) rarely use them   or 5) never use them.   (7 DK 8 NA 9 RF)

OK, now I'd like know <u>who you talk to</u> when you call these public and private organizations for information on environmental stories.

24a. For example, how about **public information officers.**
In your environmental reporting, would you say you talk to public information officers
1) always   2) often   3) sometimes   4) rarely   or 5) never.
(7 DK 8 NA 9 RF)

24b. How about **scientists?** In your environmental reporting, would you say you talk to scientists
1) always   2) often   3) sometimes   4) rarely   or 5) never.
(7 DK 8 NA 9 RF)

24c. How about **administrators** of the government agency or private group. In your environmental reporting, would you say you talk to administrators
1) always   2) often   3) sometimes   4) rarely   or 5) never.
(7 DK 8 NA 9 RF)

Finally, we want to know whether you **value the time you spend with each of these sources**.

25a. How about the **public information officers?** Would you say the time you spend with them on a story has
1) no value   2) little value   3) some value   4) fairly high value
or 5) very high value.   (7 DK 8 NA 9 RF)

25b. How about **scientists?** Would you say the time you spend with them on a story has
1) no value   2) little value   3) some value   4) fairly high value
or 5) very high value.   (7 DK 8 NA 9 RF)

25c. How about **administrators?** Would you say the time you spend with them on a story has
1) no value   2) little value   3) some value   4) fairly high value
or 5) very high value.   (7 DK 8 NA 9 RF)

> *Now a few questions about your background and we'll be through.*

26. In what year did you become a full-time employee of
(NAME OF ORGANIZATION)?
YEAR: _____   (9997 Not full-time; 9998 Don't Know; 9999 RF)

27. How long have you worked in journalism?
YEARS: _____   (DK/Can't estimate 97 NA 98 RF 99)

28. In looking back, why did you become a journalist?
(PROBE IF NECESSARY: "Any other reasons?")
a.

b.

c.

d.

e.

29. For how many years now have you been covering the environment?
_____ years

30. Which newspapers do you read regularly -- that is, at least once a week?
(LIST EACH PAPER -- FULL NAME, CITY AND STATE OF PUBLICA-
TION.) (ON-LINE VERSION COUNTS IF "read regularly -- that is, at least
once a week?")
a.

b.

c.

d.

e.

f.

g.

31. How many days a week do you usually watch the early evening **network**
newscasts on TV–that is CBS, NBC or ABC?
(Circle one)   0   1   2   3   4   5   6   7 DK--8   RF--9

32. How many days a week do you usually watch CNN or other cable TV news?
(Circle one)   0   1   2   3   4   5   6   7   DK--8   RF--9

33. Please tell me **the <u>magazines you read regularly -- that is, almost every issue</u>**.
(LIST FULL NAMES OF ALL MAGAZINES.)

a.

b.

c.

d.

e.

34. What is the highest grade of school, or level of education, you have completed? (Ask open ended; circle best category)
01 No school or kindergarten
02 Grades 1 - 11
12 Completed high school
13 1-3 years of college
16 Graduated from college
17 Some graduate work, no degree
18 Master's degree
19 Doctorate, law, or medical degree
20 Vocational or technical school beyond high school
(DK 97 NA 98 RF 99)

(IF RESPONDENT ANSWERS "18" to Q34, ASK FOLLOWING QUESTION. OTHERWISE GO TO Q36)

35. What field were you in graduate or professional school?
FIELD_____

36. What was your undergraduate major?
   1   Journalism
   2   Journalism and other major (SPECIFY Other: _____)
   3   Other major(s) – what was it? (SPECIFY Other: _____)
   6   Did not have a major
   (DK 7 NA 8 RF 9)

37. What was your undergraduate minor, if any?
    1   Journalism
    2   Journalism and other minor (SPECIFY)_____
    3   Other minor(s)--what was it? (SPECIFY)_____
    6   Did not have a minor
    (DK 7 NA 8 RF 9)

38. Do you feel you need additional training in journalism or other subjects?
    1   Yes
    2   No
    (DK 7 NA 8 RF 9)

(IF NO, GO TO Q40)
(IF YES:
Q39. In what subjects?   (RECORD ANSWER VERBATIM:)

_____

40. Have you had any short courses, sabbaticals, workshops or
fellowships since becoming a journalist?
    1   Yes
    2   No
    (DK 7 NA 8 RF 9)

(IF NO: GO TO Q42)
(IF YES
41.What were they:
a.
b.
c.

42. In what year were you born?_____
Don't know. 9998
Refused. 9999

43. In which one of the following groups would you place yourself? (Read list
slowly until person responds to category)
    1   White (Caucasian)
    2   Black or African-American
    3   Hispanic or Latino
    4   Asian or Asian-American
    5   Native American or Indian
    6   Other (SPECIFY: _____)
    (DK 7 NA 8 RF 9)

44. In what religion, if any, were you brought up? (Read list slowly until person responds to category)
    1   Protestant
    2   Catholic
    3   Jewish
    4   Other
    5   None at all
    (DK 7 NA 8 RF 9)

44a. How important is religion or religious beliefs to you? Would you say:
    1   Very important
    2   Somewhat important
    3   Not very important, or
    4   Not at all important
    (DK 7 NA 8 RF 9)

45. What is your marital status? (Read list slowly until they respond)
    1   Married
    2   Cohabiting
    3   Divorced
    4   Separated
    5   Widowed, or
    6   Single, that is, never married
    (DK 7 NA 8 RF 9)

46. As of today, are you a Democrat, a Republican, or what?
    1   Democrat
    2   Republican
    3   Independent/no party
    4   Other (SPECIFY BELOW)
    (DK 7 NA 8 RF 9)

46a.(OTHER OR IF INDEPENDENT OR NO PARTY) Which of the following best describes your political leanings?
    1   Lean toward the Republican party
    2   Lean toward the Democratic party, or
    3   Lean toward neither major party
    4   (VOLUNTEERED: Other (SPECIFY) _____
    (DK 7 NA 8 RF 9)

47. I'd like to mention once again that all information you give us will be treated in strict confidence, and neither you nor your organization will ever be reported by name.

I want to read you a list of three categories. Please tell me what your total personal income was, before taxes, from your <u>work in the communications field</u> during 1999. Was it:
> 1   Less than $35,000
> 2   Between $35,000 and $60,000, or
> 3   Over $60,000
> (DK 7 NA 8 RF 9)

48. (INTERVIEWER: RECORD RESPONDENT'S SEX. ASK ONLY IF NECESSARY.)
I'm required to ask all questions. Are you:
> 1   Male, or
> 2   Female
> 9   DK/Refused

We're all done. Thank you very much for your help. We will be using the answers only in the aggregate, adding up the responses and reporting what percentage of environmental journalists feel a certain way.

---

49 Do you have any additional comments?
> Yes ....1 (SPECIFY)
> No 9

50. Are there any other people at your news organization we should survey?

51. How about in your news market or statewide. Are there other knowledgeable reporters covering the environment on a regular basis that we should talk to?

Record time ended: _____

Version 3   Cover sheet

__ __ __ __

(Number if confirmed participant)

1. State:____

2. Respondent: _____   Phone: _____

E-mail: _____

3. News organization: _____

4. Name obtained from (check all that apply):
a. SEJ list
b. E&P Yrbook
c. Bdcast Yrbook,
d. pr list 33
e. pr list 2
f. state env agency
g. fed env agency
h. from another journalist; (name:_____)

5. TYPE OF NEWS ORGANIZATION:
1. Daily newspaper . . . .
2. News agency (wire service) . . . .
3. Local tv station . . . .
4. regional or network tv . . . .

5a. If print, circulation: _____

6.
a. Contact 1: date/time/result _____

b. Contact 2: date/time/result _____

c. Contact 3: date/time/result _____

Instructions to interviewers:

1. Call news org, ask for news room, then ask for contact person. If unavailable, ask any full-time reporter and note their name.

Read the questions exactly the way they are listed. If a respondent requests clarification, reread the question back to them but do not make any effort to interpret the information for them.

The success of this project is based, in part, on there being no variation in the way the following questions are asked. Any variation in the answers, therefore, is the result of differing opinions of the subjects, not differences in the way questions are asked.

2. The one exception to this is the introduction to the survey. Here you have the freedom to use whatever persuasive skills you possess to convince the respondent to take part. Use the attached script or modify it to use your strengths.

3. The material in parentheses is there only for your instruction and is <u>not to be read.</u> The question numbers and the number before each potential response (e.g., **1**. Strongly agree, **2**. Agree, etc.) also are not to be read.

4. Underlined material is to be stressed or "punched" when reading. The underlined material is usually the most important concept in a question and should be emphasized.

5. When you do a set of related questions with the same five-part answers, the respondent will pick up on the pattern of the questions and begin to answer succeeding questions before you have a chance to read all the categories.

This is OK, as long as you are sure you listed all options in the initial questions in that list.

6. Most questions offer
    7   don't know
    8   no answer
    9   refused to answer

Be sure to circle most appropriate answer if these are relevant.

Appendix B

Sources Used by Environment Reporters

The reporters were asked how often they used 29 types of sources, ranging from federal agencies to state and local government offices, environment groups and environmentalists, to business groups, plus academics. They rated them using a five point scale running from 1 = always used as a source to 5 = never used. The following tables are a continuation of the data found in Chapter 5 and contain the complete data for the use of sources by environment reporters.

Table 1
Sources Used by Environment Reporters, Grouped by Type of Source
(Raw numbers and percentages represent the actual number of respondents in each category.)

Environment Reporters…	Always	Often	Sometimes	Rarely	Never	Total	Mean*
1. Federal							
Environmental Protection Agency	21 / 3.2%	222 / 34.1%	307 / 47.2%	89 / 13.7%	12 / 1.8%	651[a] / 100.0%	2.77
Centers for Disease Control and Prevention	7 / 1.1%	102 / 15.7%	308 / 47.4%	177 / 27.2%	56 / 8.6%	650[b] / 100.0%	3.27
Department of Energy	6 / 0.9%	73 / 11.2%	228 / 35.1%	241 / 37.1%	101 / 15.6%	649[c] / 99.9%**	3.55
Department of Transportation	8 / 1.2%	61 / 9.4%	217 / 33.4%	255 / 39.2%	109 / 16.8%	650[d] / 100.0%	3.61
Food and Drug Administration	4 / 0.6%	26 / 4.0%	155 / 23.9%	316 / 48.8%	147 / 22.7%	648[e] / 100.0%	3.89
National Science Foundation	2 / 0.3%	22 / 3.4%	188 / 29.0%	213 / 32.9%	223 / 34.4%	648[f] / 100.0%	3.98
Agency for Toxic Substances and Disease Registry	5 / 0.8%	47 / 7.3%	145 / 22.4%	177 / 27.4%	273 / 42.2%	647[g] / 100.1%**	4.03
National Health and Safety Council	1 / 0.2%	18 / 2.8%	152 / 23.4%	216 / 33.2%	263 / 40.5%	650[h] / 100.1%**	4.11
2. State							
Department of Environment Quality	57 / 8.9%	417 / 65.3%	130 / 20.3%	20 / 3.1%	15 / 2.3%	639[i] / 99.9%**	2.25
Department of Natural Resources	51 / 8.7%	329 / 56.0%	163 / 27.7%	32 / 5.4%	13 / 2.2%	588[j] / 100.0%	2.37
Department of Health	23 / 3.6%	276 / 42.7%	268 / 41.4%	60 / 9.3%	20 / 3.1%	647[k] / 100.1%**	2.66
Legislative offices	18 / 2.8%	253 / 39.0%	287 / 44.3%	74 / 11.4%	16 / 2.5%	648[l] / 100.0%	2.72
Governor's office	15 / 2.3%	155 / 23.9%	299 / 46.1%	142 / 21.9%	38 / 5.9%	649[m] / 100.1%**	3.05
Department of Transportation	20 / 3.1%	154 / 23.8%	254 / 39.2%	174 / 26.9%	46 / 7.1%	648[n] / 100.1%**	3.11
Department of Food and Agriculture	11 / 1.7%	120 / 18.8%	299 / 46.7%	151 / 23.6%	59 / 9.2%	640[o] / 100.0%	3.20

3. Local

Departments of Health	29 4.6%	224 35.4%	269 42.5%	79 12.5%	32 5.1%	633[p] 100.1%**	2.78
Mayor/top official	34 5.2%	205 31.6%	254 39.2%	130 20.1%	25 3.9%	648[q] 100.0%	2.86
City/town council	30 4.6%	185 28.6%	264 40.8%	141 21.8%	27 4.2%	647[r] 100.0%	2.92
County administrators	24 3.9%	180 29.2%	263 42.7%	111 18.0%	38 6.2%	616[s] 100.0%	2.93

4. Environmental Organizations

Local environmental groups	59 9.1%	377 58.2%	182 28.1%	18 2.8%	12 1.9%	648[t] 100.1%	2.30
Individual citizens	60 9.5%	346 54.7%	191 30.2%	28 4.4%	7 1.1%	632[u] 99.9%**	2.33
Sierra Club	4 0.6%	106 16.3%	299 46.1%	151 23.3%	89 13.7%	649[v] 100.0%	3.33
Audubon Society	4 0.6%	83 12.8%	267 41.1%	180 27.7%	115 17.7%	649[w] 99.9%**	3.49
Natural Resources Defense Council	1 0.2%	33 5.1%	247 38.1%	175 27.0%	193 29.7%	649[x] 100.1%**	3.81
Greenpeace	1 0.2%	2 0.3%	76 11.7%	251 38.7%	319 49.2%	649[y] 100.1%**	4.36

5. Business

Local manufacturers, developers, business leaders	21 3.2%	247 38.1%	300 46.3%	60 9.3%	20 3.1%	648[z] 100.0%	2.71
Chamber of Commerce	10 1.5%	106 16.4%	299 46.2%	141 21.8%	91 14.1%	647[aa] 100.0%	3.30
Chemical Manufacturers Association	2 0.3%	48 7.4%	148 22.8%	160 24.7%	291 44.8%	649[bb] 100.0%	4.06

6. Academic

Academic officials, professors, researchers	32 4.9%	340 52.6%	219 33.8%	45 7.0%	11 1.7%	647[cc] 100.0%	2.48

Q: Now I am going to read you a list of potential <u>sources</u> that you might use on environmental stories. Please tell me if you always use the source in your reporting, often use it, sometimes use it, rarely use it or never use it.

Federal:
Q: For example, the federal Environmental Protection Agency. Would you say that you…
Q: The Centers for Disease Control and Prevention. Would you say that you…

Q: The Department of Energy. Would you say that you…
Q: The Department of Transportation. Would you say that you…
Q: The Food and Drug Administration. Would you say that you…
Q: National Science Foundation. Would you say that you…
Q: Agency for Toxic Substances and Disease Registry. Would you say that you…
Q: National Health and Safety Council. Would you say that you…

State:
Q: Your Department of Environmental Quality (or Environmental Management). Would you say that you…
Q: Your Dept. of Natural Resources. Would you say that you…
Q: Your state Department of Health (or Public Health). Would you say that you…
Q: Legislative offices. Would you say that you…
Q: The governor's office. Would you say that you…
Q: Your state Dept. of Transportation. Would you say that you…
Q: Your state Department of Food and Agriculture. Would you say that you…

Local:
Q: Local departments of health. Would you say that you…
Q: The mayor or top municipal official in local cities and towns. Would you say that you…
Q: Local City or town council offices. Would you say that you…
Q: County administrators. Would you say that you…

Environmental Organizations:
Q: Local environmental groups. Would you say that you …
Q: And how about individual, local citizens who are active on the environment? Would you say that you…
Q: Sierra Club. Would you say that you…
Q: Audubon Society. Would you say that you…
Q: Natural Resources Defense Council. Would you say that you…
Q: Greenpeace. Would you say that you…

Business:
Q: Local manufacturers, developers or other business leaders. Would you say that you…
Q: The Chamber of Commerce. (local or national if they ask) Would you say you…
Q: The Chemical Manufacturers Association. Would you say that you …

Academic:
Q: Academic officials, professors and researchers at colleges and universities. Would you say that you

* Sources are ranked by mean score, lowest to highest. Index ranged from: Always = 1.0 to Never = 5.0.
** Percentage does not total 100 because of rounding.

[a] Total does not include reporters who responded no answer (1).

[b] Total does not include reporters who responded no answer (1) or refused to answer (1).

[c] Total does not include reporters who responded don't know (1), no answer (1) or refused to answer (1).

[d] Total does not include reporters who responded no answer (1) or refused to answer (1).

[e] Total does not include reporters who responded no answer (2) or refused to answer (2).

[f] Total does not include reporters who responded no answer (2) or refused to answer (2).

[g] Total does not include reporters who responded no answer (2) or refused to answer (3).

[h] Total does not include reporters who responded no answer (1) or refused to answer (1).

[i] Total does not include reporters who responded don't know (3), no answer (3), or refused to answer (7).

[j] Total does not include reporters who responded don't know (2), no answer (25), or refused to answer (37).

[k] Total does not include reporters who responded don't know (1), no answer (3), or refused to answer (1).

[l] Total does not include reporters who responded no answer (3) or refused to answer (1).

[m] Total does no include reporters who responded no answer (2) or refused to answer (1).

[n] Total does not include reporters who responded don't know (1), no answer (2), or refused to answer (1).

[o] Total does not include reporters who responded don't know (1), no answer (7), or refused to answer (4).

[p] Total does not include reporters who responded don't know (4), no answer (14), or refused to answer (1).

[q] Total does not include reporters who responded don't know (1), no answer (2), or refused to answer (1).

[r] Total does not include reporters who responded don't know (2), no answer (2), or refused to answer (1).

[s] Total does not include reporters who responded don't know (16), no answer (19), or refused to answer (1).

[t] Total does not include reporters who responded don't know (2) or no answer (2).

[u] Total does not include reporters who responded don't know (2), no answer (13), or refused to answer (5)

[v] Total does not include reporters who responded don't know (1) or no answer (2).

[w] Total does not include reporters who responded don't know (1) or no answer (2).

[x] Total does not include reporters who responded don't know (1) or no answer (2).

[y] Total does not include reporters who responded don't know (1) or no answer (2).

[z] Total does not include reporters who responded don't know (2) or no answer (2).

[aa] Total does not include reporters who responded don't know (2) or no answer (3).

[bb] Total does not include reporters who responded don't know (1) or no answer (2).

[cc] Total does not include reporters who responded don't know (1), no answer (3), or refused to answer (1)

Table 2
Sources Used by Environment Reporters, Grouped by Type of Source, by Region
(Raw numbers and percentages represent the portion of respondents who said they use the source always, often, or sometimes.)

Environment Reporters...	New England	Mountain West	South	Pacific West	Mid Atlantic	Mid Central	West Central	National*
1. Federal								
Environmental Protection Agency	51 92.7%	80 87.9%	130 86.1%	94 81.0%	46 86.8%	85 85.0%	64 75.3%	550/651 84.5%
Centers for Disease Control and Prevention	37 67.3%	45 49.5%	102 68.0%	63 54.3%	40 75.5%	68 68.0%	62 72.9%	417/650 64.2%
Department of Energy	22 40.0%	57 62.6%	64 43.0%	58 50.0%	22 41.5%	42 42.0%	42 49.4%	307/649 47.3%
Department of Transportation	18 32.7%	47 51.6%	64 42.7%	42 36.2%	21 39.6%	54 54.0%	40 47.1%	286/650 44.0%
Food and Drug Administration	19 34.5%	16 17.6%	46 30.9%	28 24.1%	15 28.3%	33 33.3%	28 32.9%	185/648 28.5%
National Science Foundation	17 30.9%	31 34.1%	39 26.0%	46 40.0%	14 26.4%	29 29.0%	36 42.9%	212/648 32.7%
Agency for Toxic Substances and Disease Registry	14 25.5%	23 25.3%	48 32.2%	39 33.6%	23 43.4%	24 24.0%	26 31.3%	197/648 30.4%
National Health and Safety Council	10 18.2%	17 18.7%	44 29.3%	28 24.1%	12 22.6%	34 34.0%	26 30.6%	171/650 26.3%
2. State								
Department of Environment Quality	55 100.0%	88 96.7%	140 94.6%	106 93.0%	46 90.2%	89 92.7%	80 95.2%	604/639 94.5%
Department of Natural Resources	35 94.6%	69 93.2%	126 90.6%	95 88.0%	44 91.7%	97 98.0%	77 92.8%	543/588 92.3%
Department of Health	52 94.5%	82 91.1%	134 89.3%	90 77.6%	45 86.5%	93 93.9%	71 83.5%	567/647 87.6%
Legislative offices	51 92.7%	76 83.5%	128 85.3%	103 88.8%	45 86.5%	81 81.8%	74 87.1%	558/648 86.1%
Governor's office	44 80.0%	71 78.0%	115 76.7%	88 75.9%	37 71.2%	62 62.0%	52 61.2%	469/649 72.3%
Department of Transportation	41 74.5%	61 67.0%	101 67.3%	71 61.2%	31 59.6%	71 71.7%	52 61.2%	428/648 66.0%
Department of Food and Agriculture	32 59.3%	56 62.2%	104 69.8%	75 65.2%	31 60.8%	69 71.1%	63 75.0%	430/640 67.2%
3. Local								
Department of Health	38 74.5%	66 72.5%	128 85.9%	89 81.7%	42 84.0%	94 94.9%	65 77.4%	522/633 82.5%
Mayor/top official	42 76.4%	73 80.2%	116 77.3%	75 64.7%	45 86.5%	76 76.8%	68 80.0%	493/648 76.1%
City/town council	39 70.9%	65 71.4%	112 74.7%	85 73.3%	41 78.8%	78 78.8%	59 70.2%	479/647 74.0%
County administrators	10 32.3%	75 82.4%	120 81.1%	91 79.8%	34 66.7%	77 79.4%	60 71.4%	467/616 75.8%

4. Environmental
    Organizations

Local environmental groups	55 100.0%	91 100.0%	141 93.4%	114 98.3%	48 92.3%	90 91.8%	79 92.9%	618/648 95.4%
Individual citizens	55 100.0%	86 96.6%	137 93.2%	104 93.7%	49 92.5%	93 94.9%	73 92.4%	597/632 94.5%
Sierra Club	30 54.5%	73 80.2%	96 63.6%	83 71.6%	30 56.6%	49 50.0%	48 56.5%	409/649 63.0%
Audubon Society	39 70.9%	56 61.5%	77 51.0%	63 54.3%	32 60.4%	45 45.9%	42 49.4%	354/649 54.5%
Natural Resources Defense Council	22 40.0%	35 38.5%	63 41.7%	63 54.3%	26 49.1%	37 37.8%	35 41.2%	281/649 43.3%
Greenpeace	6 10.9%	10 11.0%	20 13.2%	13 11.2%	9 17.0%	15 15.3%	6 7.1%	79/649 12.2%

5. Business

Local manufacturers, developers, business leaders	40 72.7%	83 91.2%	132 87.4%	105 90.5%	44 83.0%	88 89.8%	76 90.5%	568/648 87.7%
Chamber of Commerce	30 54.5%	53 58.2%	107 70.9%	66 57.4%	30 56.6%	70 71.4%	59 70.2%	415/647 64.1%
Chemical Manufacturers Association	11 20.0%	33 36.3%	56 37.1%	34 29.3%	21 39.6%	25 25.5%	18 21.2%	198/649 30.5%

6. Academic

Academic officials, professors, researchers	53 96.4%	80 87.9%	138 92.0%	105 90.5%	47 88.7%	88 90.7%	80 94.1%	591/647 91.3%

* In the National categories, the first number is the total of respondents in that category who said always, often, or sometimes. The second number is the number of reporters who answered always, often, sometimes, rarely, or never (but does not include those responding no opinion, don't know, no answer, or refused to answer). The percentage is the percentage of respondents in each category who said they use the source always, often, or sometimes. Each type of source is rank ordered nationally by mean, rather than the percent answering always, often, or sometimes.

Appendix C

Three Factors in Environmental Reporter Analysis: Objective/Fair Reporters, Workplace Critics, and Advocates/Civic Journalists

In Chapter 6, twelve questions were used to judge the responses of environmental reporters on the central issues of objectivity, fairness, and advocacy. Using factor analysis to identify underlying variables, or factors that might explain the pattern of responses, three factors were identified (among the ten questions with sufficient loadings): "Objective/Fair Reporters," "Workplace Critics," and "Advocates/Civic Journalists." The following table identifies the breakdown on the three factors used in the environmental reporter analysis.

Component	Initial eigenvalues			Extraction Sums of Squared Loadings			Rotation Sums of Squared Loadings	
	Total	% of Variance	Cumulative %	Total	% of Variance	Cumulative %	Total	% of Variance
1	2.233	22.334	22.334	2.233	22.334	22.334	2.126	21.260
2	2.005	20.052	42.385	2.005	20.052	42.385	2.002	20.023
3	1.365	13.651	56.036	1.365	13.651	56.036	1.475	14.753
4	.941	9.411	65.447					
5	.877	8.774	74.221					
6	.728	7.279	81.499					
7	.667	6.666	88.165					
8	.554	5.545	93.710					
9	.520	5.198	98.907					
10	.109	1.093	100.000					

Extraction Method: Principal Component Analysis.

Index

ABC (American Broadcasting Company), 56, 211
Ader, Christine R., 34 n71
advocacy, xiii, 12-15, 26-27, 33 n62, 39, 42, 47 n25, 97, 104, 115, 117, 119-126, 132, 136-137, 149, 155, 157, 183-184
Advocate, The, 93
Agency for Toxic Substances and Disease Registry, 98-99, 100 table 5.4, 206, 220-222, 224
AIDS, 19, 44
Albany Union, The, 190
Alexander, Lamar, 131
Altman, Larry, 187
American Association for the Advancement of Science (AAAS), 3, 30 n5, 133
American Enterprise Institute, 117
American Journalist in the 1990s: U.S. News People at the End of an Era, The, xvi, 33 n64, 38, 46 n3
Anderson, Ronald B., xvi n6, 33 n62, 46 n5, 47 n25
Arizona State University, 192
Arkansas Democrat Gazette, 117
Associated Press, The, 150, 174 n10, 175 nn15, 16, 19, 26, 42, 187
Association of Alternative Newsweeklies, 159
AT&T, 3
Atlanta Constitution, The, 39, 66
Atlantic, The, 66, 186, 192 n6
Atwater, Tony, xvi n6, 33 n62, 46 n5, 47 n25
Audubon, 191
Audubon Society, 97-99, 208, 221-222, 225
autonomy, *see* environment reporters.

Babbit, Joel, 190
Barchie, Lisa, 35 n103, 139 n20
Bauer, Martin W., 140 n31
Beam, Randal A., xvi n4, 38, 46 n10, 72 n14
beat, *see* environment beat.
Beeman, Perry, 116, 138 n6
Belli, Brita, 158-173, 174 nn43, 44, 47, 49, 62, 176 nn79, 85, 86, 87, 88, 177 nn91, 103, 112
Best AltWeekly Writing and Design 2006, 159
Bhopal, India, 147
bias, 27, 35 nn91, 98, 36 n106, 115-118, 132-133, 135-138, 139 nn14, 22, 154, 184
    anti-business, 26, 118, 136
    "balance as bias," 113 n15, 137, 139 n22, 141 n46
    pro-business, 121
    pro-environment, 132
Bloom, Deborah, 47 n19
Bogart, Leo, 16, 32 n47
Borenstein, Seth, xviii, 116, 138 n5, 187-188, 192 n8
Boston Globe, The, 66, 149
Boston Herald, 149, 159
Bowman, William W., 46 n9
Boyd, Robert, 187
Boykoff, Jules M., 113 n15, 137, 139 n22, 141 n46
Boykoff, Maxwell T., 113 n15, 137, 139 n22, 141 n46
Bozell, L. Brent, III, 35 n97, 138 n13
Brainard, Curtis, 187
Braun, Kevin, 189
Britt, Russ, xvi n8
Broadcasting & Cable Yearbook, 42, 56
Broder, David, 131, 140 n34

Brossard, Dominique, 175 n24
Brown, Jane Delano, 30 n18
Brown, MariAn Gail, 57, 71, 72 nn9, 33
Brownlee, Bonnie J., xvi n4, 38, 46 n10, 72 n14
Bruggers, James (Jim), 31 n26, 73-74, 92, 92 n2, 146, 174 n4
Burgess, Phillip, 13, 14-15, 32 n34, 154-157, 175 nn28, 41
Burnett, R. Christopher, 16, 32 n45, 46 n16
Burton, Paul, 30 n14
Bush, George, 129
business, see bias; see covering the environment; see objectivity and fairness.
Bybee, Carl, 30 n18

"Can the World Be Saved?", 5
Cantrill, James G., 33 n62, 47 n25
Carilli, Theresa, 31 n18, 47 n25, 48 n26
Carnegie Corporation, 191
Carson, Rachel, 4, 8, 10, 21, 34 n80, 132
Caudill, Edward, 140 n40
Caudill, Susan, 140 n40
CBS, 5, 56, 211
Centers for Disease Control and Prevention (CDC), 98-100, 205, 220, 221, 224
Chamber of Commerce, see sources.
Chattanooga Times Free Press, 117
Chemical Manufacturers Association, 97-99, 100 table 5.4, 105, 182, 209, 221-222, 225
Chernobyl, 148
Cheveigne, Suzanne, 175 n24
Christian Science Monitor, 44
civic journalism, xiii, 119, 122-126, 136-137, 183-184
climate change, viii, 9-10, 14, 132, 137, 139 nn21, 22, 25, 141 n46, 146, 158-174, 192
ClimateWire, 187, 189
Clinton, Bill, 22, 24, 129, 172-173
CNN (Cable News Network), 187, 190, 212
Cohn, Roger, 191
Cohn, Victor, 20, 33 n62, 34 n75, 47 n25
Columbia Journalism Review, 66, 147, 187
Columbia University, 192
Congress, 6, 14, 21, 171, 188, 189
Connecticut Home & Garden, 159

Connecticut Post, The, 53, 57
Connecticut Society of Professional Journalists, 159
consequence, see news values.
conservationists, 4, 22
Cotter, Brianna Cayo, 162, 167
Coulson, David C., 31, 47 n26
Council of 100, 130
Council on Sustainable Development (President Clinton's), 22, 31 n18, 48 n26, 174 n2
covering the environment,
    and business angles, 9, 24, 92, 95, 104-105, 109, 136, 151, 162, 182-184, 203
    and business sources, 10-11, 93-100, 104-105, 136, 209, 221-222, 225
    and environment reporters and business issues, 104, 184
    and news angles in environmental stories, see news angles.
    and news sources used in environmental reporting, see sources.
    and potential problems affecting environment reporting, see environment reporters.
    and reporting environmental risk, see risk.
    and risk as a story angle, see risk.
Cronkite, Walter, 5
Culbertson, Hugh M., 31 n24
Cullen, Heidi, 166
Curtin, Patricia A., 32 n29

Darrow, Richard W., 6-7, 30 nn13, 16
Davie, William R., 31 n18, 33 n62, 47 n25, 48 n26
Davis, Joel J., 34 n70
Davis, Joseph A., 31 n25
Dawson, Bill, 139 n22
DDT, 10
Dean, Cornelia, 118
Dennis, Everett E., 139 n19
Department of Energy, see sources.
Department of Environmental Quality, see sources.
Department of Food and Agriculture, see sources.
Department of Transportation, see sources.
Des Moines Register, The, 116

DotEarth, 160
Dunne, Mike, 93, 95, 102, 113 n2
Dunwoody, Sharon, 34 n69, 113 n7, 175
    n24
DuPont, 3, 159
Dykstra, Peter, xviii, 187-188, 192 n10

E – The Environmental Magazine, 66, 68,
    158-160, 173
E&E Publications, 187
East Boston Community News, 160
Easterbrook, Gregg, 108, 113 n4
ecology,
    as news angle, see news angles.
    crisis, 4
Economic Council of the Forest Products
    Industry, 7, 30 n13
editors, see environment reporters.
Ehrlich, Paul, 5
Eisner, Thomas, 52
Endrey, Phyllis, 32 n48
Energy Action Coalition, 162, 167
Energy Trader, 189
environment, see news angles.
Environment & Energy Publishing, 189
environment beat, the,
    environmental risk reporting, see risk.
    gatekeepers of science, risk, and tech-
        nology,
    government: the dominant source, see
        sources.
    many different beats, 9
    medium influences the message, the,
        15-16
    objectivity and advocacy, see advocacy;
        see objectivity; see objectivity and
        fairness.
    protocol for ethical reporting, 25-26
    reliance on public relations, see public
        relations.
    setting the environmental agenda, see
        environmental.
    size matters, 16
    studying specialized environment
        reporters, see specialized environ-
        ment reporters.
environment groups, see sources.
environment reporters,
    age and experience of, xiv, 29, 39, 41,
        45, 60, 61 table 3.5, 63, 70-71, 76,
        111, 180

    and autonomy, 60, 67 table 3.8, 73-74,
        79-84, 151, 181-182, 201
    and editing, 60, 78-79, 81, 84, 203
    and job satisfaction, 74-76, 79-80, 111,
        151, 181
    and job security, 80, 80 table 4.3, 82-
        83, 182, 201
    and job titles, xiii, 58-59, 69, 77, 180
    and potential problems/barriers, 17, 73-
        74, 81, 85-88, 105-108, 111, 118
    and their beats, see environment beat.
    and U.S. journalists/reporters, see U.S.
        journalists/reporters.
    choosing journalism as a career, 68-
        69
    education of, xi-xii, 13, 38-39, 41, 60,
        63, 65, 70-71, 75-76, 111, 127, 137,
        180-181, 212
    ethnicity of, xiv, 60-62, 70-71, 76,
        180
    gender of, xiv, 60-62, 70-71, 76, 104,
        180
    income/ salary of, 62-63, 77, 79, 104,
        215
    media usage patterns of, 60, 66-67, 70
        political affiliation of, 27, 29, 61,
        62, 70, 76, 165, 214
    race of, 104
    religious affiliation of, 75, 133-135,
        214
    time constraints of, 74, 79-80, 85-88,
        105, 151, 182, 200
    where are, 53-57
    who are, 57-59
environment reporters at work,
    and the basics of the beat, 148-157
    case studies of environment reporting,
        158-174
    getting a handle on the environment,
        145-148
environment reporters in a time of
    change,
    a golden age of environment reporting?,
        xi, xiv, 45, 179-180, 185
    and environment reporting outlets,
        187-192
    the environment reporters, 180-184
    the time of change, 184-186
Environment Writer, xiv, 116
environmental,
    activists, 4, 6, 22-23, 28, 86-89, 95,

115-116, 118-121, 128, 148, 166, 190, 200, 219
activist groups, 7, 104, 119-122, 127, 129, 136, 183, 197
agenda, 18, 24, 27, 116
awareness, 6, 184
communicators, 13, 15, 154-157, 184
community, 12, 14
groups, 21, 97-100, 105, 117-118, 146, 182, 189, 208, 221-222, 225
health, 20, 23, 57
issues, xi-xii, 3-4, 7, 9, 14, 19, 23, 27-29, 37, 59, 63-65, 69, 73, 77, 87, 90-91, 127, 145-147, 149, 155, 160, 170, 171, 180, 187, 190
information explosion, 6
news, 4, 7, 8, 13, 19, 20, 27, 134, 137, 145, 148, 152, 158, 180, 184-185, 204-205
perspective, 109
policy, 146
problems, xiii, 4, 22, 42, 45, 87-88, 91, 108-109, 119, 122-129, 136-137, 146, 151, 157, 182-184, 197-198
reporters, *see* environment reporters.
risk, *see* risk.
environmental coverage, *see* covering the environment.
Environmental League of Massachusetts, 14, 155
Environmental Protection Agency (EPA), *see* sources.
Environmental Risk Reporting Project, 19
environmentalists, *see* environmental.
ethnicity, *see* environment reporters.
Exxon Valdez, 48 n26, 148

Fahys, Judy, 9-12, 31 n28
Fairfield County Weekly, 159
fairness, 97, 104, 115-138, 184, 227
Faris, Stefan, 190
"favor bank," 156
FDA (Federal Defense Agency) 98-100, 205, 220-224
feature stories, 3, 158
federal agencies, *see* sources.
Ferguson, Mary Anne, 25, 35 n93
Fialka, John, 187
Fierce Green Fire, A, 21, 34 n79, 81
Filho, Walter Leal, 31 n18, 48 n26, 174 n2

Finucane, Melissa L., 25, 35 n91, 94
Flessner, Dave, 109, 112, 113 n6, 192 n1
FOI (Freedom of Information), 57, 129, 160
Food Chemical News, 189
Forecast Cloudy, xviii, 159, 166, 176 n89, 177 nn90, 99, 101
Forecast: The Consequences of Climate Change from the Amazon to the Arctic, from Darfur to Napa Valley, 190
Friedman, Sharon M., 33 n62, 47 n25, 113 n7
"Future of Science and Environmental Journalism, The," xviii, 187, 192 nn8, 10, 11, 193 n20

Gandy, Oscar, 31 n29
Gans, Herbert, 31 n18
Gaskell, George, 140 n31
Gawker.com, 163
gender, *see* environment reporters.
general assignment reporter, 8-9, 58-59, 69, 135, 180
General Electric, 3
George, Christy, xviii, 149, 158-161, 163-167, 174 n11, 176 nn43, 46, 48, 54, 72, 83, 89
Gilovich, Thomas, 35 n91
Girotti, Gianfranco (Vatican Bishop), 135, 141 n43
Gladney, George, 32 n46
global warming, 10, 26, 35 n95, 53, 71, 113 n15, 117, 118, 132, 137, 146, 150-151, 158, 161, 167, 171, 173, 185, 187-88
GlobalPost, 190
Gochfeld, Michael, 18, 34 n68
Goidel, Robert K., 35 n103, 139 n20
Gomes, James, 14-15, 32 n37, 155-157, 175 n34
Gore, Al, 10, 22, 118, 132, 139 n21, 158, 173, 184
Great Ecological Communications War, 6-7, 28
Greenberg, Michael R., 31 n18, 32 n43, 33 nn62, 66, 67, 34 n68, 73, 75, 83, 47 n25, 26, 110, 113 nn9, 12, 13, 140 n26
greenhouse effect, 10, 146, 168-169
Greenpeace, *see* sources.
Greenwire, 145, 149
Griffin, Dale, 35 n91

Griffin, Robert J., 34 n69
Grist.org, 165, 190
Guide to Environmental Laws: From Pre-manufacture to Disposal, 153

Hackett, Robert A., 27, 36 n106
Ham, Becky, 140 n39
Hansen, Anders, 17-18, 33 n63, 47 n25
Harvard University, 192
Hauserman, Julie, 130
Hayward, Stephen F., 35 n100, 117, 139 nn16, 18
Henig, Robin Marantz, xvi n7, 46 n7, 47 n19, 174 n7
Herrmann, Benedikt, 140 n38
Hickel, Walter J., 30 n15
Hirschorn, Michael, 186, 192 n6
HIV, 40
Hornig, Susanna, 32 n48
Hotz, Robert Lee, xvi n7, 46 n7
Huffington Post, The, 186
human interest, *see* news angles; *see* news values.
Huntsman, John, 11-12
Hurricane Katrina, 93
Hussman, Walter E., Jr., 181

"IH Spends $71,900 to Be a Good Neighbor," 5
Inconvenient Truth, An, 10, 118, 132, 158
Inside NRC, 189
Intergovernmental Panel on Climate Change, 174
International Harvester, 5-6
International Social Survey, 17
Interpretative Reporting, 34 n74, 40, 48 n28
Izard, Ralph S., 31 n24

Jenkins, McKay, 39
job satisfaction, *see* environment reporters.
job titles, *see* environment reporters.
Johnson, Lyndon B., 6
Johnstone, John W.C., 38, 46 n9
journalists, U.S., *see* U.S. journalists/reporters.
Juskalian, Russ, 191, 193 n18

Kafatos, Fotis C., 33 n52
Kahneman, Daniel, 35 n91

Kallfass, Monika, 175 n24
Kamalipour, Yahya R., 31 n18, 47 n25, 48 n26
Kaylin, Jennifer, 150-151, 175 n17
Kennedy, Robert F., Jr., 116
Kim, Koang-Hyub, 32 n46
Knight Foundation, 191
Knight-Ridder Newspapers, 116
Knudson, Mary, xvi n7, 46 n7, 47 n19, 174 n7
KPTV, 164
KQED, 147, 174 n5
Krieghbaum, Hillier, 30 n2, 47 n24
Kriz, Margaret, 148, 174 n9
Kulongoski, Ted, 168
Kyoto Treaty, 26, 35 n95, 117, 173

Lacy, Stephen, 31 n18, 47 n26
LaFollette, Marcel C., 3, 30 n5
LaMay, Craig L., 139 n19
Lambert, Donald A., 31 n24
Langley, Ronald E., 35 n103, 139 n20
Leary, Warren, 187
Leavell, Chuck, 190
Leavitt, Mike, 116
Lee, Jung-Sook, 31 n18, 33 n62, 47 n25, 48 n26
LEED (Leadership in Energy and Environmental Design), 158
Leonard, Jennifer Pease, 140 n26
Lichter, Linda S., 35 nn99, 102, 139 nn15, 17
Lichter, S. Robert, 35 nn99, 102, 139 nn15, 17
Life, 4
Logan, Brian, 32 n46
Lomborg, Bjørn, 35 n101, 108, 113 n4
Look, 4
Los Angeles Times, xii, 38, 66
Louisville Courier-Journal, 73, 146
Love Canal, 147
Lovell, Ronald P., 31 n19
Luntz, Frank, 171
Lutgen, Bob, 117, 138 n9

MacClennan, Paul, 21
MacDougal, Curtis D., 34 n74, 40, 48 n28
MacGregor, Donald C., 35 nn91, 94
Marketplace, 149, 159, 162
Marston, John E., 30 n11

mass media, 3-4, 7, 15, 19-20, 24, 27, 30 n10, 33 n63, 187-192
Mathews, Cleve, 131, 140 n32
McClatchy, 187
McClure, Robert, 152, 175 n20
McClure's Magazine, 132
McPhee, John, 12
Mecklin, John, 193 n23
media competition, 110
media usage patterns, *see* environment reporters.
Meersman, Tom, 115, 118, 138 n2, 139 n24, 141 n47
Mejia, Robin, 152, 175
Melwani, Geetu, 25, 35 n93
Meyer, Philip, 32 n46, 46 n16
Mid Atlantic region, xiii, xvi, 43, 54, 58, 77, 83, 88, 90, 90 table 4.11, 91, 96, 100, 103, 107-108, 119, 121 table 6.2, 123, 124 table 6.4, 224
Mid Central region, xiii, xvi, 43, 54, 58, 77, 83, 88, 90, 90 table 4.11, 91, 96, 100, 103, 105, 107-108, 119, 121 table 6.2, 124 table 6.4, 224
Miller, Steve, 17 n24
Minneapolis Star Tribune, 115, 138
Mooney, Chris, 139 n22
Morris, Bernard R., 39, 47 n21
Motavalli, Jim, 171
Mother Jones, 152, 191
Mother Nature Network, 187, 190
Mountain West region, xiii, xvi, 43, 54, 56, 58, 59, 69, 77, 83, 88, 90, 90 table 4.11, 91, 96, 100, 100 table 5.4, 103, 105, 107, 108, 119, 121, 124 table 6.4, 180, 224
Moyers, Bill, 12
MSN, 159, 190
MSNBC, 190
Muir, John, 21
"Myth of Objectivity, The," 132, 140 n36

NASA, 188
National Association of Science Writers, 186
National Geographic, 4, 10, 66, 68
National Health and Safety Administration, 98, 182
National Journal, 148
National Public Radio (NPR), 133, 149, 166, 188, 190

National Science Board, 17
National Science Foundation, 19, 23, 98, 99, 100 table 5.4, 206, 220, 222, 224
Natural Resources Defense Council, 97-99, 208, 221-222, 225
Nature, 71, 94
Nature Conservancy, The, 12
NBC, 56, 190, 211
Nelkin, Dorothy, 16, 32 n50, 33 n51
Nelsen, Mark, 164, 172
Nelson, Peter, xviii, 145, 149-150, 152, 174 n1, 175 nn12, 23
New England Press Association, 159
New England region, xiii, xv n1, xvi 10, 43-44, 54, 56, 58-59, 69, 77, 83, 88, 90, 90 table 4.11, 91, 96-97, 100 table 5.4, 103, 107, 119, 121 table 6.2, 124 table 6.4, 180, 224
New Jersey Institute of Technology, 19
New Washington Press Corps, xviii, 188, 192 n14
New York Sun, 190
New York Times, The, xii, 4, 38, 66, 68, 118, 146-147, 153, 160, 166, 186-187, 191
New Yorker, The, 66, 68
news angles,
    business, *see* covering the environment.
    ecology, 4, 6
    economic, viii, 20-21, 24, 93-96, 104, 109, 182, 203
    government, 6-9, 27, 39, 64, 94-97, 109, 167, 182, 203
    health, viii, 9, 11, 13, 15, 16, 19-21, 23, 25, 39, 57, 94-96, 109, 112, 132, 148, 151, 182, 185-186, 204
    human interest, 7, 19, 93-96, 109, 167, 182, 203
    natural resources, vii-viii, 26
    nature or wilderness, 94-96, 109, 167, 182, 203
    political, viii, 20-24, 26-27, 93-96, 109, 182, 203
    pollution, *see* pollution.
    risk assessment, *see* risk.
    science/technology, 94-96, 109, 167, 182, 203
News People: A Sociological Portrait of American Journalists and Their Work, The, 38, 46 n9
news sources, *see* sources.

news values,
  and geographical factors/cost and convenience, 16, 18, 23, 28, 111
  and visual images, 18, 23-24
  consequence, 19-20, 24-25, 40, 108, 110, 183
  human interest, 19, 24-25, 40, 108, 149, 183
  prominence, 19, 24-25, 40, 108, 183
  proximity, 19, 24-25, 40, 108, 183
  timeliness, 19, 24-25, 40, 108, 133, 183
newspapers, vii, xi-xv, 4-5, 8-9, 16-17, 29, 37-38, 41-42, 53-60, 66-71, 75, 147, 151, 179-181, 185-189, 191, 211
Newsweek, 66, 68
newsworthiness, 27, 108, 183
Nobel Prize, 132
Northwestern University, 192
Norusis, Marija J., 113 n14
Notes from the Underground: The Most Outrageous Stories from the Alternative Press, 159
nuclear power plant, 109, 148
Nuclear Regulatory Commission, 189

Obama administration, 190
objectivity, xiii, 26-27, 29, 42, 115-138, 157, 173, 183-184, 227
objectivity and fairness,
  and advocacy, 26-27, 123-125
  and civic journalists, 125-127
    and ethical decision making in environmental journalism, 127-135
  and how environment reporters view their peers, 119
  and workplace critics, 125-127
  fairness vs. pro-environment or pro-business slant, xvii, 26-28, 30 n1, 36 nn103- 106, 104, 115-121, 136, 138 n1, 149, 157, 183, 198
  objectivity vs. fairness, 122
  should journalists stay out of stories?, 122
Oregon Museum of Science and Industry, 171
Oregon Public Broadcasting, xviii, 158-159, 161
Oregon Territory, 159
Oregonian, The, 66, 166
Ostro, Stu, 166

Pacific West region, 54, 58, 77, 83, 88, 90, 90 table 4.11, 91, 96, 100, 103, 107, 121, 124, 224
Palca, Joe, 133, 140 n37
Palmer, Lisa, xviii, 189, 192 n16
Paterno, Susan, 16, 32 n45, 39
Patterson, Philip, 131, 140 n32
Paving Paradise, 130
PBS (Public Broadcasting Service), 147
Peiser, Wolfram, 32 n41
Perlman, David, 187
Peters, Ellen, 25, 35 nn91, 94
Peters, Hans Peter, 175 n24, 153
Pew Research Center, 17
PIO (Public Information Officer), 15, 100-103, 157, 180, 210
Pittman, Craig, 127, 129-131, 135, 140 nn27, 29, 30, 141 n44
PlanetGreen, 190
Plenty Magazine, 159, 165
pollution, 4-6, 11, 18, 21-23, 26, 42, 53, 94-96, 105-109, 127, 148, 182-183, 198, 203
  air, 4-5, 11, 21-22, 26, 117, 159
  industry, 5
  water, 4-5, 11, 21, 26, 53
Population Bomb, 5
"PowerShift," 160, 162, 167
PR Newswire, 186
prominence, *see* news values.
ProPublica, 189-190
Project for Excellence in Journalism, viii, xviii, 188
proximity, *see* news values.
public health, viii, 9, 98-99, 206
public interest, 5, 130, 189-190
public relations, 4-7, 13-15, 26, 102, 117-118, 152, 180, 186

Quest, 147

radioactive material, 109
Radio-Television News Directors Association, 185
Raphael, Chad, 139 n20
Rather, Dan, 12
Revkin, Andrew, 147-148, 153-154, 174 n7, 175 n27
risk, xiii, 15-16, 18-26, 28, 40-41, 94-96, 108-112, 151, 182-185, 204
risk assessment, *see* risk.

Rivers, William L., 131, 140 n32
Rockefeller, John D., 132
Rogers, Carol L., 113 n7
Rogers, Paul, xvi n6, 46 n5, 147
Rollin, Sara Thurin, 153, 175 n25
Rothman, Stanley, 35 nn99, 102, 139 nn15, 17
Rubin, David Mark, 30 n10
Rutgers Group, 20, 34 n75

Sachs, David Peter, 30 n10
Sachsman, David B., iv, viii, xv n1, xvi nn2-3, 5, 8-12, xvii-xviii, 8, 13, 15, 18, 25, 29 n1, 30 nn4-9, 17, 31 nn18, 20-22, 24-25, 27, 32 nn30, 33, 40, 43, 47, 33 nn51, 53, 61-62, 65, 34 nn68, 72-73, 75, 77, 82, 86-87, 35 nn90, 94, 36 nn103-104, 106-107, 109-110, 112, 45 n1, 46 nn2, 4, 6, 8, 10, 15, 17, 47 n20, 23, 25, 26, 48 nn26, 27, 29, 37, 40, 42, 49 nn44, 72 nn1, 4, 10, 15-16, 27, 92 nn1, 4, 10, 15, 16, 27, 92 nn1, 4, 110, 112 n1, 113 nn5, 9, 12, 138 nn1, 4, 9, 140 nn26, 141 n45, 192 n3
Salomone, Kandice L., 15, 18, 31 n18, 32 n43, 47 nn25, 26, 110, 113 nn9, 12
Salt Lake City Tribune, 9
Salwen, Michael B., xvi n6, 33 n62, 46 n5, 47 n25
San Diego Union Tribune, 190
San Francisco Chronicle, 66, 187
San Jose Mercury News, 147
Sandman, Peter M., 15, 18, 31 n18, 32 n43, 34 nn68, 75-76, 47 nn25-26, 110, 113 nn9, 12, 40 n26
Santa Barbara Channel-Union Oil Leak, 4, 7
Saturday Review, 4
Schaffer, Jan, xviii, 191, 193 n20
Schama, Simon, 21, 34 n78
Schneider, Stephen, 133
Schwitzer, Gary, 32 n44
Science, 71, 152
Science Communication, xiii
science communication specialists, 131
science writers, 20, 40, 153
Scripps Howard, 93, 116
Seattle Post-Intelligencer, 152
SEJournal, 4, 116, 147
sensationalism, 183
Shabecoff, Philip, 21, 34 nn79, 81, 146, 174 n3

Shogren, Elizabeth, xviii, 188, 192 n12
Sierra Club, 97-99, 116, 208, 221-222, 225
Sigal, Leon V., 31 n18
Silent Spring, 4, 8, 21, 34 n80, 132
Simon, James, iv, vii, xv n1, xvi nn2-3, 5, 8-9, 10-12, xvii, 29 n1, 30 nn4, 6, 8, 17, 31 nn21, 24, 27, 32 nn33, 34, 37, 43, 47, 33 nn51, 53, 61, 65, 34 nn68, 72-73, 35 nn68, 72-73, 35 nn90, 94, 36 nn103-104, 106, 109, 110, 112, 45 n1, 46 nn2, 4, 6, 8, 10, 15, 47 n23, 48 nn27, 29, 37, 40, 42, 49 n44, 72 nn1, 2, 4, 9, 10, 15, 16, 27, 33, 92 nn1, 2, 4, 112 n1, 113 n2, 6, 16, 138 n1, 2, 4, 140 n38, 141 n45, 150, 174 n10, 175 nn15-16, 19, 26, 28, 34, 42, 176 n43
Simon, Julian L., 35 n101
Simons, Eric, 147, 174 n5
Singer, Eleanor, 32 n48, 140 n26
Singletary, Michael W., 134, 140 n40
Slawski, Edward J., 46 n9
Slovic, Paul, 25-26, 32 n48, 35 nn91, 94
Smith, Jim, 53, 72 n2
Smithsonian, 66, 68
Society of Environmental Journalists (SEJ), 3-4, 24-25, 39, 73, 110, 130, 116, 159-160, 162, 166, 186, 216
Somers, Benjamin, 140 n39
sources,
    academic researchers, 97, 105
    academics, 93, 95, 98-99, 100 table 5.4, 210, 219, 221-222, 225
    administrators, 98-103, 157, 208, 210, 221-222, 224
    business groups, see covering the environment.
    Chamber of Commerce, 97-99, 105, 118, 136, 209, 221-222, 225
    Department of Energy, 98-99, 100, 205, 220, 222, 224
    Department of Environmental Quality, 99-100, 148, 206, 222
    Department of Food and Agriculture, 98-99, 100, 205, 220, 222, 224
    Department of Transportation, 98-99, 205, 220, 222, 224
    Environmental Protection Agency (EPA), 97-100, 116, 205, 220-221, 224
    government agencies, 6, 8, 22, 57, 98, 206-207

government officials, 4, 6-7, 23, 86-89, 149, 200, 206-208, 210, 219
Greenpeace, 97-100, 182, 208, 221-222, 225
public officials, 98, 221, 224
state and local government offices, 98, 220, 224
state officials, 5, 23, 95, 97, 98-100, 105, 149, 189, 206-207, 219-220, 222, 224
South region, xiii, xvi n10, 43, 54, 58-59, 77, 83, 88, 90, 90 table 4.11, 91, 96, 100, 103, 105, 107, 121, 124, 224
specialized environment reporters, xii, 18, 28-29, 137-145
and the American journalist, *see* U.S. journalists/reporters.
method, 42-45
research questions, 41-42
specialized journalists, xi
Sports Illustrated, 66, 68
SPSS, 43, 128
St. Petersburg Times, 127, 135
staff writer, 58-59
Standard Oil, 132
Stanford University, 4, 160
State Department of Environment Quality, *see* sources.
Steiger, Paul, 189
Stein, Meyer L., 16, 39, 46 n16
stem cell, 132-135
Stocking, S. Holly, 113 n7, 140 n26
Stokstad, Erik, 140 n33
Storad, Conrad J., 30 n3, 46 n17
Straughan, Dulcie, 30 n18
Superfund, 147
Sussman, Bruce, 167
sustainability, 14, 145-146, 171, 190
Sutter, Daniel, 32 n46
Suzuki, David, 17, 33 n53

Tanner, Andrea H., 13, 32 nn31, 42
Tarbell, Ida, 132
Taylor, Claire E., 31 n18, 33 n62, 47 n25, 48 n26
Taylor, George, 161, 164, 171-172
technology, xii, 16-18, 38, 64, 94, 147
television, xi-xiv, 3, 7-8, 12-13, 15, 17-19, 23-24, 28-29, 37-38, 40-45, 53-54, 56-57, 59-60, 67-70, 75, 79, 81, 110, 147, 149, 151, 158-159, 161, 164, 166-167, 170-171, 179-181, 185, 187

Tennessee Valley Public Power Association (TVPPA), 14, 154
Thacker, Paul D., 139
Thomas, Evan, 132, 140 n36
Thompson, Paul, 138 n8
Thompson, Peter, 26, 36 n105, 117
Three Mile Island, 148
Time, 4, 66, 68
Tokunaga, Lori, 36 n103, 139 n20
Treehugger.com, 159-160, 165, 190
Tsuchida, Shoji, 175 n24
Tyson Chicken, 117

U.S. Army Corps of Engineers, 127
U.S. Environmental Protection Agency (EPA), *see* sources.
U.S. journalists/reporters, xvi n4, 29, 38-40, 41, 75
United States Rubber, 5-6
University of California, Berkeley, 192
University of Southern California, 192
University of Texas, 161
University Press of Florida, 130
Upshaw, Jim, 161
USA Today, 66, 68

Valenti, JoAnn Myer, iv, viii, xv n1, xvi nn2, 3, 5, 8-12, xvii, 25, 29 n1, 30 n1, 30 nn4, 6, 8, 17, 31 nn18, 21, 24-25, 27-28, 32 nn33, 43, 47, 49, 33 nn51, 53, 61, 62, 65, 34 nn72-73, 88, 35 nn89-90, 93-94, 36 nn103-104, 106, 109-110, 112, 45 n1, 46 nn2, 4, 6, 8, 10, 15, 47 nn23, 25, 48 nn26, 27, 29, 37, 40, 42, 44, 72 nn1, 4, 10, 15, 16, 27, 29, 35, 41, 45, 174 n2
Voakes, Paul S., xvi n4, 38, 46 n10, 72 n14

Wai, Christina, 36 n103, 139 n120
Waite, Matthew, 130
Wakefield-Albers, Julie, 113 n8
Wall Street Journal, The, 66, 68, 189
Ward, Bud, v, ix, xiv, 26, 31 n23, 36 n104, 46 n18, 116, 138 n4, 139 nn21, 22, 23, 141 n46, 147, 153, 174 n6
Washington Post, The, 68, 190
Wearden, Stanley, 30 n18
Weather Channel, The, 166, 190
Weaver, David H., xii, xiv, xvi n4, 18, 29, 33 n64, 36 n111, 37-40, 46 nn3, 10, 11, 60, 62, 66, 69, 72 nn14, 16, 26, 74

table 4.1, 78, 84
WEHCO Media, 181
Welch, Jack, 140 n41
Wesleyan College, 163
West Central region, xiii, xvi n10, 43, 48
    n41, 54, 56, 58, 69, 77, 83, 88, 90, 90
    table 4.11, 91, 96, 100, 100 table 5.4,
    103, 107-108, 121-122, 124, 180, 224
West Nile encephalitis, 57
Westinghouse, 3
wetlands, 93, 127, 129-130
WGBH-TV, 159
White, H. Allen, 140 n40
White, Matthew,
Wilford, John Noble, 187
Wilhoit, G. Cleveland, xvi n4, 18, 29, 33
    n64, 38, 40, 46 nn3, 10, 62, 65-66, 72
    n14, 74, 84
Wilkins, Lee, 25, 34 n87, 47 n25, 110, 113
    n10, 131, 140 nn26, 32
Wilks, Russell, 30 n12
Wilson, Kris, 161, 166, 170
wise-use, 22-23
WNYC, 190
work environment, the,
    and autonomy in the newsroom, 81
    and barriers to reporting on environ-
        ment stories, 81-85
    and job satisfaction by characteristics of
        environment reporters in, 75-79
    and judging jobs in journalism, 79-81
    environment reporters and job satisfac-
        tion in, 74-79
    reporters' perceptions of editors and the
        audience, 85-92
Woodrow Wilson International Center for
    Scholars, 187, 191
World War II,   5
WTNH TV, 151

Yale Environment 360, 191
Yale Forum on Climate Change and the
    Media, ix, xiv, xviii, 189, 192 n16
YouTube, 13

Zajonc, Robert B., 25, 35 n92